For my dear niece Shane — 12/00
You are the rock of Femininity
Here's a book to help you
remember who you truly are.
Merry Christmas.
Love
Aunt Jody

D0435162

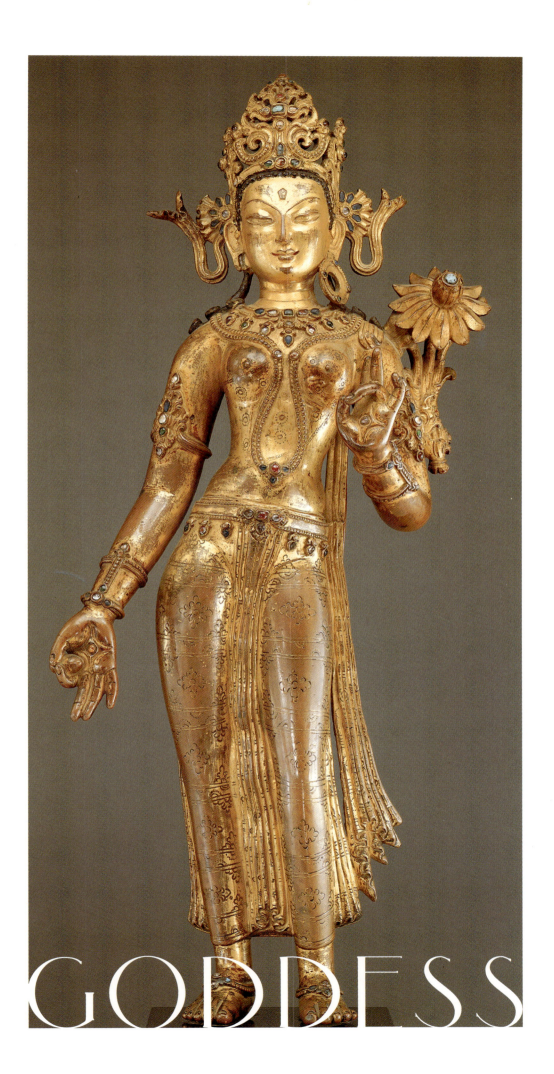

GODDESS

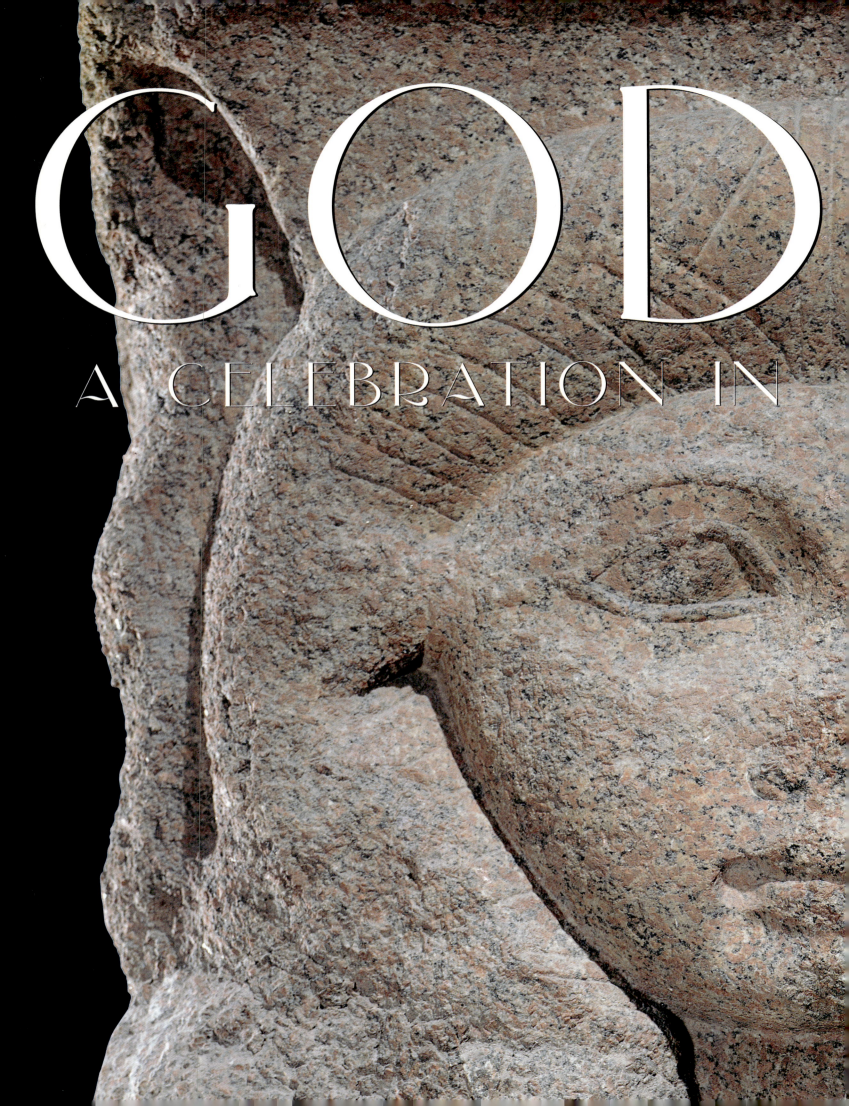

GOD

A CELEBRATION IN

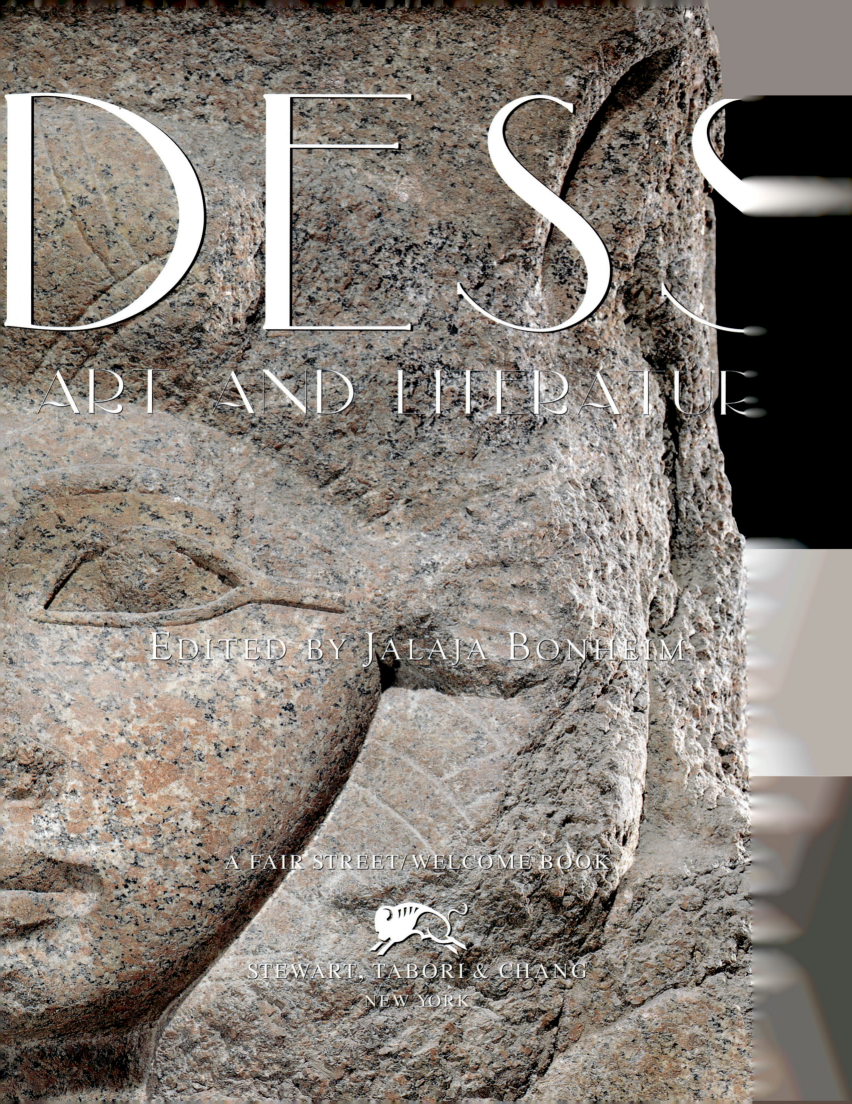

DES[IRE]

ART AND LITERATURE

EDITED BY JALAJA BONHEIM

A FAIR STREET/WELCOME BOOK

STEWART, TABORI & CHANG
NEW YORK

4

INTRODUCTION

ABOVE: *Venus with Ceres and Juno*, Raphael, c. 1518. Farnesina Palace, Rome.

I will never forget the moment when I stumbled upon the four-thousand-year-old Sumerian story of Inanna's descent to the underworld. I was in a bookstore, idly browsing through a pile of books that had been damaged by recent flooding. The copy of *Inanna: Queen of Heaven and Earth* was in bad shape, and the wavy pages crackled in protest as I pulled them apart and began reading:

> From the Great Above she opened her ear to the Great Below.
> From the Great Above the goddess opened her ear to the Great Below.
> From the Great Above Inanna opened her ear to the Great Below.
> My Lady abandoned heaven and earth to descend to the underworld.
> Inanna abandoned heaven and earth to descend to the underworld.
> She abandoned heaven and earth to descend to the underworld.

The words sent shivers down my spine. I closed the book, purchased it and took it home, little knowing what an integral part of my life the goddess Inanna was to become. I found myself thinking about her, talking to friends about her, and finally leading workshops in which I would tell her story to groups of women. What I came to realize was that we all have a piece of Inanna in us; in some way, we all relive her journey. Inanna's story—like any great myth—tells our own story, the story of the human soul. For this reason, myths are valuable to us, even if we do not share the religious beliefs that spawned them.

In recent decades, there has been an immense surge of interest in the goddess. Why? What is the meaning of this strange phenomenon? The first and most obvious answer is that the goddess reveals to us the feminine face of God, long neglected in Western religion. Less obvious, but equally important, is the fact that unlike the transcendent Judeo-Christian God, goddesses are generally immanent powers who act *within* the world and are one with the world. Today many people, tired of the extreme materialism of contemporary life, seek the divine. We hunger for spiritual communion, for contact with something holy and profound—not in a distant after-life, but in the here and now. And therein lies the appeal of the goddess, who not only creates the world, but rather *is* the world. Thus, an ancient Indian chant affirms:

> Salutations to the goddess who dwells in all things as their inner-
> most nature, salutations again and again.

The goddess is earth and sky, sun and moon. She is a spider, a bear, a whirl of snowflakes. She is the beauty of dawn, the innocence of a child, and the love that draws man to woman. "Things are not what they seem," she assures us. "Now as always, sacred power surrounds you on all sides." Her stories remind us, living in a mechanical, demystified world, of the mysterious and magical spirit that dwells in trees and rivers, mountains and animals.

The first goddess introduced in the following pages is a much-loved Native American figure called Spider Woman, or Grandmother Spider. It seems appropriate to begin a book about goddesses with Spider Woman, because the world of the goddess is like a giant web in which all things are interconnected and interdependent. Like a spider, the goddess spins the strands of creation out of her own body and weaves them into the intricate patterns that sustain our life. She is an infinitely resourceful shapeshifter and trickster who pulls orchids, antelopes, and elephants out of stardust. She dictates the orbits of the planets and stations the sun at exactly the right distance from the earth, so that people neither burn nor freeze. Not only does she transform everything she touches, but also she herself continually transforms, appearing now in the guise of a thundercloud, now as a whirling mass of snowflakes, now as an ugly old hag. So complex and varied are her manifestations that the Navajo, in fact, call her Changing Woman. She is generally less interested in the hereafter than in the present. And as weaver of the cosmic web, the goddess is naturally concerned with relationships—the relationships, for example, that bond mother and child, lover and beloved, or husband and wife, as well as the relation-ships between people and their land, or between sun and moon.

Western religion tends to describe nature as finite and limited. Yet many other spiritual traditions disagree and say that such limitations exist only in the eye of the beholder. The words of the seventeenth-century visionary poet William Blake are relevant to one of the central messages of goddess mythology: "If the doors of perception were cleansed, every thing would appear to man as it is, infinite." Many myths emphasize the fact that though the goddess is everywhere, in everything, only those whose minds and hearts are pure can perceive her. We encounter such a test of perception when we read about the African goddess Mbaba Mwana Waresa who, wanting to challenge her future husband's purity of heart, appears before him in rags and tatters. As it turns out, she has chosen well. Because the young man has cleansed the doors of his perception, he is not misled; he recognizes and bows down to the divinity of the disheveled, dirty woman who stands before him. In another story, the Native American goddess Buffalo Woman makes the same point when she insists that her people relate to all beings with reverence and respect, conscious of the sacred presence within them.

The images in this book represent just a few of the thousands of goddesses, from every culture and era. Amazingly, each goddess has her own unique personality, her preferred colors, scents, and locales; each has her own style of relating to the human world. Goddesses rarely come alone; just as Aphrodite interacts with the entire Greek pantheon, so most goddesses belong to a complex polytheistic system.

Adherents of monotheism (the belief in a single godhead) often consider polytheistic religions primitive and unsophisticated. They tend to assume that people who worship many deities have failed to realize that God is one and that there is only *one* source, *one* ultimate truth, *one* eternal mystery which underlies and sustains everything. In fact, most polytheistic cultures are very much aware of the unity of life. However, the focus of their mythologies lies in the workings of sacred power *within* creation, where divinity necessarily assumes many forms. As an Indian proverb puts it, "God is one, but many are the names."

To better understand this point, we might think of God the One as brilliant white light, which fractures into a rainbow spectrum of divine powers. People envision these powers as "deities," a word related to the Sanskrit root *div*, which means "to shine." A goddess, then, is a luminous being, a being of light. Many goddesses, in fact, are associated with specific colors. For example, Mary as the Queen of Heaven belongs to a long lineage of sky goddesses, all of whom are cloaked in blue robes. The goddess of love always comes bathed in golden light, whether she appears in her Greek form as Aphrodite, her Hindu form as Lakshmi, or her Haitian form as Erzulie. Warrior goddesses are generally red, the color of passion, anger, and blood. The black goddesses, whom we present in the section "A Terrible Beauty," preside over the processes of destruction, dissolution, and death.

If the goddess is light and color, she is also rhythm, one of the fundamental expressions of relationship. Many of the stories in this book celebrate the goddess as the source of all natural rhythms. Consider that the first sound every embryo hears is the steady, reassuring heartbeat of its mother. Night and day, month after month, the heartbeat remains the center of the baby's world and serves as its first lullaby. The fact that life is inherently rhythmic may well be the very first lesson every human being learns; in a sense, the mother's heartbeat acts as the child's first spiritual teacher. "You are about to enter a world of rhythm and pulsation," it says. "This is a world of alternating opposites, sound and silence, light and darkness, male and female." We can appreciate, then, why rhythm plays such an important role in the stories of the goddess.

Nature *is* rhythm. Just as rhythm defines the relationship between mother and child, so it defines our relationship with nature. For example, the rhythms of day and night and of the seasons are determined by the relationship between earth and sun. Our whole world is comprised of myriad rhythms, from the spinning galaxies to the infinitely fast waves we perceive as light or the particles that compose all matter. No wonder, therefore, that the goddess is a lover of music and dance. "Oya moves her body in an enormous dance," says a song of praise to the Yoruban goddess. The Greek goddess Eurynome dances the universe into being, while the Hindu goddess Kali dances wildly upon the prone body of her husband Shiva.

Indigenous people, who were acutely aware of their dependency on nature's benevolence, dedicated enormous time and energy attuning the rhythms of their lives to those of the cosmic powers. This process always involved storytelling, often in conjunction with drumming and dancing. By evoking the image of a particular goddess and telling her stories, one could harmonize oneself with her—get on her rhythmic wave length, so to speak—attract her attention, and win her support. In all goddess-worshiping cultures, rhythm was held sacred, and in many religious ceremonies, very specific

musical rhythms were played to propitiate certain deities. In India and Bali, the stories of the deities are to this day simultaneously told, sung, and danced. Throughout human history, rhythmic chanting, singing, drumming, and dancing have served as a means of connecting with the steadying, unwavering heartbeat of the cosmic mother.

Although a goddess belongs to a specific culture—with its own values, beliefs, and religious customs—all goddesses are expressions of the sacred feminine. To speak of "the goddess," is to refer to the totality of energies, powers, and forms

ABOVE: *The Venus of Willendorf*, 30,000–25,000 B.C.E. Naturhistorisches Museum, Vienna.

attributed to the sacred feminine. For centuries, people have worshiped the goddess in one form while simultaneously acknowledging her many other forms as equally valid. For example, the second-century Roman Apuleius speaks of Isis as a cosmic power who is worshiped in many different places under many names. Similarly, Hindus reverently chant 1008 names of the goddess in recognition of the fact that her names, as well as her forms, are infinite.

The selections in this book are organized to render a portrait of the goddess as a universal spirit, without downplaying the differences that distinguish one goddess from another. Each section focuses on one important aspect of her being. The first three sections celebrate her as the source of the cosmos, and as the cosmos itself. In Part I, she appears in her most ancient and universal aspect as the great mother who creates the world and nurtures her creatures. Part II honors her as earth, water, fire, and air, the elements that sustain us throughout our lives. Part III celebrates her luminous presence in the sky as sun, moon, and stars.

Beginning with Part IV, we turn to the emotional and psychological forces through which the goddess becomes manifest in our lives. Perhaps the greatest of these forces is the power of love, essential to existence. Yet she who loves will also suffer; this is true not only of human beings but also of goddesses. Thus, Part V explores the suffering of the goddess and its causes. Part VI reveals the fascinating archetype of the black goddess, whose function is to help us come to terms with the "dark" realities of violence, destruction, and death. Part VII celebrates the marriage of the goddess, either to a god or to a worthy mortal. For us who have no religious images of the sacred marriage, the concept of an equal partnership between the divine feminine and masculine is an important and healing concept.

Judaism, Christianity, and Islam have no "official" goddesses. And yet, as revealed in Part VIII, the goddess still survives within these traditions, albeit in disguise. Finally, the selections in Part IX evoke the goddess as a faithful friend who accompanies the soul through all of life's vicissitudes and lovingly guides it towards the light of truth.

Like the writings, the images we selected for this volume seek to convey, not only how various goddesses are envisioned, but also (and perhaps even more importantly) what they *feel* like—what mood they evoke, what qualities they embody, who they are beyond their surface appearance. The art is not meant to illustrate the stories. Rather, our intention was to let images and stories become equal partners in a mutually inspiring dialogue. Our hope is that each will deepen and enrich our appreciation of the other.

Besides celebrating the goddess, this book also celebrates the enduring, timeless power of storytelling. Goddesses have always fed our imaginations, comforted our hearts, and awakened our souls with their captivating stories and alluring images. Today, their images continue to inspire storytellers, writers, and poets such as Clarissa Pinkola Estés, Carolyn Edwards, and Lucille Clifton.

Many of the stories in this book come from cultures which, even to this day, maintain a rich oral tradition. In these societies, storytelling is much more than a form of entertainment. Stories are the principal means of communicating religious, ethical, and mythological heritage. Through stories, the elders educate the youth; and through stories, the young remember and preserve the wisdom that has been passed down to them from the elders. Stories create community and, in times of

10

crisis, often enable us to endure and survive. Many of the stories and hymns gathered in this book were once told or chanted in a ritual context. Pieces like the Tibetan "Homages to the Twenty-One Tārās," the Egyptian "Hymn to Nut," the Yoruban "Traditional Praise of Oya," or the Sumerian hymn to the goddess Inanna as "Lady of the Evening" were designed to propitiate and invoke the goddess.

The world of mass media has made us voracious consumers of stories. We gobble them up, discard them, and are hungry for more. But this approach does not work with myths. A myth needs to be lived with for a long time. It must be looked at from different perspectives, digested, absorbed, and folded into the imagination. In a sense, each one of us must recreate a myth for ourselves. Then, its meaning and its particular significance for each personal journey will gradually emerge. Sacred stories are not intended to be told once, but to be told and retold over and over so that they acquire a patina. Why do Christians tell the story of Christ's birth every year? Surely not because they have forgotten it, but because they know that telling the old, familiar story is a way of evoking the Christ spirit in their minds and hearts, and because the retelling brings a special balm to the soul.

In choosing selections for this book, I essentially used the criteria of a storyteller; I aimed to intrigue the reader and, at the same time, reveal the complexities of the goddess, who might inspire love or arouse loathing but who should never leave us cold. In one way or another, her world should mirror our own. For example, few of us have ever fallen in love with a snow goddess, as one man does in the Japanese tale "Shiratamahime"; but we may have experienced a love affair that appeared like a mira-culous blessing, then melted away, leaving us both grateful and saddened.

But is Shiratamahime really a goddess? That depends on the definition of the term. A dictionary defines a goddess as "a female being of supernatural powers or attributes." But many cultures do not conceive of matter and spirit as separate, nor do they distinguish between "natural" and "supernatural" phenomena. Read the stories of indigenous tribes, and you will soon realize that to them, everything, from the flight patterns of birds to the cycles of the moon, is miraculous, sacred, and suffused with spiritual presence. In their world, nothing is "supernatural," least of all a goddess, who represents the very essence of natural power. They perceive spirit as a stream that flows through all things, uniting plants, animals, humans, and spirits. This unity makes it possible for different species to communicate with each other and allows one species to transform into another. "Huiio the Rainbow Snake," for example, is both an ordinary human being, a snake, and a goddess. In Huiio's story, as in many other myths, the goddess cannot be clearly distinguished from nature, spirits, fairies, animal allies, and heroines.

O ver the years, I have developed great respect for the power that sacred stories and sacred images exert upon us. Sometimes, as happened with my encounter with Inanna, a particular story haunts us like a strange dream. Then, we know it has spoken to our unconscious. It has held up a mirror in which we have caught a glimpse of ourselves. If you see nothing of yourself reflected in a myth, you may want to put it aside—it is probably not a useful mirror. But if you feel a spark of interest in a certain story, pursue it. Unlike the transcendent Western father-god, who tends to be distant and inaccessible, the goddess invites our identification, for her function is to mirror the hidden wellsprings of our own nature.

In recent Western history, the psychologist Carl Jung was one of the first to use

OVERLEAF: *Sarsavati,* Goddess of Learning, c. 1860. Victoria & Albert Museum, London.

myths as mirrors of the human psyche, thereby building a bridge between religion, mythology, and psychology. He found that the human psyche contains what he called archetypes, powers that affect us all and are evoked by certain symbols or images. For example, Aphrodite is the Greek version of a universal archetype who is worshiped as Lakshmi in India, as Erzulie in Haiti, as Oshun in Africa. Wherever this goddess appears, she is associated not only with love, luxury, pleasure, and beauty, but also with water, flowers, and gold.

The way similar stories and deities tend to appear in quite diverse cultures is one of the most intriguing aspects of goddess mythology. As you peruse this book, you will begin to see that goddesses are not really the clearly defined entities we might take them to be. They are more like powerful currents that flow through the depths of human consciousness, sometimes mingling and merging with other currents, sometimes forking off and going their separate ways. From the perspective of Jungian psychology, we might define a goddess as an archetypal power, as perceived through the eyes of a particular people, at a given point in space and time. By approaching myths as mirrors of the human psyche, archetypal psychology has done much to help us appreciate the goddesses of the world.

In Part III, we tell an old Japanese myth about how Amaterasu the sun goddess gets insulted and withdraws into a cave, leaving the world in darkness. She refuses to emerge until she catches sight of her own reflection in a mirror, overjoyed by the recognition of her own radiant beauty. Amaterasu's story, like all goddess myths, is also a story about the soul. In times of trial, transition, or crisis, sacred stories and images can draw forth the soul and entice it to re-engage in life. For tens, perhaps hundreds of thousands of years, people have used storytelling and art in this way, as medicine for the soul, and, even today, this medicine has lost none of its potency.

For women in particular, the images and stories of the goddess act like mirrors that reflect their innermost essence. Mirrors are, in fact, sacred to the Greek goddess Aphrodite, who is often shown gazing at the reflection of her own beauty with evident delight. This is more than mere vanity. We all need mirrors that reveal our true beauty to us. Women need images that validate their femininity, their sensuousness, and their mysterious magic and that reveal the sacred dimensions of their own gender. It is therefore only natural that the goddess should have a special significance for women who long to know that they, too, are made in the divine image. In India, for example, where the worship of the goddess is still strong, women experience her not as a distant, abstract idea, but as a living reality to which they feel intimately connected. Their religion teaches them to believe that every woman is a manifestation of the goddess.

As you look through this book, you will see a wide variety of female shapes and forms, all of them sacred, all objects of great devotion and worship. Such images provide a much-needed reminder that if we can only look beyond the narrow (and usually unobtainable) standards that our culture upholds for women, we will find many alternative images of beauty. In other ways, too, the stories of the goddess encourage women to own the full breadth of their potential. Figures like Durga the Warrior Queen, for example, honor qualities that our society often considers "unfeminine," such as anger, physical strength, and courage.

But the goddess also speaks to men, as well as to women, and many men feel deeply connected to her. We must remember that those qualities which our culture considers typically feminine (such as gentleness, nurturance, compassion, and tenderness) are actually the birthright of all human beings, male *and* female. The recent

OPPOSITE: *Artemis*, from the Parthenon, 5th B.C.E. Acropolis Museum, Athens.

interest in the goddess reflects a growing awareness that our culture is out of balance and that, at this point in history, we need to consciously reconnect with the "feminine" aspects of our being.

Because most goddesses are human as well as divine, they are often far from perfect, even by the standards of their own culture. Some are tender and compassionate, while others, like Athena and Artemis, may treat the unfortunate mortals who displease them with outright cruelty. As we suffer, so do goddesses, and for a similar variety of reasons. They have physical problems, emotional ups and downs, moments of doubt and confusion, failure and defeat. Like ourselves, they struggle and sometimes fail to achieve their goals, and can be moody and difficult. Even their immortality is no sure thing; like the moon, their life force waxes and wanes.

Such human qualities make it easy to feel a sense of kinship with certain goddesses. Our heart aches for Demeter as she grieves over the abduction of her daughter Persephone, or for Macha who is publicly humiliated at the height of her pregnancy. Such vulnerabilites hold the key to the nature of the goddess and reflect the fact that her worshipers conceive of her as both human and divine. In a Gnostic scripture called *The Thunder, Perfect Mind*, the goddess points out her own paradoxical nature: "I am the first and the last. I am the honored one and the scorned one. I am the whore and the holy one."

And so, the image of the goddess—not as a substitute for the male god, but as his complement and counterpart—invites us to contemplate the possibility that divinity and humanity can coexist. Texts like the Hindu "Tantric Praise of the Goddess" emphatically declare that the goddess resides within all of us, which means that we, too, are both human and divine—we are gods and goddesses who have merely lost sight of our own divinity.

Patriarchal religion might appear to have banished the goddess for good, but this is not so; great shapeshifter that she is, she has simply changed forms once again. To recognize her within our contemporary world, we must remember what she represents—the web, the principle of relationship, the universe as a hologram, in which every particle reflects and interconnects with every other particle, the intelligence that creates and animates the entire universe. During the last decades, these ancient concepts have sprung to life again.

Surprisingly, subatomic physics is, in fact, one of the most important arenas in which concepts of ancient goddess religion have re-emerged. Ever since the great physicists Heisenberg and Einstein advanced their theories, science has been reconceptualizing the universe as a whole in which every particle relates to every other particle and which, in Einstein's words, "reveals an intelligence of such superiority that, in comparison with it, the highest intelligence of human beings is an utterly insignificant reflection." Similarly, physicist Fritjof Capra claims that quantum theory "reveals a basic oneness of the universe," which is one of the basic tenets of many goddess-centered religions. He goes on to describe nature "as a complicated web of relations between the various parts of the whole." Such declarations, coming from a modern scientist, make us appreciate the Navajo vision of a spider goddess who weaves the universal web.

One cannot speak of the return of the goddess without mentioning ecology. In recent decades, Gaia, the Greek Goddess of the Earth, has become the symbol and focal point for a wide array of scientists, ecologists, and philosophers who are seek-

16

ABOVE: *Mother and Child*,
12th century. Indian
Museum, Calcutta.

ing ways to heal the damaged ecosystems of the earth. This "Gaia" movement began when James Lovelock offered his hypothesis that our planet might be a giant, self-regulating, intelligent organism—or, in other words, a goddess.

The strength of the sacred feminine lies in her capacity for communion, communication, and connection. Today, her voice is calling us to remember our connection with nature and our oneness with the cosmos. It is therefore no coincidence that the re-emergence of the goddess in our times has coincided with an urgent call to stop exploiting and polluting the environment and to mend our wounded relationship with nature. Forced to grapple with the planetary crisis, we are realizing that our own survival depends upon the survival of the earth's forests, oceans, and ecosystems. Simultaneously, we are realizing how much we can learn from the wisdom of indigenous people, many of whom lived in harmony with their land for thousands of years.

The love of goddesses is deeply ingrained in our collective psyche. Even though Western religion has seemingly done away with the goddess, people stubbornly continue to create and worship new goddesses, and the sacred feminine continues to return in ever new forms. The goddess is indeed immortal, and her ability to inspire us is as strong today as it was thirty thousand years ago, when our ancestors painted her on the walls of caves and sculpted her out of rock. We may no longer believe in an external goddess, yet the compelling power of the archetype will never cease to inspire and move us.

17

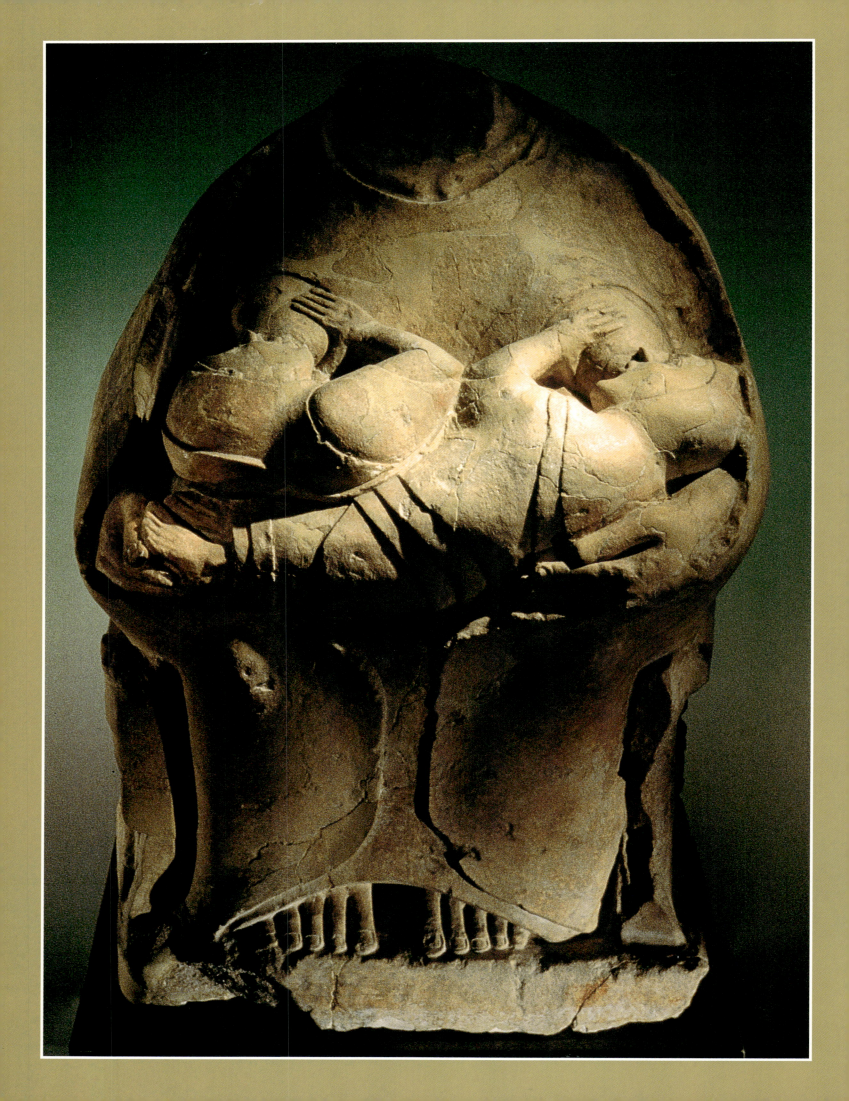

I

Mother of the Universe

ILLIONS OF YEARS OF EVOLUTIONARY HISTORY HAVE IMPRINTED
the memory of woman as source of life, sustenance, and protection deep within our
collective psyche. To a child, the mother is everything—protection, food, love, and intimacy.
The closeness of a child's bond with the mother is rarely matched by the father, for not even
the most devoted father can carry a baby within his belly or feed it from his own body. The
mother, the child's first image of divinity, leaves an unequaled and lasting imprint on her child's psyche. "As a
mother at the risk of her life watches over her only child," the Buddha told his followers, "so let everyone cultivate
a boundlessly compassionate mind toward all beings."

Humanity's first images of divine power were great mother goddesses with wide hips, fertile bellies, and full
breasts. Nearly all human images dating from 30,000 to 5000 B.C.E. are female, a reflection of the fact that our
prehistoric ancestors revered women and conceived of the divine as a maternal power who nurtured and provided
for them. To them, the Great Mother was the source of life and sustenance. She was nature, and she was the
creative mystery made manifest in every birthing mother. In "Spider Woman Creates the World" she is the
primordial power that sings the universe into life, while in the South American myth "Coadidop" she creates
man by puffing smoke and forms the earth by squeezing milk from her breast. To this day, the Tibetan people
worship the goddess Tārā as an eternal mother who gives their lives "a foundation like the earth."

Approximately four thousand years ago, patriarchy became the dominant social model, and the ancient
mother gods were rejected in favor of male father gods. Still, traces of more ancient beliefs endured. Eurynome,
for example, was originally a goddess of the Pelasgian people, pre-Hellenic inhabitants of Greece who came from
Palestine to Greece around 3500 B.C.E. Similarly, the Aztecs continued to revere Coatlicue, the ancient mother of
the gods, alongside more prominent male gods; and Native Americans never ceased to honor the first mothers of
the people.

You may note that many snakes slither through the myths of the goddess. Ngalyod and Huiio are serpents,
as is Eurynome's lover Ophion. Because snakes shed their skin, they symbolize nature's regenerative powers, a
power that is held sacred in all goddess religions. As the divine is the source of both life and death, so a snake's
venom can both heal and harm. Universally worshiped as emblems of divinity, snakes are the special allies of
the goddess.

19

OPPOSITE: Statue, possibly *Night feeding her children Sleep and Death*. Regional Archaeological Museum, Syracuse, Sicily.

Spider Woman
Creates the World

———◆———

NAVAJO

Told by Paula Gunn Allen

Ooma-oo, long ago. The Spider was in the place where only she was. There was no light or dark, there was no warm wind, no rain or thunder. There was no cold, no ice or snow. There was only the Spider. She was a great wise woman, whose powers are beyond imagining. No medicine person, no conjurer or shaman, no witch or sorcerer, no scientist or inventor can imagine how great her power is. Her power is complete and total. It is pure, and cleaner than the void. It is the power of thought, we say, but not the kind of thought people do all the time. It's like the power of dream, but more pure. Like the spirit of vision, but more clear. It has no shape or movement, because it just is. It is the power that creates all that is, and it is the power of all that is.

In that place where she was alone and complete with her power, she thought about her power, how it sang to her, how she dreamed from it, how she wished to have someone to share the songdream with her. Not because she was lonely, but because the power's song was so complete, she wished for there to be others who could also know it. She knew this was the power's wish just as it was hers. For she and her power were together and of one mind. They were two, but they were the same thing.

So she thought to the power once and knew a rippling, a wrinkling within. Then she knew she was old, and wrinkled, and that the power's first song was a song of great age. The wrinkling became tighter, more spidery, stronger. It became in one place. She named that place Northwest. She knew the wrinkling had folded up on itself, enfolded on itself. She knew much of the universe, the great power, was contained within. Later the earth would be ripples and wrinkles, spidery lines of power folded and enfolded into a tight moving shape, and it would also hold the great power within, like a mother holds new life. Others would also imitate this time: walnuts and acorns, apples and pineapples, cactuses and mountains, even the oceans would be like that. And humans, five-fingered beings, would grow wrinkled in their skin and brains, in honor of this time when she and the power made a song to form new life, new beings.

She was so happy with what she knew, so full of awe at the beauty of the song, that she thought again. And again she knew the rippling, the wrinkling, the running of spidery lines along the edges of the forming pouch of the power's song, the folding and enfolding into a shape that held some of the power of all that is within. She knew that the place of that pouch, that bundle of her thought, her song, was in the Northeast. So humming and singing, she shaped them. Humming and singing, she placed them where they

OPPOSITE: *Corn Prayer Paths I,*
Dan V. Lomahaftewa, 1994.

belonged. That was how the directions came into being. How the seasons came to be.

She thought in her power to each of the bundles and continued singing. She sang and sang. She sang the power that was her heart, the movement that is the multiverse and its dancing. The power that is everywhere and that has no name or body, but that is just the power, the mystery. She sang, and the bundles began to move. They began to sing, to echo her song, to join it. They sang their heart's song, that was the same as Spider's heart song, that was the heart song of great mystery, the power that moves. The song seemed to deepen as she heard other hearts singing. The song seemed more free, it seemed stronger. The two who rose up from the bundles with their singing each had a bundle of her own. And in each bundle the life of the universe rested, waiting until it was sung into life.

Spider named each of the beings; one she named Ic'sts'ity and the other she named Nau'ts'ity. They were not human beings, but supernatural beings. They did not have physical bodies because they were much vaster than even a planet, even a star. A star couldn't contain all they were and knew, all they thought.

Spider told each of them that they were to make more beings, so that the song could go on and on, so that she and the power could share the beauty with more and more beings. She told them that they would take from their pouches a part of the song and would sing it into fullness, into ripeness. They would need to sing the mystery in the way of thought to bring the lives in their bundles into being. They understood her directions because they were the song and the mystery. All of it and only a small piece of it. It was much vaster than they, and yet they could sing it into different shapes of being, different ways of singing, different parts of the great being song.

Ic'sts'ity began to sing a new chant: *way-a-hiyo, way-a-hiyo, way-a-hiyo, way-a way-ay-o*. She sang and sang, thinking to her bundle, and around them as she sang swirling, whirling globes of light began to form. They began pushing outward in a great whirling

spiral, a great wheeling multitude of stars, all singing as they circled and wheeled like great geese upon the void. As they spiraled outward, they grew larger and brighter. Around and around the still, invisible center where Spider, Ic'sts'ity and Nau'ts'ity sang. They whirled, the outer ones flinging themselves farther and farther from the center, great arms forming in the spiral dance, following the lines of the song, the lines of the power, reaching out farther and farther into the mystery, carrying the song in their light, in their fingers, making both the darkness and the light as they danced, finding the power coming to them from the darkness, flinging it out from them in the light. The power danced in the void, in the light, in the midnight reaches of the gleaming dark. It sang.

Then Nau'ts'ity began to sing her thought to her bundle. *Aam-i-humm, humm, humm, aam-i-humm, humm, humm, aam-i-o, o, o, o, aam-i-o, o, o, o, aam-i-o.* The song changed again as Spider and Ic'sts'ity joined her song, and from the brilliant globes of light new shapes spun out, dancing around and around the lights, giving shape and solidity to the darkness, carrying the spin of the song into new places, more solid, more full. The planets sang, new beings awakening, joining their minds and hearts to the huge chorus, singing their parts of the heart song. The power shaped and dipped, wheeled and danced, and over vast reaches it took on forms it hadn't known.

Satisfied with their work, Spider turned to her granddaughters and smiled as she chanted. In their begetting they would make many worlds, and upon some of them human beings would sing in the same way as she and her granddaughter-sisters sang. On those same worlds, feathered beings would swoop and wheel as the great fires around her did. And on them, life would press its way from the place of the Spider singing into the place of individual songs. And that would be far away from the place where the three stood. It would be right among them as they stood and sang in the void, surrounded by the wheeling lights and the great swooping dark.

EURYNOME

GREEK

Told by Erica Meade

LEFT: *Goddess*,
Myceneaen, 14th
century B.C.E.
Louvre, Paris.

In the beginning there was only Chaos . . . coiled serpents in cold darkness. In the beginning there was only cold and tangled Chaos in the dark. The only sound was Eurynome's breath skirling through the twisted nothing where it all began. The only heat was the breath steaming in her breast. The only notion was the no-notion of her dream. She reached out and seized hold of two tails of Chaos, one in each hand. She stretched and awoke from her dream. The first tail of Chaos was fluid and light. She released it above and called it Sky. Sky spread across the Great Above covering all. "It is good!" cried Eurynome, Sky Maker. She held the second tail of Chaos in her other hand. She released it below and called it Sea. Sea tumbled downward. Fluid and heavy, falling across the Great Below, covering all. "It is smooth, and it is good!" sang Eurynome, Sea Maker.

Then Eurynome began to dance. She danced along the Sea, whirling and kicking, casting water beads against Sky. She reeled harder and faster, plow-

OPPOSITE: *The Island of Gold*
(The Island of Hyeres),
Henri-Edmond Cross, late 19th or early
20th century. Musée d'Orsay, Paris.

ing deep furrows where water meets air. "It is good!" sang Eurynome, First Dancer. The faster she danced, the higher the wake rose up behind her. When she danced swiftly, the air followed, caressing her skin, tickling her. When she leapt swiftly to the North, she produced the North Wind. The swifter she turned, the harder the wind whipped and furled her hair. She seized hold of the wind, fought it, twisted it, kneaded it, braided it. Out of wind she made bone and flesh: the great serpent of the North Wind, Ophion.

Eurynome and Ophion danced together on the Sea. She changed herself into a dove and flew high above to swoop down to him. He surged from under the waves to rise up to her. He entered and entwined her. She enfolded him with her wings and engulfed him with her dark folds. Swooping and surging. Entering, entwining, enfolding, engulfing. Eurynome, First Dancer, played and coupled with Ophion, until exhausted, she floated on the Sea and fell asleep. Eurynome swelled large and ripe with the fruits of their bond. She awoke alone, spread her dove wings and cried. Spasms churned through her, opening her flesh, thrusting the egg of the universe from her womb. It floated on the waves of the Sea. Eurynome, First Mother, sang, "Open, sweet egg, open." She ached to see what would hatch. She nudged the egg, pushed it, tapped it, kicked it. But the egg held firm.

Eurynome called at the top of her voice, summoning the serpent of the North Wind. Ophion came to her from across the Sea. "Ophion," she sang. "Coil 'round the egg. Rend it in two!" The great serpent coiled 'round: one, two, three. He squeezed tightly, but the egg held firm. "Ophion, coil 'round again." The serpent wound again: four, five, six, squeezed tightly, but the egg held firm. "Ophion, you have one length left. Coil 'round again and squeeze!" The great serpent coiled 'round. The seventh time he wrapped around, the world egg cracked in two. The seventh time the serpent wound, the world egg fell in two.

The two halves of the world egg floated like pearly bowls on the Sea. Eurynome watched to see what emerged. The stars flew out and scattered like seeds across the Sky. The Moon drifted up to center Sky shedding infinite, ghostly petals on the Sea. Then the bold Sun shot out, blinding the Sky. The planets drifted up and found their places. Earth spilled forth with its mountains, valleys, plains, and rivers. Eurynome stepped upon the Earth. "It is firm, and it is good!" sang the Mother of All Things.

Eurynome and Ophion climbed to the highest peak in the center of creation, Mt. Olympus. They basked under Sky's new brilliance. They savored the fragrance of Earth, adored the sweetness of honey, and the songs of mating birds and rushing brooks.

But Ophion grew bored with beauty and pleasure—bored with the drone of bee to poppy, hummingbird to lupine, stag to hind, blossom to fruit, fruit to seed, seed to Earth, sprout to tree and 'round. He wanted more than to be part of creation. He wished to claim authorship. He began whispering to birds, "Creation is mine." Soon he hollered from hilltops, "I am Ophion, Maker of All Things! I rose up from Chaos. I made Sky and Sea. I produced the egg of the universe! I am Ophion, creator of Heaven and Earth. All things come from me!"

Eurynome—she who separated the limbs of Chaos, produced the wind, created the serpent, laid the egg of the universe, and gestated all things—had no patience for the braggart or his false claims. Right then and there, she kicked him in the teeth and banished him to a pit at the edge of the world. He may be there still.

Eurynome looked out from Mt. Olympus, and gazed upon creation. For the first time she noticed something was missing. Earth's creatures lived with mates and families. The mare had the stallion, the goose had the gander, and the lion had her pride, but the great eternal planets stood alone. They kept to their solitary, sterile courses in the Sky. Eurynome, too, stood alone. Ophion was not with her, he was of her. Her true companion was longing, and out of longing, she completed creation.

She made a queen and a king to rule each planet, crafting pairs to meld poles: She and He, north and south, attracting, gravitating, whirling, uniting. Male enveloping female, female penetrating male—one gestating the other's seed—ruling together in harmonic dissonance, tender disagreement, fiery union.

Eurynome stood back to look at the planets. "It is good!" said the Mother of All Things. "They dance and turn—they quarrel and make up. It is good." Then Eurynome was satisfied. She gazed out from Mt. Olympus and she rested.

The Making of the World

HURON

In the beginning there was nothing but water, a wide sea, which was peopled by various animals of the kind that live in and upon the water. It happened then that a woman fell down from the upper world. It is supposed that she was, by some mischance, pushed down by her husband through a rift in the sky. Though styled a woman, she was a divine personage. Two loons, which were flying over the water, happened to look up and see her falling. To save her from drowning they hastened to place themselves beneath her, joining their bodies together so as to form a cushion for her to rest on. In this way they held her up, while they cried with a loud voice to summon the other animals to their aid. The cry of the loon can be heard to a great distance, and the other creatures of the sea heard it, and assembled to learn the cause of the summons. Then came the tortoise, a mighty animal, which consented to relieve the loons of their burden. They placed the woman on the back of the tortoise, charging him to take care of her. The tortoise then called the other animals to a grand council, to determine what should be done to preserve the life of the woman. They decided that she must have earth to live on. The tortoise directed them all to dive to the bottom of the sea and endeavor to bring up some earth. Many attempted it—the beaver, the musk-rat, the diver, and others—but without success. Some remained so long below that when they rose they were dead. The tortoise searched their mouths, but could find no trace of earth. At last the toad went down, and after remaining a long time rose, exhausted and nearly dead. On searching his mouth the tortoise found in it some earth, which he gave to the woman. She took it and placed it carefully around the edge of the tortoise's shell. When thus placed, it became the beginning of dry land. The land grew and extended on every side, forming at last a great country, fit for vegetation. All was sustained by the tortoise, which still supports the earth.

When the woman fell she was pregnant with twins. When these came forth they evinced opposite dispositions, the one good, the other evil. Even before they were born the same characters were manifested. They struggled together, and their mother heard them disputing. The one declared his willingness to be born in the usual manner, while the other malignantly refused, and, breaking through his mother's side, killed her. She was buried, and from her body sprang the various vegetables which the new earth required to fit it for the habitation of man. From her head grew the pumpkin-vine, from her breasts the maize, and from her limbs the bean.

OPPOSITE: *Celestial Germinators,*
Dan V. Lomahaftewa, 1992.

COATLICUE

AZTEC

Translated by Edward Kissam

The Aztecs called Coatlicue the mother of all the gods and worshiped her as "Lady of the serpent skirt," mistress of both life and death. This hymn expresses the reverence and awe Coatlicue inspired.

Oh, golden flower opened up
     she is our mother
whose thighs are holy
     whose face is a dark mask.
She came from Tamoanchan,
     the first place
where all descended
     where all was born.
Oh, golden flower flowered
     she is our mother
whose thighs are holy
     whose face is a dark mask.
She came from Tamoanchan.
Oh, white flower opened up
     she is our mother
whose thighs are holy
     whose face is a dark mask.
She came from Tamoanchan,
     the first place
where all descended
     where all was born.
Oh, white flower flowered
     she is our mother
whose thighs are holy
     whose face is a dark mask.
She came from Tamoanchan.
She lights on the round cactus,
     she is our mother
the dark obsidian butterfly.
     Oh, we saw her as we
          wandered
Across the Nine Plains,
     she fed herself with deers'
          hearts.
She is our mother,
     the goddess earth. . . .

OPPOSITE: *Coatlicue*, the Earth Mother, late 15th century A.D. National Museum of Anthropology, Mexico City.

THE MYTH OF NGALYOD

AUSTRALIAN

Told by Louis A. Allen

Ngalyod, also known as the Old Mother,
is an archaic goddess of the Gunwinggu tribe in Australia.

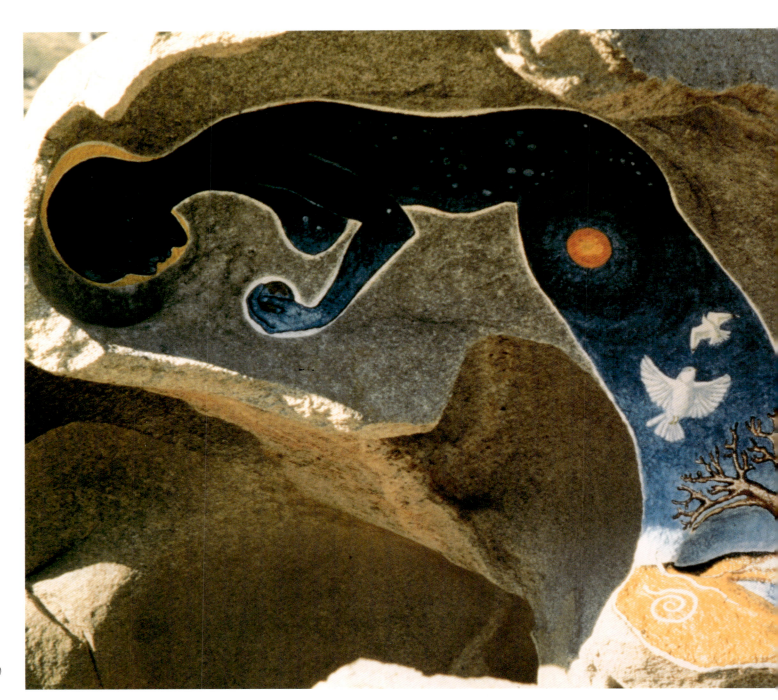

In the earliest days when time began, the sun brightened the earth and made it warm. Spirit beings lived then who sometimes transformed themselves into human form.

Chief among these spirits was the Great Rainbow Snake, Ngalyod, the Mother who created the world and who even today causes the plants and animals to multiply and the Gunwinggu women to bear many children. Sometimes, after the rain, you can see her arch her body and take on the colors of the rainbow where the water washes from sky to earth.

In the Dreamtime, Ngalyod turned herself into a woman called Waramurungundji and took Wuragog for her husband. The couple went from place to place in the Gunwinggu country, she carrying a digging stick and a net bag. Wuragog wished to have intercourse more often than Waramurungundji was willing, and they quarreled often about the matter. Finally, when Wuragog sought to lie with her, Waramurungundji turned herself into her snake form. However, Wuragog persisted, and from their union came the first people. The children grew quickly, and soon there were many camps of the Gunwinggu people. Waramurungundji continued to quarrel with Wuragog, but she cared for her children and tended to their needs even when they became men and women. "Be kind. Help one another," she told them as she traveled among their camps.

When drought came and her people hungered, Ngalyod sent food. When the water holes dried up, Ngalyod plunged her digging stick into the ground

LEFT: Cosmic Woman, Vijali, 1989. World Wheel Site 5, Tinos Island, Greece. Courtesy of the artist.

and spring water gushed forth. But this did not bring happiness to the people. They fought with one another, and the noise of their bickering was loud and unpleasant. Ngalyod heard and was concerned. "My children have not learned to live peacefully even though I have given them all they need," she said. She went to the camps to show them how to live together harmoniously. "I shall teach you songs and dances so that you may know how to live in peace," she told them. "You shall teach them to your children, and they also will know." So the people gathered and learned the sacred songs and rituals which their mother, Ngalyod, taught. But some quickly forgot her words.

Close by a tree-bordered lagoon lived an old man who had lost his wife. In the same camp lived a girl, his granddaughter, long of limb and firm-breasted. The old man hungered after her. One day he found a bee tree and brought back a bark container brimming with honey. "Come with me," he coaxed his grandchild. "You and I will eat the honey." They went into the bush, and the old man coaxed the girl into making love to him.

Ngalyod's anger was awakened, for this she had forbidden. She appeared to the old man in the form of the Rainbow Snake. "What you have done is bad," she rebuked him. "This place shall be taboo to you and to all men so that the people shall remember what I have said." So she drove him from that place.

The old man wandered about for many days. Finally, he encountered a group of people gathered to perform a sacred ceremony. The ritual was to last for a day and a night, so the people had caught many fish and cooked them in advance.

"These fish are sacred; they may be eaten only during the ceremony," the song leader announced.

The men danced the ritual dances, and the women sang the sacred songs far into the night. Their noise rose to a clamor. The mothers neglected to feed their children, who began to cry from hunger. Their wails finally reached the hearing of Ngalyod. "This is not right," she decided and called to the people to moderate their noise and feed their children. But they paid no attention. The dancing quickened, the songs intensified.

A little orphan boy stood up and began to wander about the fire, sobbing from the pangs that gripped his empty stomach. Seeing the fish that had been prepared, he reached out for it. But one of the men caught his hand and pushed him aside, saying, "It is sacred. You may not eat it." All through the night and well into the morning the orphan cried.

Ngalyod saw the child's suffering, and her anger

was great. She sent a flood to punish the people. The ground became soft and wet. The water rose higher and higher. The dancers stopped. The singers fell silent. The water became a flood. Some of the people climbed rocks, others trees, as they tried to escape. The old man scrambled up a tall ironwood tree and huddled in its highest branches. He continued to chant the sacred songs, trusting their power to arrest the flood.

Ngalyod came through the water to survey her handiwork. The old man broke off his song and clung close to the tree, hoping the great snake would not notice him. Just then a mosquito flew by and began to buzz around his nose. The old man slapped at it as gently as he could, but even that small noise Ngalyod heard. She lifted her head and saw the old man. "You shall die, for you have done wrong," she pronounced and swallowed him.

Ngalyod, the Great Rainbow Snake, continued to travel across the country teaching her children. At one place, a river fell over a cliff and made a waterfall. A large pool had formed at the top where the people came to fish. Often an unwary fisherman would lose his footing on the steep banks of the pool and be carried over the falls to his death.

"My children must learn to avoid this place," Ngalyod said.

She went to the pool and swallowed the first fisherman she saw. Then she approached his companion and swallowed him. The third fisherman saw her coming and turned to flee.

"This place is forbidden to you and your people. You shall fish only at the stream below the falling water," called out Ngalyod after him.

From that time on, fishermen went to the stream below and never returned to the pool.

Ngalyod continued her travels among the camps of her children. At another place, two girls had gathered some round yams, *mangindjak*, and had lit a fire to cook them. As they were slicing the yams, their brother stopped by.

"What are you doing?" he inquired.

"Cooking yams," they replied.

"I am hungry. I will share your yams," suggested the brother. He sat down and began to fondle one of the sisters. "Come into the bush with me," he invited.

The girl resisted. "I cannot. It is forbidden. You are my brother."

When he tried to force her, both sisters set upon him and beat him. "Let me be!" he cried at last. "I would do you no harm."

As soon as they released him, the infuriated

brother ran to the pile of yams and urinated on them. "You are spoiling our food, brother," cried the girls. They picked up the yams and carried them to the stream to wash. But no matter how vigorously they scrubbed, the yams remained bitter and inedible.

The brother ran off into the bush, where he met Ngalyod. "Brother shall not lie with sister," she pronounced and promptly swallowed him.

Then Ngalyod returned to the sisters, who were still lamenting the loss of their yams. "Make a bag of

reeds and place the yams in it. Put it in the quiet water by the side of the stream to soak. Tomorrow the bad taste will be gone." The sisters did as Ngalyod directed, and by morning the yams were once again sweet in the mouth.

Later, the sisters told their people what had happened. So well did they listen and remember that even today the story is repeated around Gunwinggu camp fires, and all know what their mother, Ngalyod, the Great Rainbow Snake, said and did in the Dreamtime.

ABOVE: *Rainbow Serpent Dreaming*, Ginger Tjakamarra, painted with the assistance of his wife, Wingie Napaltjarri, 1989. Courbally Stourton Contemporary Art, London.

COADIDOP

TARIANA

Adapted by John Bierhorst

When earth did not yet exist, they say, a young girl, a virgin, lived alone in the empty space. Her name was Coadidop (grandmother of the days).

She said, "I live alone in the world, I want earth and people." She looked for tobacco, for smoke. She took the two large bones from her right and left legs to make the cigar holder, drew the tobacco from her body, and made a large cigar. She squeezed her milk onto the cigar, which she placed in the holder. She puffed on the cigar, wanting to give birth to people. She also created *ipadú* (the coca plant). She took the *ipadú* and smoked the cigar.

The smoke produced a thunderclap and a flash of lightning. The image of a man appeared and immediately vanished. She puffed again. Thunder and a flash of light came, then disappeared. The third time she puffed, the smoke changed into a human body. "This one is Thunder," she said. "You are son of Thunder and Thunder itself. You are my grandson. I have created you. I will give you power. You will be able to make everything you wish in the world." This Thunder was called Enu.

The two lived alone. She said, "I have made you as a man. As a man you will be able to do everything, good and evil. I am a woman. I command you to create companions for yourself in order to live well. And I will create my own companions."

When Enu had made three brother Thunders and the Creator had made two female companions for herself, she took a cord, circled her head, laid the cord down, divided it in half, and squeezed her breast. Her milk fell into the circle and formed the earth. The next day a large field had taken shape in that earth. Then she gave the earth to the women so that they could work it. She said, "With this earth you can live."

LEFT: *Untitled,* Francisco Toledo, c. 1966.
David Douglas Duncan Collection.
Courtesy of Associated American Artists.

35

HUIIO THE RAINBOW SNAKE

—◆—

ORINOCO

Told by Marc de Civrieux
Translated by David M. Guss

This creation myth begins with a god called Wanadi, who lives in Kahuña, the highest regions of heaven. There he guards a stone-like egg called Huehanna, which contains the unborn people of the earth.

Nuna, the evil, voracious moon, was hungry and devised a plan to steal Huehanna and devour the people. Nuna went up to Kahuña, to the highest part, up to the door of the Wanadi from there. It never opens. No one goes in the house. No one sees Wanadi. You can only speak with the guards at the door.

Nuna lied when he got there. "I'm Wanadi, the one from the Earth," he said. "I came for Huehanna. I'm going to make people there." . . .

The guards called Nuna to the door and they gave him Huehanna.

Now Nuna went back down, happy. He wanted people like Wanadi, but just to eat them. He was hungry. He was evil. He thought like Mado, the jaguar: "There's no food. Okay. I'll eat people."

That's the way his evilness got started.

When Nuna got home, he thought: "I'm going to eat." That man's sister lived in the same house. She was a beautiful young girl. Her name was Frimene.

"Where were you? What's that?"

"In Kahuña," he said. "That's Huehanna."

"It's beautiful. It looks like a tinamou egg," the girl said.

Huehanna was buzzing like a beehive. People were dancing and singing in there. You could hear voices.

"I want it!" the girl thought. "It's filled with people who haven't been born." She knew Nuna had stolen it.

"I can't let him eat them. I'll save them. I'll keep them myself. I don't want to give them back to Wanadi. I'm going to raise them. I'll hatch them. I'll be their mother." That's what the girl thought to herself when she saw Huehanna. She didn't say anything; she just thought it.

Now Nuna said: "I'm going over there. Keep Huehanna in the house. Watch it. Wanadi may come looking for it. If he comes, say: 'I don't know anything. I haven't seen a thing.'"

"Okay," said the sister.

When the man left, the girl hid Huehanna in her vagina, thinking: "It's done. I'll keep them all in my belly. They'll be born. I'm going to be their mother." She rubbed her stomach. She was happy. She listened to the dancing and the shouts of laughter of Wanadi's little people. They were going to populate the Earth.

When the man returned, he looked for Huehanna. It wasn't there. He got angry, really angry.

"Did Wanadi come? Did he take it?"

"I haven't seen anyone," she said. "I don't know anything."

He beat her. Then Nuna saw his sister's stomach. It was round as if she were pregnant. He just looked and looked. He knew what it was. He didn't say anything.

She turned her back. She didn't want him to hear or see. "I'm going," she said. "I'm tired. I'm going to get in my hammock."

She left. Night came. Now she was alone. She listened to her stomach. She listened to the voices and the drums, the songs and the horns. It was her children. She fell asleep.

Then she woke up. She opened her eyes. She couldn't see anything. There was no sun. Everything was dark and quiet. She heard a dull sound, very faintly. It was like steps. They were coming closer. She couldn't see. She just heard them. She was frightened. "Who could it be?" she thought. The steps were coming toward the hammock. They were coming very, very slowly.

When they arrived, a big object, like a body, fell on the hammock. It was a man. That girl was scared. He didn't say anything.

She didn't hear anything. Hands were moving all over her, landing here and there like bees on the girl's body. They were feeling and groping and searching.

You could just barely hear Huehanna softly humming below. The girl squeezed her legs shut to protect her children. The hands tried to spread them. Impossible. They couldn't.

The sun hadn't come up when that man jumped out of the hammock and went away. He didn't say anything, just that sound, like very, very slow steps. Now the sun rose. Then the girl got up.

"What happened?" she thought. "Was it a dream? Who was it? Odosha? Wanadi looking for his children? Nuna hungry? Now I'm going to find out."

She went to find some *caruto* oil. She put it in a gourd.

Now, in memory of that time, our women paint the inside of their gourds with *caruto*.

When night came, the girl painted herself. She painted her face, her legs, her entire body with *caruto*. She turned black with *caruto*. Then she got in her hammock and went to sleep.

When she woke up, she heard the steps in the dark. They were slowly coming toward her again. The man fell on her. Hands were feeling and groping and searching. They took hold of the girl's legs. They wanted to force open the cave. They wanted Huehanna. The girl squeezed her legs shut. The people inside Huehanna were spun around. A hand reached up. It touched Huehanna. It tried to grab it. The girl fought back. She started to bleed. She bled a lot.

That's why our women bleed each time Nuna passes, as a reminder.

When the sun came up, the girl jumped out of her hammock. She was alone again. "Now I'm going to find out," she thought. She went out to look.

On her way, she met her brother, hidden in a field, crouched down beside a trap.

"What are you doing?" she asked.

"Don't make any noise," he answered. "I'm hunting. I'm hungry. Some people are coming."

He was hunting people as if they were animals.

As he spoke, he showed his face. It was stained with *caruto*, his body too. His hands were all black with *caruto*.

"It was him," the girl said to herself. "I've found him out."

She didn't say anything. She just left.

Now that girl thought: "I can't live in Nunaña anymore."

She went back home. She gathered up her things

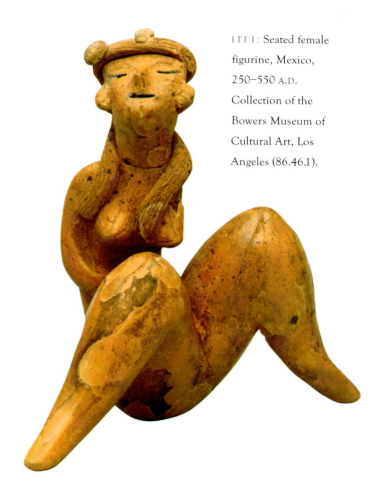

LEFT: Seated female figurine, Mexico, 250–550 A.D. Collection of the Bowers Museum of Cultural Art, Los Angeles (86.46.1).

and she fled.

Now Nuna has a stained face. When it's full, we look at the moon. We can still see those stains on his face. They're a reminder of the beginning. I've seen them. You can too.

That's the way the old ones tell it. Okay.

That woman fled into the jungle, her children in her stomach, her arms filled with gourds and baskets. She was running. As she ran, she dropped a gourd. When it hit the ground, it turned into Wiwiio, the tree duck. Another one fell. It turned into Kahiuwai, the anhinga. That's the way they were born. The woman went on running and came to the Uriñaku (Orinoco). She couldn't get across it.

"Okay," she said. "I can't get across. The water will be my path."

She went into the water. She fled from her brother's house swimming.

She said: "I'm the Water Mistress, the River Mother." Then she changed into Huiio, the Great Snake, the Water Mistress. She went beneath the water and hid. You couldn't see her anymore. Now she built her house at the bottom of the rapids.

The Orinoco had just been born. All the rivers

were just starting to flow then. . . . Now Huiio was born. She made herself mistress of the new water which was flowing everywhere.

Wanadi was angry. His Huehanna had been stolen. He went looking for it. He asked the people. He went around asking. No one knew.

He went to Nuna's house. He asked him about Huehanna. "I don't know where it is," Nuna said. "My sister knows. She has it hidden in her stomach. That's why she ran away at dawn." That's what Nuna told Wanadi. He told him to get back at her. He thought: "This way she'll be punished."

Wanadi went to find the girl. He called everywhere for her. She didn't answer. He asked the people. "We haven't seen her," they said. Each one went on his way, looking and calling. Nothing. Then they got tired.

LEFT: *The Twin Rainbows*, Joe Herrera, 1952. From the collection of James Bialac, courtesy of the Heard Museum, Phoenix.

They couldn't find her. They came back.

Wanadi had a brother. His brother's name was Müdo. When he wanted to, he turned into a great potoo.

"You're engaged to her," Wanadi said. "She'll come out if you call her. Then we can catch her."

"She's beautiful. With my big bill and tiny little eyes, she doesn't want me. I'm ugly. She's not going to come out if I call her."

"Let's try," said Wanadi. "I don't want to lose Huehanna. Help me."

"Okay, brother," Müdo answered. He called his friend Höhöttu, the owl. "Help me," he said. "Let's call her."

They both turned into night birds. They called and shrieked the entire night. When the sun rose she came out. She lifted her body out of the water, up above the river, high in the air, saying: "Here I am." But it wasn't the girl who came, it was the Great Snake, Huiio.

"Who are you?" asked Müdo. "I don't know you. I didn't call you." And he squinted his eyes to get a better look at her.

"Sure you called," she answered. "I'm her, your betrothed. That's why I came. I recognized your call."

When she came out, they heard the music from Huehanna. You could hear those children of Wanadi's singing and dancing inside the snake's belly. They were waiting to come out.

Müdo said to the Great Snake: "Wanadi wants you to give Huehanna back."

"I can't," she answered. "I have my children in it."

"They're not yours. They're Wanadi's."

She didn't want to give them back.

Now Müdo and Höhöttu called the people, yelling in every direction. Many came. They made bows and arrows and spears. Müdo and Höhöttu were giving everyone orders. "We'll catch her and kill her," they said.

Now the first hunt began, when they chased Huiio along the river. They could see the rainbow, the snake's feather crown, from far off. She was spreading her feathers in the air, drying them in the sun. "There she is!" the hunters shouted. They were looking at the rainbow.

They were close now. They spoke to Dede, the bat. "We're going to shoot our arrows," they told him. "We're going to kill the snake and get Huehanna out. You stay here and just watch quietly. When Huehanna drops, catch it, so it doesn't fall in the water."

"Okay," said Dede. "I'll wait right here."

The hunters went to shoot the Great Snake. There were really a lot of them. They all shot at the same moment. Their arrows flew. Now Huiio looked like a porcupine with all those arrows stuck in her body. She fell over. She let go of Huehanna. Huehanna shot up in the air. Dede was watching, ready to catch Huehanna with his fishnet so it wouldn't fall.

"Grab it!" they shouted. "Don't lose it!"

Now Ficha, the cuckoo, came zooming up, headed straight for Dede. He had a long tail. He shoved Dede aside with that tail and took the fishnet.

"Move over," he said. "Let me get it. Your eyes are too small. You can't see."

Ficha was vain and wild. No one could tell him anything. He did whatever he wanted to. That's why the accident happened.

As he took the net, Huehanna was coming by. He tried to catch it. There wasn't time. Huehanna flew right by. It fell in the water.

"It's gone!" they all screamed. "Because of you, we've lost it!"

There was a huge rock in the water. Huehanna burst on it. The unborn people flew all over. They didn't drown. They just turned into fish eggs. When the eggs opened, hundreds of fish came swimming out. They were the first ones. Crocodiles came out too, and caimans and anacondas; all the animals you see today living in the rivers and lakes. Huiio was the mother of them all. They killed her. She collapsed on the shore. She died there, covered with arrows.

She didn't really though. She was too powerful. She just left her form, her body here. The rainbow is a reminder. Now she lives in the highest Heaven, in Lake Akuena. Now she's the mistress of Akuena, of eternal life.

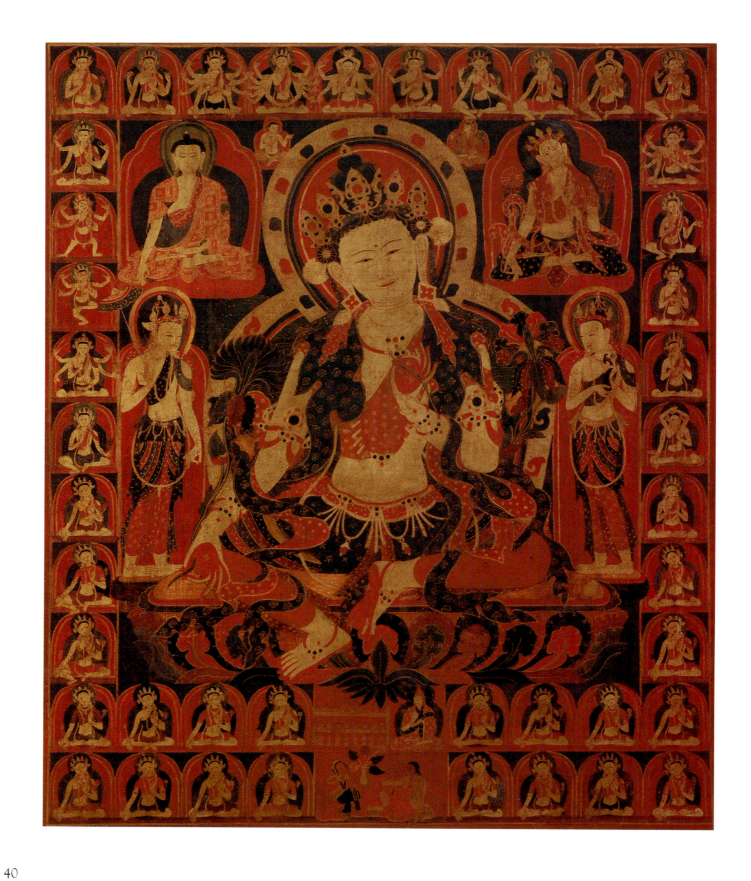

Homage to
Tārā Our Mother

TIBETAN

Homage to Tārā our mother:

great compassion!

Homage to Tārā our mother:

a thousand hands, a thousand eyes!

Homage to Tārā our mother:

queen of physicians!

Homage to Tārā our mother:

conquering disease like medicine!

Homage to Tārā our mother:

knowing the means of compassion!

Homage to Tārā our mother:

a foundation like the earth!

Homage to Tārā our mother:

cooling like water!

Homage to Tārā our mother:

ripening like fire!

Homage to Tārā our mother:

spreading like wind!

Homage to Tārā our mother:

pervading like space!

OPPOSITE: *Green Tārā*, Tibet, 14th century. The Asia Society, New York, Mr. and Mrs. John D. Rockefeller 3rd Acquisitions Fund (1991.1).

ELEMENTAL MAGIC:
EARTH, WATER, FIRE, AND AIR

THE STORIES IN THIS SECTION CELEBRATE THE INVISIBLE SPIRITUAL powers that underlie the visible manifestations of nature, and invite us to look at the river, the volcano, and the hurricane as expressions of the one great mystery that abides in all things. Indigenous people, who have an intimate connection with the land, invariably perceive the earth as sacred and alive. Any landmark—a mountain, a river, a tree—is likely to be viewed as a spiritual entity, and such landmarks are often revered as goddesses. In "Traditional Praise of Oya," the Yoruban goddess of wind and fire is associated with the River Niger; Pele, the fiery Hawaiian volcano goddess, supposedly lives in Mount Kilauea.

The goddesses we meet in these stories do not live in distant, transcendent heavens; they make their homes right here on earth, where they govern the intricate processes whereby spirit enters into manifest form. They are the fertile earth, a flurry of snow, the flooding river, or a precious spark of fire. Like Shiratamahime, the elusive Japanese snow maiden, they appear and disappear with the seasons.

The message of the following stories is that the goddess is everywhere. She may show up anywhere, at any time, and in any shape or form; the potential for an encounter with the sacred is always present. Any moment, a doorway may open up from our world into other dimensions, and the luminous face of a goddess may become visible.

Some of the pieces included here are very ancient. Others, like the Zulu tale, "Two Water Goddesses," and the Caribbean, "Anancy and the Hide-Away Garden," are contemporary. Yet a reverence for the earth pulsates through them all, uniting the peoples of the world. As the Greek poet Homer proclaims, "Whoever you are, it is she who nourishes you from her storehouse."

OPPOSITE: *The Elements (Los Elementos)*, Diego Rivera, 1926–27.
Universidad Autonoma Chapingo, Mexico.

HYMN TO GAIA

GREEK

Homer, translated by Jules Cashford

Gaia
mother of all
foundation of all
the oldest one

I shall sing to Earth

She feeds everything
that is in the world

Whoever you are
whether you live upon her sacred ground
or whether you live along the paths of the sea
you that fly

it is she
who nourishes you
from her treasure-store

Queen of Earth
through you

beautiful children
beautiful harvests
come

The giving of life
and the taking of life

both are yours

Happy is the man you honour
the one who has this
has everything

His fields thicken with ripe corn
his cattle grow heavy in the pastures
his house brims over with good things

These are the men who are masters of their city
the laws are just, the women are fair
happiness and fortune richly follow them

Their sons delight
in the ecstasy of youth

Their daughters play
they dance among the flowers
skipping in and out

they dance on the grass
over soft flowers

Holy goddess, you
honoured them
ever-flowing spirit

Farewell
mother of the gods
bride of Heaven
sparkling with stars

For my song, life
allow me
loved of the heart

Now
and in my other songs
I shall remember you

OPPOSITE: *Gaia, Goddess of the Earth,*
600 B.C.E. Archaeological Museum,
Corfu, Greece.

Grandmother Spider Gets the Fire

———◆———

NAVAJO

Told by Paula Gunn Allen

Long ago the people were in the dark, and they were tired of not knowing when to go to sleep and when to get up. They didn't have Six Killer (the fire of the sun) to pray to in the mornings when they went to the water to greet Long Man and prepare for the new day. True, there was a place of greater heat during some hours, and the air around them was more gray than dark, but they didn't have much light by which to work and play.

They were also yearning for a cozy fire to sit next to when they told stories after the little ones went to sleep, after the daily activities ended. Besides, they knew that fire was very powerful, and they wanted the joy and growing that came to people who had fire to grace their lives.

They really liked to pass the time companionably, and the only reason they didn't do as much of it as they liked is that when the darkness got a little darker some of them insisted it was time to go to sleep. They believed that if they had fire and some regular daylight, they'd be able to spend even more time telling stories and gossiping and being together. Maybe they would even have new ceremonies to hold and go to.

The people learned about some other people in a distant country who had firelight. They heard that those people got to spend all day and all night telling stories, singing, dancing, and generally carousing till all hours.

Well, they thought about all this for a long time. They thought about what they needed and wanted. They thought about those rumors, and they even sent some men to see if they were true. They listened to each other's ideas about what they might do if they had some firelight, and they dreamed up all sorts of interesting activities. Even those who liked to sleep early got caught up in the goings on. They began to think that maybe they could sleep more in light time, when there was true light, so they could also enjoy the fire when it was very dark.

There were a few, of course, who had some reservations about the whole affair. But aside from mumbling a bit, mostly among themselves about possible dangers and hazards from such a volatile and untested force, especially when it was in the untrained hands of the would-be merrymakers, they kept their reservations to themselves. And this, of course, is how reservations first got started.

After a proper length of time planning and dreaming, discussing and surmising, mumbling and wondering had gone by, the people settled into the serious business of strategy. "How will we get some firelight?" they asked. "The people over in that other country who have some won't give us some. We tried."

"H'mmm," they sighed. They stopped discussing for a long pause.

"I know," one of the people finally said. He was a tall skinny man who decorated himself magnificently with feathers. He was especially proud of his luxurious thick hair fashioned in a spiky style. He kept it in place with a nice sticky clay that came from the nearby clay bed. His name was Buzzard.

Buzzard uncoiled his lanky form and stood.

OPPOSITE: *Earth Mother (Red Cap),* Frank LaPena, 1990. Courtesy of the artist.

"Maybe someone will take a little jaunt over there long after it gets dark, maybe just before light, and try to snag some," he intoned sonorously.

"Yeah, you need practice snagging," someone hooted. The others laughed.

After the general merriment at Buzzard's expense subsided, it was agreed that Buzzard would go. When the first rays of light were just emerging over the saddle-back rise near the village, Buzzard came limping in. He was definitely the worse for wear, his fine feathers matted and blackened. He sported a bald spot right at his crown. The hair there never did grow back. "I blew it," he said resignedly. "Maybe someone else should try."

Well, a couple of others went, but with the same result.

Everyone was feeling pretty glum about how matters stood. They were trying to reconcile themselves to doing without the exciting firelight—which meant adjusting their plans, dreams, and hopes to fit their accustomed circumstances. Most were disappointed, except for the few who were relieved. They went whistling and giggling about their tasks, relieved that nothing fearful and different was going to unsettle their equilibrium just yet.

But Spider got to thinking. She was always doing that. She couldn't help it, of course, any more than Buzzard could help swooping, strutting, and snagging. She spun out her thought and wove implications, extrapolations, and a few elegant daydreams into a satisfying pattern. Her Dreaming done, she joined the folks sitting dejectedly around the empty place where they could almost see the firelight snapping cheerily on the sticks and branches they had carefully laid out in such anticipation just a few days before.

"Well," Spider began softly. "Maybe someone might try to get some firelight," she said to no one in particular. She sat down carefully so as not to jar her fragile joints unduly. "It's true I'm old and slow," she continued. She paused again for a silence, breathing it in and out comfortingly.

No one looked at her. As was their way, they just kept on sitting as they had been, doing whatever they had been doing even if that was just brooding or wishing over their regrets. But of course, they were all attending carefully to what she said.

"It's true I'm a very small person and not very strong," she said at last. "But I think I could give it a try. My old body would appreciate some firelight at night sometimes. And I wouldn't mind having a little brightness to tend." They sat companionably in silence after that, some wandering off, some coming over to join the group from time to time.

So Spider set out, much earlier than Buzzard and the others had because she was much slower. Along her way she stopped off at the clay bed and dug up some smooth, damp clay. She took some time to shape it into a tiny pot with a lid that she kept separately so they wouldn't stick together while they were drying. Her Dreaming had told her that the firelight would dry them more quickly and more finely than Heat Giver in the sky could. She had seen some fine potteries in her Dream, and she was looking forward to making and firing them.

The last one of her folks watched her make her slow way across the rise beyond the saddleback on her way to the Fire People's land. Her tiny figure soon disappeared in the grayness that met the top of the rise and clung to it like a *u'tinaatz*, a woman's short, light cloak.

As the next day was well advanced, the people saw her returning. She had a round lamp on her back and looked a bit misshapen in the gray distance. Their hearts fell to the ground in dismay when they saw this. "Oh, no," they said. "It's one thing for Buzzard to get a new hairstyle, but if something so horrible has happened to Spider!"

They were too heartsick to finish the thought, but waited as calmly as they might, busying themselves with whatever came to hand as was their way when worried or anxious.

At long last Spider was close by, grinning a satisfied grin. "Well," she said, "looks like I got it." She reached up and took the clay pot from her back, revealing a change such as they had feared. For on her back pulsed a bright red-orange design that hadn't been there the day before. But it was a very handsome and wise design, one she had dreamed of herself, and it exactly matched the one her pot lid sported, and she seemed happy to wear it.

She set the tiny pot down in front of her, sighing a small sigh of satisfaction as she removed the lid to reveal the bright glowing ember she had carefully carried so far. "Look," she said. "Firelight."

And there was a hot time in the old town that night.

OPPOSITE: *Sacred Fire*, Frank LaPena, 1987. Courtesy of the artist.

TRADITIONAL PRAISE OF OYA

NIGERIAN

Translated by Judith Gleason

*Sometimes identified with the great river Niger,
Oya also takes the form of tornadoes, lightning,
and raging fires. Oya embodies an aspect of the
feminine that is wild, untamed, unpredictable,
and potentially destructive. At the same time,
her joy and zest for life are infectious.*

Complete Oya, strolling along with full
confidence and importance

She takes a basket of kola to place before
her husband

Owner of the place of worship

Oya, deep in thought, carving out
concepts

Complete Oya, come receive your offering
without offense

Owner of the place of worship

May those who have prepared food begin
to serve it

Oya who causes the leaves to flutter

Oya, strong wind who gave birth to fire
while traversing the mountain

Oya, please don't fell the tree in my
backyard

Oya, we have seen fire covering your body
like cloth

If you are looking for Oya and can't find
Oya

Maybe you'll meet her at the kola nut stall

Where Oya enjoys throwing little pieces
into her mouth

Maybe you'll meet her at the bitter kola
nut stall

Where Oya enjoys throwing little pieces
into her mouth

Maybe you'll meet her at the camwood stall

Where Oya enjoys rubbing red salve onto
her body

Maybe you'll meet her at the batá drum stall

Where Oya moves her body in an
enormous dance

Mother, mother, I will always respond to
Oya's call

They warned me not to respond to her call

Father, father, I will always respond to
Oya's call

They warned me not to respond to her call

Where can I go, what can I do?

They said I should offer little pieces of
cloth to Oya

They said I should offer kola nut and
pounded yam to Egungun [ancestral spirits
who are Oya's progeny]

They give a sword to Oya but she doesn't
use it to kill an animal

To Mother they should present a sword but
 not for killing any animal

They give her a sword but not for
beheading people

She said, "What can I do with my sword?"

Oya saw fire as a body covering, like cloth

Strong wind who knocks down trees
everywhere in the wilds

Egungun deserves pampering and respect
from cult members

Mother, pour into me as from your breasts,
world-mother

Egungun worshiper, owner of bush rat

Oya, owner of Egungun

Ashe! (vitality, authority, so be it!)

BELOW: Kneeling female figure
probably representing Oya,
c. 1900, Republic of Benin,
Yoruba. Staatliches Museum für
Völkerkunde, Munich.

51

Frigga, Eostre, and Holde

GERMANIC

The Germanic goddess of the earth and the atmosphere was called Frigga, queen of the gods. Frigga was usually portrayed "as a tall, beautiful, and stately woman, crowned with heron plumes and clothed in pure white robes, secured at the waist by a golden girdle." She was also known as Ostara or Oestre whose holy day was Easter, and as Holde, who later became the formidable Frau Holle of Grimm's fairy tales—a model housewife who sends down snowflakes as she shakes out her great down comforters. In former times, Frau Holde was a mighty weather goddess. The following is an old Tyrolean story about a peasant's encounter with the goddess.

There was once a peasant who daily left his wife and children down in the valley to take his sheep up the mountain to pasture; and as he watched his flock graze on the mountain side, he often had the opportunity to use his crossbow and bring down a chamois, whose flesh furnished his larder with food for many a day.

While pursuing some fine game one day he saw it disappear behind a boulder, and when he came to the spot, he was amazed to see a doorway in the neighboring glacier, for in the excitement of the pursuit he had climbed higher and higher until he was now on top of the mountain, where glittered the everlasting snow.

The shepherd boldly passed through the open door, and soon found himself in a wonderful jeweled and stalactite-hung cave, in the center of which stood a beautiful woman, clad in silvery robes, and attended by a host of lovely maidens crowned with Alpine

RIGHT: *Bigbury Bay, Devon,* Arthur Rackham, 1915. Harris Museum & Art Gallery, Preston, England.

roses. In his surprise, the shepherd sank to his knees, and as in a dream heard the queenly central figure bid him choose anything he saw to carry away with him. Although dazzled by the glow of the precious stones around him, the shepherd's eyes constantly reverted to a little nosegay of blue flowers which the gracious apparition held in her hand, and he now timidly proffered a request that it might become his. Smiling with

pleasure, Holde, for it was she, gave it to him, telling him he had chosen wisely and would live as long as the flowers did not droop and fade. Then giving the shepherd a measure of seed which she told him to sow in his field, the goddess bade him begone; and as the thunder pealed and the earth shook, the poor man found himself out upon the mountain side once more, and slowly wended his way home to tell his adventure

LEFT: *Mountain in the Fog*, Caspar David Friedrich, 19th century. Staatliches Museum Heidecksburg, Rudolfstadt, Germany.

seed enough for several acres.

Soon the little green shoots began to appear, and one moonlight night, while the peasant was gazing upon them, wondering what kind of grain they would produce, he saw a mistlike form hover above the field, with hands outstretched as if in blessing. At last the field blossomed, and countless little blue flowers opened their calyxes to the golden sun. When the flowers had withered and the seed was ripe, Holde came once more to teach the peasant and his wife how to harvest the flax stalks and spin, weave, and bleach the linen they produced. Of course all the people of the neighborhood were anxious to purchase both linen and flaxseed, and the peasant and his wife soon grew very rich indeed, for while he plowed, sowed, and harvested, she spun, wove, and bleached her linen. When the man had lived to a good old age and seen his grandchildren and great grandchildren grow up around him, he noticed that his carefully treasured bouquet, whose flowers had remained fresh for many a year, had wilted and died. Knowing that his time had

to his wife and show her the lovely blue flowers and the measure of seed.

The woman reproached her husband bitterly for not having brought some of the precious stones which he so glowingly described, instead of the blossoms and seed; nevertheless the man sowed the latter, and often lingered near the field at nightfall to see his new crop grow, for to his surprise the measure had supplied

come and that he too must soon die, the peasant climbed the mountain once more, came to the glacier, and found the doorway which he had long vainly sought. He vanished within, and was never seen or heard of again, for the legend states that the goddess took him under her care, and bade him live in her cave, where his every wish was gratified.

PELE THE VOLCANO GODDESS

HAWAIIAN

Told by Carolyn McVickar Edwards

When the center of the Earth swells red hot and roars to meet the sky and rivers of fire race down the mountain, the people cry in terror. Even the old ones who know the name of Volcano Woman bring Her presents of silk and tobacco with their knees trembling. At the edge of Her mouth they set their gifts, and though Her steaming cry does not sound like She is grateful, more than once Her liquid fire has stopped at the edge of the village and the people and their animals are left alive.

Pele is the name of Volcano Woman, and no one really knows why She comes from the center of the Earth dressed in Her terrible beauty.

Some people say it is not really Pele that comes from the center, but Her children instead. Long ago, they say, when Pele was young, the center of the Earth glowed with Her loveliness. Her skin was black as coal and Her hair red as flames. Singing Her song that hissed like steam through a small opening, She was content for a million years to putter in Her house, stirring Her red pepper soup in Her huge iron pot. Sometimes She would sleep for a hundred years at a time, Her arms wrapped around Her brown and yellow snakes.

Then one day, Pele walked to the edge of the center and pushed Her hands upward. That was the day Pele met Ocean. For in pushing upward, Pele made a crack in the center, and through the crack came Ocean's voice, deep and soft. "Pele, may I come in?" asked Ocean. Pele drew back. "I don't know you," She said. "Then let us meet here again and again and talk until we do know each other," said Ocean.

That was how the conversations began. For a thousand years, Pele came to the crack and talked with Ocean. Some days Ocean didn't answer Her call. But She could hear his voice boiling and dark in the distance. And some days Pele didn't come at Ocean's call. But every day they did talk, Pele's heart swelled with curiosity and wonder. For Ocean asked Her about Her soup and Her snakes. He asked Her what She dreamed when She slept. He asked Her about the shapes of Her rocks. Ocean told Her about his wet purple world. He told Her about the color green, and he told Her about the sky. One day, Pele whispered to Ocean that She loved him.

"Oh, my Pele," said Ocean. "My wonderful friend," said Ocean. "Will you let me come in now?"

Pele felt Her skin prickle. "Ocean, I am afraid," She said. But She curled Her fingers into the edges of the crack and pulled. Her muscles rippled and the crack opened wide. Ocean fell into Her arms.

That was the beginning, the people say, of the marriage of Pele and Ocean. Some say it is when Pele is fighting with Her husband that the volcano bursts. Others say that lava is the offspring of Pele and Ocean. It is the fire of Pele that makes the lava red hot, and the water of Ocean that makes it flow like a mighty river.

But some of the old ones shake their heads. No one knows the Volcano Woman, they say—not even Ocean. The volcano explodes only when Pele comes up from the center to balance the great scale of life and death. The Volcano Woman is the Great Balancer, they say. But that is another story.

OPPOSITE: *Pele*, the Volcano Goddess, Hawaii, late 18th century. British Museum, London.

Two Water Goddesses

ZULU

Told by Jan Knappert

These two contemporary tales bear witness to the important role of the goddess in Zulu culture. Regarding the second tale, author Jan Knappert comments, "In Zululand, at least in the old days, beer was mainly brewed by women, some of whom could make theirs quite strong and sweet. I was told the following story as a true report of the facts."

I.

Once upon a time a man was caught by the Inkanyamba who, according to some Zulu wise men, is female, a goddess of the waters, of hail and storm. She picked him up and carried him through the air many miles away to her own pool where she hid, together with her quarry. Police searches were fruitless: the man remained missing, until a man from the Nyanga tribe offered to find him. He dived in a certain pool and persuaded the man who was now living in it to come back with him to the world of earthlings. Finally both men emerged from the water. The missing man had become as white as a fish under water, with long hair looking like seaweed and a long white beard. He seemed to be strong and healthy, but he refused normal human food. He only ate seafood, crabs and toads.

Not long afterwards the Inkanyamba came back to her pool, missed the old man and went in search of him. This caused such a terrible storm that the authorities requested the old man to give himself up to Inkanyamba. This he did willingly, since he no longer liked living on earth, but preferred life with the water-goddess.

II.

One day a beer-woman decided that she did not have enough customers in her beer-shop, so she went to the bank of the river Umgeni near Durban, after due preparations, and performed an elaborate ceremony, throwing much food as offerings in the water. She was calling the River Mother, and she succeeded. She watched carefully and after a long time she found what she had hoped for: a piece of wood no bigger than a matchstick came floating down the river. She picked it up and took it to her modest brewery in the firm faith that it was the River Mother. She placed the piece of wood on the bottom of the barrel in which she kept her beer. Then she made fresh beer and poured it into the barrel. From that day her beer-shop was always full of customers; her fame spread throughout the city. Nowhere was the beer so delicious. As they drank more of the famous beer, the patrons would feel ever happier, forgetting their worries at home and at work. They would just sit and sing nostalgic songs. This attracted the attention of the police. Brewing beer without a license is illegal, so the police invaded the premises in search of illicit liquor. They found the barrel and opened it, knowing it was there to store beer. However, it was empty. On the bottom they saw a long snake, all coiled up, hissing at them. They quickly went away. That was Mamlambo, the River Goddess, protecting the beer-woman and her customers. The latter returned soon after the police had left. The beer barrel was full again, for Mamlambo had temporarily drunk the beer and now regurgitated it again. The beer was even better than before. Customers pawned their possessions to buy it. In this way the goddess ruled them.

OPPOSITE: Ponou female funerary mask, Gabon, 19th century. Musée des Arts Africains et Oceaniens, Paris.

ABOVE: *Eden Noon*, Romare Bearden, 1988. © 1997 Romare Bearden Foundation/Licensed by VAGA, New York, NY.

Anancy and the Hide-Away Garden

AFRO-CARIBBEAN

Told by James Berry

Anancy is a trickster figure who originally hails from Africa. Witch-Sister is one of the many "red" goddesses found all over the world, whose blood-red color denotes the power of the life force.

The garden belongs to Old Witch-Sister. Nobody is really ever supposed to see this garden. But Anancy keeps on hearing about the garden grown on rocks.

"It's the world's most glorious garden," people whisper to Anancy.

"If allowed at all, not more than one stranger is ever supposed to see the garden," people also whisper to Anancy.

Anancy sets out alone to find the garden.

Anancy finds himself in a desert of rocks. He climbs up a hillside of rocks. Getting up to the top, Anancy breathes like a horse pulling hard.

At the flat top of the hill, the garden is open wide to blue sky. Anancy stands fixed in surprise. Anancy is amazed.

"True-true. This is the richest garden in the whole world!" Anancy whispers to himself. "The garden is growing, is fruiting, is ripening, is blossoming. Look at fattest vegetables! Look at shining fruits and flowers! Look at a garden of all reds, all oranges and browns, all yellows and purples!"

Anancy walks along the edge of the garden. Anancy can't help keeping on talking to himself. "What a garden of fat vegetables. What a garden of flowers that stay in your eyes. What a garden of little fruit trees ripening and blossoming. What a garden sweet-smelling of plenty-plenty!"

Anancy bends down. He examines the rocky ground. Roots are gone down, hidden in rocks,

61

shaped like smooth mounds of earth.

Anancy stands. He looks in wonder at the colourful garden in bright hot sunshine. Anancy whispers, "Sunshine takes roots. Sunshine takes roots and grows like garden."

Anancy turns round. He goes back down the rocky hillside singing:

> Sunshine 'pon rocks gets dressed up like
> garden.
> Sunshine 'pon rocks gets dressed up like
> garden.
> Seeds get wings in a breeze-blow.
> Seeds get wings in a breeze-blow.
> Catch them, pocket them, plant them
> back of house, O!
> Piece-piece luck comes quiet in one-one.
> Breeze-blow seeds raise up stone-land!
> Oh, catch them, pocket them, plant them
> back of house.
> Oh catch them, pocket them, plant them
> back of house.
> Sunshine 'pon rocks gets dressed up like
> garden, O!

Anancy stops singing. As he walks along, he begins to think again how the garden is rich and fat and colourful.

Anancy begins to think the garden should be his. He begins to feel how it feels having the garden. Anancy begins to count up what the garden can do for him. He reckons up that the garden can get mountains of praises for him. And in the heat of the day, he can lie back in a shade in the beautiful garden. He can stay there and listen to birds singing, and go off to sleep.

"Old Witch-Sister needs nothing beautiful!" Anancy says aloud.

Then Anancy laughs a funny laugh of excitement. In himself now he feels, he knows the Hide-Away Garden shall belong to him—Anancy!

But, Anancy remembers—nobody can just take away the garden easily. For one thing, the garden has a Gardener-man. He cares for the garden. He's also watchman of the garden. Then, some mysterious ways work with the garden that cannot ever be explained. Any food stolen from the garden makes the eater keep being sick till the robber is found out. Then, of great-great importance, there is the flute-playing by Gardener-man, who walks with a stick taller than himself.

With his stick lying beside him, Gardener-man sits on a comfortable pile of rocks at sunset every day.

Sitting there, he plays his flute to the garden. He gives the garden his music till darkness covers him.

While the flute is playing, Old Witch-Sister always comes and listens. Dressed in red completely, Old Witch-Sister creeps up into the garden, unseen. Sometimes she just listens and goes away again.

Other times, she begins to dance straightaway, on a flat rock near the centre of the garden. But there is one big-big rule you see, that must be kept.

Gardener-man must never-never play his flute over a certain length of time. If Gardener-man should ever go on with the music over a certain length of time, he will not be able to stop playing. Also, if Old Witch-Sister happens to be dancing, she too will not be able to stop dancing.

Anancy goes and sees his son.

"Tacooma," Anancy says, "I want you to get Bro Blackbird KlingKling to get nine Blackbird KlingKling-cousins together with himself. I want them to do a careful-careful clever job. I want them to hide, to listen, to learn Gardener-man's music of the flute, exact-exact. I want them to learn, to know, to remember every, every slightest bit."

The Blackbird-people creep up and listen unseen, as Anancy asks. Bro Blackbird KlingKling and cousins have sharp ears. They take in every sound of Gardener-man's flute music, quick-quick.

Anancy sends a message to Gardener-man. The message invites Gardener-man to come and eat with him. But, you see, Anancy goes and collects Gardener-man himself. And because he's setting a trap for Gardener-man, just listen to that Anancy. "Oh, Mister Gardener-man, I just happen to be passing this way. And my good memory says we are eating together. And as you know, Bro Nancy isn't a man to miss a friendly company a little longer. So I come and call for you."

Gardener-man walks with his stick taller than himself beside Anancy, towards Anancy's house. At this exact time, Anancy's son Tacooma makes his way to the Hide-Away Garden.

Quick-quick. Tacooma collects up some food from the garden.

Sunset comes. The Blackbird-people come and sit in Gardener-man's place, on the pile of rocks. The Blackbird-people begin to sing Gardener-man's flute playing, all to the garden.

The Bird-people work the singing in groups of three. When one group is stopping, the other group comes in smart-smart. Like that, the Blackbird-people carry on and on with Gardener-man's music, perfect-perfect.

With really sweet throats of the flute, the Blackbird-people sing and sing to the garden. Flute music fills the garden and the whole sunset evening, sweeter than when the Gardener-man himself plays.

Dressed all in red, slow-slow, Old Witch-Sister creeps up into the garden. On her flat rock, Old Witch-Sister begins to dance, slow-slow. Her long red skirt sways about a little bit at first. The skirt begins to sway about faster. Then the skirt begins to swirl and swirl. From head to toe, with arms stretched wide, Old Witch-Sister spins and spins and spins. Darkness comes down. Darkness finds Old Witch-Sister swirling as fast as any merry-go-round.

Last to sing, on his own, Bro KlingKling takes over the flute-singing. As Bro KlingKling's voice spreads over the garden, Old Witch-Sister drops down dead, in a heap of red clothes. Then, at Anancy's house, Gardener-man is the only one to eat the stolen food from the garden. Same time as Old Witch-Sister, Gardener-man drops down dead too.

Anancy gets himself busy. Anancy sees to it that Old Witch-Sister and Gardener-man get buried as far apart as possible. He sees to it too that Gardener-man's walking stick is buried with him.

Then Anancy jigs about. Dancing, Anancy says:

> Sunshine 'pon rocks gets dressed up like
>   garden.
> Catch them, pocket them, plant them
>   back of house, O!

ABOVE: *Eden Midnight*, Romare Bearden, 1988. © 1997 Romare Bearden Foundation/Licensed by VAGA, New York, NY.

Anancy begins to plan making a feast for himself, family and friends. He begins to plan too how he'll get Bro Dog, Bro Pig and Bro Jackass to work the garden.

Next day, early-early, Anancy starts out with Dog, Pig and Jackass and others to see the Hide-Away Garden.

They come to the garden. Anancy cannot believe his eyes. Every fruit and vegetable and flower and blossom is dried up. Every leaf is shrivelled and curled crisply. Anancy whispers, "The whole garden is dried up. The Hide-Away Garden is dead. Dead! Really dead!"

Anancy sings:

> Whai-o, story done, O!
> Whai-o, story done, O.
> The garden dead.
> The garden dead.
> The garden dead, O!

Everybody is sad. Even people who have never seen the garden get sad and very sad.

"That should never ever happen again," people say.

Nobody likes people who play bad tricks.

63

THE STORY OF SHIRATAMAHIME

JAPANESE

Told by Patrik Le Nestour

Le Nestour, a French poet and Orientalist, offers a poetic retelling of an ancient Japanese legend.

Visiting with the first snow
when the mountain night
is already impenetrable,
her body sparkles with purity
that gives itself until spring,
       until she herself is melted.

From the droplets of her disappearance
grows the snowflower,
the sazanka.

Before the snow's advent last year, a forester living alone in the highlands worked without respite, through mountains and valleys, preparing for the winter. He knew the snow that comes without warning and in one great brush-stroke paints moor and mountain, spraying even the underside of the low branches of the towering cryptomerias, blowing under the low eaves and around the wooden shutters of houses to bleach a corner of each small square of the paper windows. He knew how everything slumbers under this damp mantle.

That year autumn still lingered late. But the forester, this particular evening, sensed that the snow was near. Perhaps the television set had made him aware of it: on a map of Japan small circles filled with flakes, becoming more numerous each day in their southward descent, announced the imminence of snowfall in the region. In reality, however, this news served only to confirm that ability the people of the vicinity possess to read the air and the wind.

Always working from dawn to dusk, he was accustomed to retire early each night. And besides, the incessant firing of the small blinking screen upon which his eyes were nightly fixed was quick to make his eyelids heavy. Now he turned the knob and, in the reestablished silence, opened the door a moment to

LEFT: *Snowy Night*,
Shinsui Itō, July 1923.
© British Museum,
London.

OPPOSITE: *Snowstorm
in the mountains and
rivers of Kiso*, Ando or
Utagawa Hiroshige, early
19th century. Fitzwilliam
Museum, University of
Cambridge.

ABOVE: *Pink Peony*, Taiyo,
c. 1950. Color woodblock
print. Private collection.

feel the rush of this silence against that of night. He let the door slide open and was ready to take a full swallow of cold fresh air. But he had to check his breath: the snow had come.

It had evidently been snowing for some time already. The forester hazarded a few steps out of doors. Softly the "flower without fragrance" set its petals upon his face. For this man who lived alone, it was like something of the softness of a mistress with whom he was reunited after nearly a year's separation. . . .

Other petals fluttered, then settled on the edges of the windowpanes, weaving curtains of fluff. He put the shutters in place and returned to the door. But before reaching it he saw, in the diaphanous snowy light, a silhouette. It was approaching his house.

The elegance of its bearing revealed to the forester that the silhouette was that of a woman. She greeted him with a bow that showed her slightly disheveled hair, and when she raised her head he saw that a few strands of the threads of her black hair had strayed over the shoulders of her travel kimono. This garment was pure white with a pattern of a few birds in gold or silver, sober as the nuptial robe of a Buddhist ceremony.

She was young and astonishingly beautiful. He invited her in and helped her brush away the snow, which was already embedded in the folds of the kimono, and especially in the hollows of the obi's knot at her back. They had scarcely climbed the step when she went to her knees to bow again, as a sign of apology. She was in fact excusing herself, either for arriving at such a late hour, or else for coming unexpectedly. According to her explanation—to which the forester hardly listened, so fascinated was he by her face with its color of snow—she had come from Shiranuka on the last bus in order to visit her grandmother, of whom she had had no news recently, and she had been unable to find the old woman's house in the snow.

The forester knew old Aratae, whose house was less than an hour from his own. But, since the previous spring, the old woman was no longer of this world. The young stranger burst into tears upon hearing this news. She found herself tragically alone, for her parents had died, she explained, in the Aomori earthquake.

The forester comforted her, and gave her food and good hot tea. Later the two fell asleep. He took her in marriage in the morning.

His story, their story, could end there. And yet the Nine Stages of Winter passed, and they passed them away together, simply. Her name was Shiratae. When the women of the valley spoke of her, with an air of mystery, they changed her name to one still more classic and noble, Shiratamahime. In so doing they veiled her person in a delicate humor, for this name, for centuries, has served only to evoke "a certain mist" in the form of a young noblewoman with the name White-Pearls. Or perhaps they too had been struck by the rarity of her words, so precious that all who heard wanted to keep them like jewels in a treasure box of mystery.

And then approached the Month of the Melting of the Snows, as the Second Month used to be called in these wooded mountains. The snow withdrew reluctantly. It remained only as islets that held up their purity with great difficulty to the invading warmth, and they were suffocating already, slowly being undermined by the emanations of spring.

One morning the forester awoke strangely late, oppressed by a narcotic heaviness. He attributed it to the sun, already warm through the window. He looked out the window and was surprised to see Shiratae outdoors, barefoot and dressed only in a long white under-kimono. She was leaping from one beach of snow to the next, and her unbelted robe fluttered open with every bound to reveal her skin, which the sun made even whiter. She seemed to be playing like a child.

But suddenly he saw her stumble. Her robe had slipped down, and she made no attempt to pull it up again. She was immobile on the ground, as if breathing in the earth with her long hair. Intrigued and perhaps anxious, he dressed with great haste and went out to join her. She was gone.

He found the robe in the place where she had let it fall. On either side there were two islets of snow that were too far apart for the wash of ground between them to be spanned at a single bound. He looked around. She was probably hiding, to play. This was certainly not in keeping with her character, which was rather serene and withdrawn, but then, he had known her only a short time. The winter had been rigorous, and at last the spring had come to set her free.

He picked up the robe. Underneath it he discovered a plant which was already full-grown and in flower, very beautiful, very fascinating. As Shiratae had certainly done, he bent down very low to contemplate it. It had no fragrance.

67

ELEMENTAL MAGIC: EARTH, WATER, FIRE, AND AIR ● 11

HEAVENLY BODIES

THE ABILITY TO CAST LIGHT HAS ALWAYS BEEN SEEN AS A MARK of divinity. As previously mentioned, the word "divine" is related to the Sanskrit root *div*, which means "to shine." Quite naturally, people in all parts of the world have revered the sun, moon, and stars as divine beings whose blessing bathes the planet in light.

For thousands of years, poets, storytellers, and myth makers have explored the nature and identity of the heavenly bodies. Their words take us back to a time before electric lights transfigured the night, before pollution obscured the atmosphere, before children were taught to view the moon as a barren chunk of rock. Their voices remind us of the quiet wonder, awe, and reverence that we all have felt while walking outside on a clear night and gazing up into the silent depths of our inconceivably vast universe.

As these stories show, not all cultures share the Western habit of viewing the sun as masculine and the moon as feminine—in the Australian tale "Sun Dreaming," for example, the sun is a goddess. Stories about a talkative sun or an amorous moon may seem childish if we make the mistake of taking them literally; but if we look deeper, we see that behind such apparent naiveté lies a very sophisticated understanding of the universe as a living, breathing entity that speaks to those who listen. Myths about the heavenly bodies remind us that only by entering into relationship with the universe can we find meaning in it; relationship is the key that allows us to experience all things as interconnected, spirited, and alive. This knowledge is the gift that the ancient storytellers give us today.

OPPOSITE: *Luna*, Sir Edward Burne-Jones, 19th century. The Maas Gallery, London.

Hymn to Usha, Goddess of Dawn

HINDU

Translated by Jean Le Mée

LEFT: *Celestial Being*, India, c. 1000. Williams College Museum of Art, Museum purchase, with funds provided by John T. Winkhaus, Jr., Class of 1935 (69.45).

OPPOSITE: *Woman Dressing Her Hair*, India, 18th century. Private collection.

Blessed, bearing the sun, the eye of the Gods,
Leading her white horse, magnificent to see,
Dawn reveals herself, arrayed in beams of light,
And with boundless glory she transforms the world.

O fair one, banish the enemy with light!
And prepare for us broad pastures free from fear!
Ward off hatred, bring us your priceless treasure!
O bountiful, shower blessings on the singer!

Illumine us with your glorious splendor,
O divine Dawn! Enrich and lengthen our lives,
O Goddess full of grace! Grant us fulfillment
And cows, horses, and chariots in abundance!

O Daughter of Heaven, Dawn of noble birth,
Whom the men of glory celebrate in hymns,
Establish in us wealth sublime and mighty!
O Gods, protect us always with your blessings!

This hymn is from the Rig-Veda, an ancient Hindu text that dates back to c. 1500–1000 B.C. and consists of 1,028 hymns addressed to various deities.

HYMN TO SELENE, GODDESS OF THE MOON

GREEK

Homer, translated by Apostolos N. Athanassakis

Muses, sweet-speaking daughters of Zeus Kronides
and mistresses of song, sing next of long-winged Moon!
From her immortal head a heaven-sent glow
envelops the earth and great beauty arises
under its radiance. From her golden crown the dim air
is made to glitter as her rays turn night to noon,
whenever bright Selene, having bathed her beautiful skin
in the Ocean, put on her shining raiment
and harnessed her proud-necked and glistening steeds,
swiftly drives them on as their manes play
with the evening, dividing the months. Her great orbit is full
and as she waxes a most brilliant light appears
in the sky. Thus to mortals she is a sign and a token.
Once Kronides shared her bed and her love;
she became pregnant and gave birth to Pandeia,
a maiden outstanding for beauty among the immortal gods.
Hail, queen and white-armed goddess, splendid Selene,
kindly and fair-tressed! Beginning with you I shall sing
of the glories of demigods, whose deeds are ennobled by bards,
who serve the Muses with their lovely mouths.

ABOVE: Drinking vessel with Selene, 5th–4th century B.C.E. Archeological Museum, Florence.

OPPOSITE: *Diana* or *The Moon*, Agostino di Cuccio, c. 1450. Chapel of the Planets, Tempio Malatestiano, Rimini.

Sun Dreaming

AUSTRALIAN

Translated by Catherine H. Berndt

When the world was new, the Sun woman made a little baby girl. She was not like other babies, because all her body was shining with light. As she grew older, away in the west in the land beneath the ground, she was still the same. When some other women tried to touch her, her body burned their fingers like fire.

"Why does your daughter carry fire like this?" they asked the Sun woman.

"We are Sun Dreaming, both of us," the girl's mother told them.

"When all the land is dark, my daughter will bring you light. But I, myself, can't come up above the ground. I'm too strong. If I came up and looked at you, up there, I would burn you to ashes."

Still the girl lived with her mother. At first there was darkness everywhere, but when the girl came up into the sky she lit up all the country. "It's true," people said, looking up at her. "She brings light to us all." They were happy to see her there above them.

Every day, she does just the same. When the first birds start to talk, she comes up into the sky and stands there alone to give us light. Then she begins to think of her mother, lonely and waiting for her, and she moves down in the west on her way home. Down she goes, under the ground, to be with her mother, and

darkness covers the land. They sleep there together until it is time for the birds to waken again. Then the Sun woman sends her back to us.

"You must go now," she says. "Go and light all the men and women and children, all our relatives up there. It's all right for you to go, but my light is too strong. If I came, I would kill them."

So she takes her daughter on her shoulders, and they hurry across to the east. There she lifts her daughter up until she touches the sky.

"It's all right now, Mother," says the girl. "I'm here. You go back and wait for me." So away she goes under the ground, back to the west.

In the beginning the Sun was a woman like us, but today she is different. Her body looks just like the Rainbow Snake, all bright and shining; and the Sun girl has light and fire all over her body.

They made themselves Dreaming for us, so that we would have light every day to move about, and hunt for our food. If we had no sun and there was night all the time, we couldn't find our way and we couldn't see any animals or plants. We would starve to death.

The moon and the stars give us only a weak light, and the Sun woman is too dangerous for us to see. But the Sun's daughter always looks after us; and every day she makes the country bright, to keep us alive.

OPPOSITE: *Dream of Two Women*, Ronnie Tjampitjinpa, 1990. Musée des Arts Africains et Oceaniens, Paris.

75

HYMN TO NUT

EGYPTIAN

*Translated by Anne Baring
and Jules Cashford*

*To the Egyptians, the luminous blue sky was the vast body of a goddess called
Nut, who protectively overarched the earth. Every day Nut gave birth to the sun,
and every evening she swallowed him back into her body.*

O my mother Nut,
stretch your wings over me.
Let me become like the imperishable stars,
like the indefatigable stars.
May Nut extend her arms over me
and her name of
　　"She who extends her arms"
　　chases away the shadows
　　and makes the light shine everywhere.
O Great Being who is in the world of the Dead,
At whose feet is Eternity.
In whose hand is the always,
Come to me,
O great divine beloved Soul,
who is in the mysterious abyss,
Come to me.

BELOW: *Separation of Heaven and Earth*, 1080–950 B.C.E. Egyptian Museum, Cairo.

Where the Frost Comes From

AUSTRALIAN

Told by Langloh Parker and Johanna Lambert

Important mythical themes tend to appear simultaneously in apparently unrelated cultures. In Greece, people told of seven maidens who were transported to heaven after being pursued by Orion the hunter; in Hindu mythology, we have the Seven Mothers, who were pursued by Agni, the god of fire. This example is from Australia.

The Meamei, or Pleiades, once lived on this earth. They were seven sisters remarkable for their beauty. They had long hair to their waist, and their bodies sparkled with icicles. Their father and mother lived among the rocks away on some distant mountain, staying there always, never wandering about as their daughters did. When the sisters used to go hunting, they never joined any other tribes, though many tried from time to time to make friends with them. One large family of boys in particular thought them so beautiful that they wished them to stay with them and be their wives. These boys, the Berai-Berai, used to follow the Meamei about and, watching where they camped, used to leave offerings there for them.

The Berai-Berai had great skill in finding the nests of bees. First they would catch a bee and stick some white down or a white feather with some gum on its back between its hind legs. Then they would let it go and follow it to its nest. The honey they found they would put in wirrees (bark containers) and leave at the camp of the Meamei, who ate the honey but listened not to the wooing.

But one day old Wurrunnah (fiery Ancestor) stole two of the girls, capturing them by stratagem. He tried to warm the icicles off them but succeeded only in putting out his fire.

After a term of forced captivity, the two stolen girls were translated to the sky. There they found their five sisters stationed. With them they have since remained, not shining quite so brightly as the other five, having been dulled by the warmth of Wurrunnah's fires.

When the Berai-Berai found that the Meamei had left his earth forever, they were inconsolable. Maidens of their own tribe were offered to them, but as they could not have the Meamei, they would have none. Refusing to be comforted, they would not eat and so pined away and died. The spirits were sorry for them and pleased with their constancy, so they gave them, too, a place in the sky, and there they are still. Orion's sword and belt we call them, but to the Daens (Aborigines) they are still known as the Berai-Berai, the boys. . . .

At one time of the year, in remembrance that they once lived on earth, the Meamei break off some ice from themselves and throw it down. When, on waking in the morning, the Daens see frost everywhere, they say: "The Meamei have not forgotten us. They have thrown some of their ice down. We will show we remember them, too."

Then they take a piece of ice and hold it to the septum of the noses of children who have not already had theirs pierced. When the septums are numb with the cold, they are pierced, and a straw or bone is placed through them. "Now," say the Daens, "these children will be able to sing as the Meamei sing.". . .

When thunder is heard in the winter time, the Daens say: "There are the Meamei bathing again. That is the noise they make as they jump, doubled up, into the water, when playing Bubahlarmay, for whoever makes the loudest flop wins the game, which is a favorite one with the earth people, too." When the noise of the Bubahlarmay of the Meamei is heard, the Daens say, too, "Soon rain will fall, the Meamei will splash the water down. It will reach us in three days."

OPPOSITE: *Night*, Edward Robert Hughes, late 19th or early 20th century. Whitford and Hughes, London.

79

AMATERASU

JAPANESE

Told by Jalaja Bonheim

Let me tell you a story, an old, old story. You know that Amaterasu is the sun goddess. And you know how beautiful she is. Plants leap out of the earth just to see her, and the flowers are always begging her to kiss them. Animals and people feel happy when they see her shining face. When she touches the water it shimmers with joy, and when she touches the ice it sparkles like a thousand stars.

You know, when you were born, Amaterasu hid a spark of her light inside your heart. She is always there, always shining in your heart. But sometimes, she feels bad, and then she withdraws into a cave deep inside of you. Listen carefully to this story, and you will understand how to comfort her when that happens, and how to make her happy.

Once, long ago, Amaterasu got angry. You see, Amaterasu had a brother called Susanowo who was the god of the oceans, of thunder, lightning and rain. Unfortunately, Susanowo was a drunk, and when he drank he would get angry and belligerent. On one of his drunken rampages, he convinced himself that Amaterasu's powers were rightfully his. Like a dark thundercloud, he puffed up with resentment, until his rage burst forth in a furious storm. He crushed underfoot the tender rice plants that Amaterasu had been so carefully nourishing with her light, and he threw excrement into Amaterasu's temples. When the goddess saw what her brother had done, she was truly upset, sad as well as angry. She stormed away and shut herself off in a cave.

Amaterasu's cave was filled with her light. But outside, it was dark, pitch dark, coal-black dark, for when the sun withdrew, the moon too covered her face and hid. It was cold. No food, nothing to eat—nothing would grow. People gathered outside Amaterasu's cave and talked about how they might bring her out again. More and more people arrived, until soon there were thousands.

Inside the cave, Amaterasu sulked. "No, no, no," she said, "I won't come out. I've had it, I'm fed up. I don't care what they say, I'm staying here." But in the meantime, the people had hatched a plan. Or, let us say, a plan had arrived in their midst, perhaps a gift from the gods, for who knows where good ideas really come from. Things had become quite gloomy without Amaterasu's light, and the people needed to lift their spirits. So, they began having a party. Everyone started singing, not love songs, mind you, but songs about Amaterasu and her great, heart-stopping beauty. And they started beating the drums and dancing wild, whirling dances that imitated the wild, whirling dances of the planets around the sun. And all this time, they carefully guarded a large octagonal mirror, making sure no harm came to it.

Amaterasu could not help but hear the commotion outside her cave. She was depressed, yes, and she was stubborn. But also, she was curious. She listened. She stood up, then she scowled and sat back down again. But the truth was, she hated missing out on a good party. Finally, she could no longer bear it. She tiptoed to the cave entrance. "Just a peek," she whispered, sure that no one would notice. But how could no one notice the sun? The instant Amaterasu peeked out, rays of her light burst forth like arrows.

This was the moment everyone had been waiting for. Instantly, the people raised the mirror to Amaterasu's face. The goddess gasped in amazement. You see, she had never seen herself before. She had no idea how beautiful she was. But now, she looked at her reflection, and she was fascinated. She took a step toward the mirror, and another. And another. The crowds waited with bated breath. The more Amaterasu looked, the happier she felt. Her light was so miraculous, so beautiful, so exquisite. "Is that really me?" she asked, incredulous. "It's you, goddess, it's you!" the people cried. "Glory be to your light!" A tiny smile appeared on Amaterasu's face, and as she smiled, her light grew more radiant, and she smiled all the more to see it. Until finally, she was laughing with joy, a deep, rich belly laugh. Still laughing, she stepped out of her cave, and accompanied by the dancing, celebrating crowds, she returned to her heavenly home.

LEFT: *Amaterasu*,
(detail), c. 1800.
Victoria & Albert
Museum, London.

Nananbouclou and the Piece of Fire

HAITIAN

Told by Harold Courlander

In ancient times only the deities lived in the world. There were Shango, the god of lightning; Ogoun, the god of ironsmiths; Agwé, the god of the sea; Legba, the messenger god; and others. Their mother was Nananbouclou; she was the first of all the gods.

One day Legba came to the city and said: "A strange thing has happened. A great piece of fire has fallen from the sky." The gods went out with Legba, and he showed them where the piece of fire lay, scorching the land on all sides. Because Agwé was god of the sea, he brought the ocean in to surround the piece of fire and prevent it from burning up the world. Then they approached the fire and began to discuss how they could take it back to the city. Because Ogoun was the god of ironsmiths, he forged a chain around the great piece of fire and captured it. But there remained the problem of how to transport it. So Shango, the god of lightning, fastened it to a thunderbolt and hurled it to the city. Then they returned.

Nananbouclou, the mother of the gods, admired what they had found. And she said, "This is indeed a great thing." But the gods began to quarrel over who should have it.

Legba, the messenger god, said: "It was I who discovered it. Therefore, it belongs to me."

Agwé, the god of the sea, said: "I brought the ocean to surround it and keep it from eating up the earth. Therefore, it should be mine."

Ogoun, the ironworker, said: "Did I not forge a chain to wrap around the fire and capture it? Therefore, I am the proper owner."

And Shango, the god of lightning, said: "Who brought the piece of fire home? It was I who transported it on a thunderbolt. Therefore, there is no doubt whatsoever, it is mine."

They argued this way back and forth. They became angry with one another.

At last Nananbouclou halted the argument. She said: "This thing that has been brought back is beautiful. But before it came, there was harmony, and now there are bad words. This person claims it, that person claims it. Therefore, shall we continue to live with it in our midst?"

Nananbouclou took hold of the piece of fire and hurled it high into the sky.

There it has remained ever since. It is known by the name of Baiacou. It is the evening star.

© 1973, 1992 by H. Courlander. Reprinted by permission of The Emma Courlander Trust.

ABOVE: *Upaupa* (Tahitian Dance), Paul Gauguin, 1891. Israel Museum, Jerusalem.

LEFT: Gold-leaf necklace, Sumerian, c. 2000 B.C.E. © British Museum, London.

OPPOSITE: Antefix in the shape of a girl's head, Estruscan, 2nd half of 6th century B.C.E. © British Museum, London.

This is one of seven hymns, dating back about four thousand years, that are addressed to the Sumerian goddess Inanna. The most popular among the Sumerian goddesses, Inanna was worshipped as Queen of Heaven.

THE LADY OF THE EVENING

SUMERIAN

Translated by Diane Wolkstein and Samuel Noah Kramer

At the end of the day, the Radiant Star, the Great Light that fills the sky,
The Lady of the Evening appears in the heavens.
The people in all the lands lift their eyes to her.
The men purify themselves; the women cleanse themselves.
The ox in his yoke lows to her.
The sheep stir up the dust in their fold.
All the living creatures of the steppe,
The four-footed creatures of the high steppe,
The lush gardens and orchards, the green reeds and trees,
The fish of the deep and the birds in the heavens—
My Lady makes them all hurry to their sleeping places.

The living creatures and the numerous people of Sumer
        kneel before her.
Those chosen by the old women prepare great platters of
        food and drink for her.
The Lady refreshes herself in the land.
There is great joy in Sumer.
The young man makes love with his beloved.

My Lady looks in sweet wonder from heaven.
The people of Sumer parade before the holy Inanna.
Inanna, the Lady of the Evening, is radiant.
I sing your praises, holy Inanna.
The Lady of the Evening is radiant on the horizon.

Shining One

YUROK

Told by Theodora Kroeber

The first people were the Wogè. The world was the same in Wogè times as it is today; it has always been the same. And Umai, who was one of the Wogè, was much as our girls are now, that is to say, she was young and beautiful. But she was lonely and restless, too.

Umai's home was on the far edge of the earth by Upriver Ocean where the river begins. She liked to stand on the riverbank and look out across the world.

She could see down the full length of the river, from one side of the world to the other, and across Downriver Ocean to where the sun sets. She liked to wait on clear evenings for the little silver flash that follows the setting of the sun, making a brief crescent of light no thicker than the crescent of a fingernail along the horizon line. When darkness settled over the earth, Umai turned away from the river and went inside her house. She thought about the crescent of light, wondering what it was, and she thought she would like to go all the way down the river if only she could find some way to do it.

She searched here and there in her house until she found an old toy dugout canoe, no longer than her foot, no wider than her hand. She took it to the river and dipped it into the water. Then she patted its sides lightly and put a hand in and stretched the little canoe until it was two hands wide. She patted it front and back and put her foot into it and

stretched it until it was long enough for both of her feet, one ahead of the other. She continued to pat the canoe and to sing to it and to stretch it a little at a time, until at last it was large enough for her to sit in.

At first dawn, Umai settled herself in her canoe and pushed off from the bank. Only then did she remember about a paddle. Having none, she held onto the sides of the canoe and swayed gently back and forth, and after a moment the canoe started down the river. In smooth water, she repeated the swaying, rocking motion. When she came to rough water or to riffles or rapids or falls, she sat still, and the canoe went safely over or around them without help from her.

She passed the Center of the World. Here, the big tributaries join the river, and the water becomes much deeper and swifter. Umai went faster and faster so that soon she was all the way downstream and at the river's mouth where it empties into Downriver Ocean.

The surf, rough and forbidding, was breaking over the rocks along the shore. But Umai looked past the breakers, out across the blue ocean and she saw where the rim of the sky meets the water. And she thought she would like to ride on the ocean, too. So she sat and counted eleven waves. As the twelfth—always the smallest wave—rolled in to shore, Umai patted the sides of her canoe and sang a song to it and swayed forward and back. The canoe rode the twelfth wave out, carrying her safely onto the open ocean. During the rest of the day she went on and on across it and farther and farther away from the earth.

The sun was low in the sky when Umai came at last to the very edge of the world. She sat in her canoe alongside the world's edge, watching quietly. She saw that the sky does not rest solidly on the ocean, but that it lifts and dips and lifts and dips in an even rhythm, except that the twelfth is a slower, gentler rise and fall. And she saw that it is this dipping sky that causes the waves in Downriver Ocean which forever beat against the shores of the earth.

The sun went down behind the edge of the world and was followed by the familiar silver flash. But from so much closer up, Umai saw that it was not at all a narrow crescent but a waving, moving something with a center of living brightness.

Umai thought: her boat had taken her easily past

LEFT: *Cloud Maiden Series #5,* Linda Lomahaftewa, 1987. Courtesy of the artist.

the pounding surf and across the great ocean—might it not carry her out beyond the world as far as this brightness?

She patted her canoe and sang to it again while she counted eleven liftings and dippings of the sky. At the beginning of the twelfth and slower rise, Umai held tightly to the sides of the boat with both hands and rocked forward. The canoe went, straight and swift, through the gap. When the rim of the sky dipped again to the water, she was already some distance away in the Ocean-Outside-the-World.

Far away in the ocean which encircles the world, water gives way to pitch, and beyond the ocean of pitch, there is nothing at all. But where Umai went under the sky, she had only to cross a narrow stretch of water to find herself coming near the shore of the Land-Beyond-the-World.

On the shore of this land, a young girl stood waving to her—Laksis, Shining One, she was. And Umai saw that the silver brightness that follows the setting sun is Laksis waving from this far shore. She waved till Umai's canoe scraped bottom; then she helped her beach her canoe and welcomed her to her home and to the Land-Beyond-the-World.

Laksis was young like Umai and she too was lonely. Neither of them had had a friend before they found each other. They walked together over the barren and empty land and talked together as young girls talk. Umai told Laksis how from her home on Upriver Ocean she watched each night at sundown for the silver crescent behind the dipping sky. And Laksis told Umai how she came to the shore of her land each night at sundown to wave to the distant earth.

When it was time for Umai to go home, they said good-bye as friends do who will see each other again before the day is done. Together they counted eleven liftings of the sky. At the beginning of the twelfth, Laksis launched the canoe with a strong push which sent Umai back into the world under the lifted rim.

The trip home seemed very short to Umai because she was busy and happy with her thoughts. She saw that from the far side of the ocean, the earth itself looks no wider than the shore of Laksis' home. She came close to her own shore and recognized its rocks and the wide mouth of the river. It was good to see these familiar things again. Without trouble, swaying

gently and singing a little, she rode a low wave through the surf and went on up the river; past its falls and rapids and riffles and into its quiet water; on to its source and her own home.

Umai belongs up where the river begins; she is known as Upriver Ocean Girl. She made no more trips in her canoe, and it shrank until it was a toy again, and Umai stored it carefully in her house. But each evening at sundown, she goes to the riverbank and she and Laksis face each other across the width of the world, and Laksis, Shining One, signals to her friend from behind the moving sky. You may see her for yourself after the sun has set—a silver streak where the sky meets the ocean, seeming no wider than the crescent of one of your fingernails.

When you are going out on the river or the ocean, it is well to sing to Umai, up there by Upriver Ocean. Put your hands on the sides of your canoe and pat it as you sing:

> *Umai!*
> *You rode the rapids.*
> *You crossed the Ocean.*
> *Lend me your canoe—*
> *This is your canoe!*
> *Now I too*
> *Shall have no trouble*
> *From the River.*
> *No trouble*
> *From the Ocean.*
> *Thank you, Umai!*

You will then go safely anywhere: on the river or through the surf or out on the ocean; to the edge of the world if you want to. It will take you longer than it took Umai: many days instead of one. And you will need a paddle, for these are not the ancient Wogè times and you are not a Wogè.

> But you will go safely and you will
>   come home safely:
> If you have followed the customs and
>   the rules;
> And if your heart is pure.

OPPOSITE: *Cosmic Hands*, Linda Lomahaftewa, 1980. Courtesy of the artist.

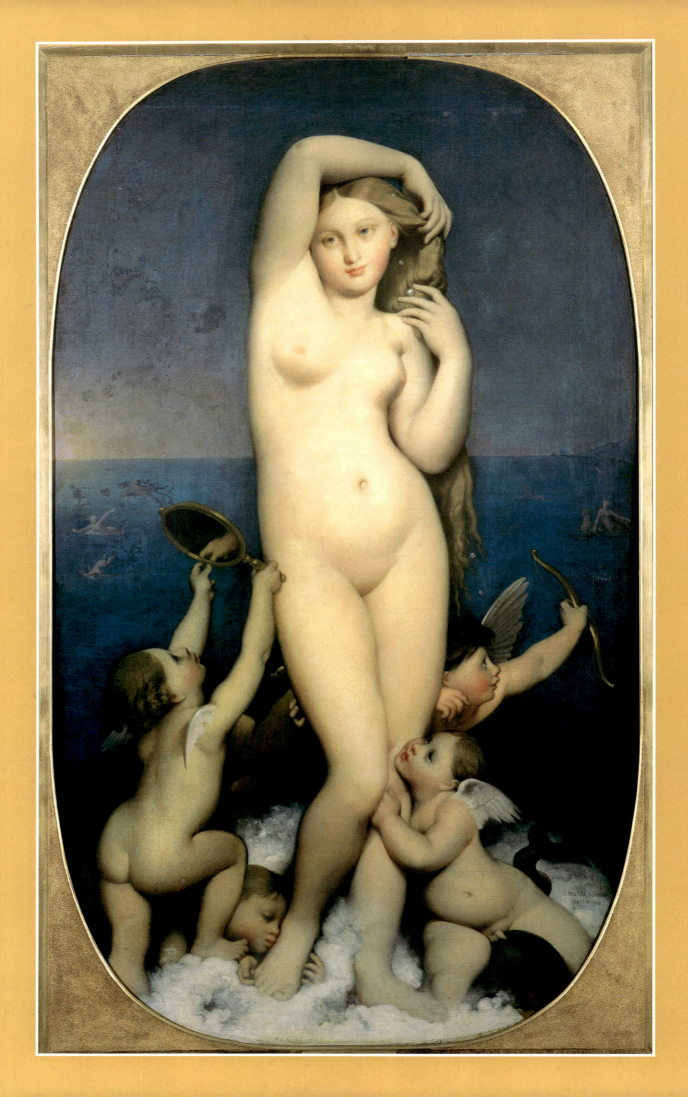

90

IV

THE GODDESS OF LOVE AND PLEASURE

ALL CELLULOID "GODDESSES," FROM MARILYN MONROE TO Madonna, evoke the goddess of love, and derive their power over the masses from this fact. Sensuous, alluring, and magnetic, the goddess of love is a flirtatious, irresistible temptress whose favorite game is sweet seduction. But she is far more than a mere sex symbol. Aesthetic harmony, refined sensuality, luxury, and elegance are of the utmost importance to her, whereas asceticism and martyrdom are abhorrent. The Egyptian goddess Hathor delights in music and dance, the Germanic goddess Freya loves sparkling gemstones and jewelry, while Aphrodite cannot resist the sensuous beauty of a young shepherd.

Instead of judging our desires as sinful and unworthy, the goddess of love invites us to embrace our natural instincts and make peace with them. These are strange yet immensely healing ideas for those of us raised with standards of perfection that could never be attained by ordinary human beings.

Always, the goddess of love is associated with water, that gentlest and strongest of all elements, element of the womb and source of all life. Aphrodite is born from the cosmic ocean, and so is the Hindu goddess of love, Lakshmi. The Canaanite goddess Asherah was called the "Lady of the Sea," and in Egypt, Isis was said to have been "born in the all-wetness." Similarly, the Yoruban goddess Oshun is a Nigerian river as well as a much-beloved goddess. All these goddesses remind us, who often tend to think of pleasure and beauty as unnecessary and frivolous luxuries, that beauty is as essential to the soul as water to the body.

OPPOSITE: *Venus Anadyomene,* Jean-August-Dominique Ingres, early 19th century. Musée Condé, Chantilly.

Hymn to Aphrodite

GREEK

Sappho, translated by Jane Hirshfield

Leave Crete,

Aphrodite,

and come to this

sacred place

encircled by apple trees,

fragrant with offered smoke.

Here, cold springs

sing softly

amid the branches;

the ground is shady with roses;

from trembling young leaves,

a deep drowsiness pours.

In the meadow,

horses are cropping

the wildflowers of spring,

scented fennel

blows on the breeze.

OPPOSITE: *The Birth of Venus,*
Odilon Redon, 1912. Petit
Palais, Paris.

In this place,

Lady of Cyprus, pour

the nectar that honors you

into our cups,

gold, and raised up for drinking.

APHRODITE AND ANCHISES

GREEK

Homer, translated by Apostolos N. Athanassakis

Anchises was a mortal who had the honor of making love to the goddess of love herself and fathering the great hero Aeneas. However, Anchises' encounter with Aphrodite ultimately led to his ruin. When he carelessly ignored her command not to boast of their union, Zeus struck him down with a thunderbolt. Aphrodite saved Anchises' life, but he remained a cripple.

Sing to me, O Muse, of the works of golden Aphrodite,
the Cyprian, who stirs sweet longing in gods
and subdues the races of mortal men as well as
the birds that swoop from the sky and all the beasts
that are nurtured in their multitudes on both land and sea. . . .
She even led astray the mind of Zeus who delights in thunder
and who is the greatest and has the highest honor.
Even his wise mind she tricks when she wills it
and easily mates him with mortal women,
making him forget Hera, his wife and sister,
by far the most beautiful among the deathless goddesses
and the most illustrious child to issue from crafty Kronos
and mother Rhea. And Zeus, knower of indestructible plans,
made her his modest and prudent wife.
But even in Aphrodite's soul Zeus placed sweet longing
to mate with a mortal man; his purpose was that even she
might not be kept away from a mortal's bed for long,
and that some day the smile-loving goddess might not
laugh sweetly and boast among all the gods
of how she had joined in love gods to mortal women,
who bore mortal sons to the deathless gods,
and of how she had paired goddesses with mortal men.
And so he placed in her heart sweet longing for Anchises
who then, looking like an immortal in body,
tended cattle on the towering mountains of Ida, rich in springs.
When indeed smile-loving Aphrodite saw him,
she fell in love with him, and awesome longing seized her heart.
She went to Cyprus and entered her redolent temple
at Paphos, where her precinct and balmy temple are.
There she entered and behind her closed the shining doors;
and there the Graces bathed her and anointed her

OPPOSITE: *Venus Before a Mirror*, Peter Paul Rubens, 1614–15. Sammlungen des Fuersten v. Liechtenstein, Vadur, Liechtenstein.

OPPOSITE: *Venus de Milo*
(detail), c. 100 B.C.E.
Louvre, Paris.

with ambrosian oil such as is rubbed on deathless gods,
divinely sweet, and made fragrant for her sake.
After she clothed her body with beautiful garments
and decked herself with gold, smile-loving Aphrodite
left sweet-smelling Cyprus behind and rushed toward Troy,
moving swiftly on a path high up in the clouds.
And she reached Ida, rich in springs, mother of beasts,
and over the mountain she made straight for the stalls.
And along with her, fawning, dashed gray wolves
and lions with gleaming eyes and bears and swift leopards,
ever hungry for deer. And when she saw them, she was delighted
in her heart and placed longing in their breasts,
so that they lay together in pairs along the shady glens.
But she herself reached the well-built shelters
and found the hero Anchises, whose beauty was divine,
left alone and away from the others, by the stalls.
All the others followed the cattle on the grassy pastures,
but he was left alone by the stalls, and away from the others
he moved about and played a loud and clear lyre.
And Aphrodite, the daughter of Zeus, stood before him,
in size and form like an unwed maiden,
so that he might not see who she was and be afraid.
When Anchises saw her, he pondered and marveled
at her size and form, and at her glistening garments.
She was clothed in a robe more brilliant than gleaming fire
and wore spiral bracelets and shining earrings,
while round her tender neck there were beautiful necklaces,
lovely, golden and of intricate design. Like the moon's
was the radiance round her soft breasts, a wonder to the eye.
Desire seized Anchises, and to her he uttered these words:
"Lady, welcome to this house, whoever of the blessed ones you are. . . ."

FREYA

GERMANIC

Told by H. A. Guerber

Freya, the fair Northern goddess of beauty and love, was the sister of Frey and the daughter of Niörd and Nerthus, or Skadi. She was the most beautiful and best beloved of all the goddesses, and while in Germany she was identified with Frigga, in Norway, Sweden, Denmark, and Iceland she was considered a separate divinity.

As Freya was inclined to lend a favorable ear to lovers' prayers, she was often invoked by them, and it was customary to compose love songs in her honor, which were sung on all festive occasions, her very name in Germany being used as the verb "to woo."

Freya, the golden-haired and blue-eyed goddess, was also, at times, considered a personification of the earth. She therefore married Odur, a symbol of the summer sun, whom she dearly loved, and by whom she had two daughters, Hnoss and Gersemi, so beautiful that all things lovely and precious were called by their names.

So long as Odur lingered contentedly at her side, Freya was smiling and perfectly happy; but, alas! this god was a rover, and, wearying of his wife's company, he suddenly left home and wandered far out into the wide world. Freya, sad and forsaken, wept abundantly, and her tears fell down upon the hard rocks, which softened at their contact. We are even told that they trickled down to the very center of the stones, where they were transformed to drops of gold. The tears which fell into the sea, however, were changed into translucent amber.

Weary of her widowed condition, and longing to clasp her beloved in her arms once more, Freya finally started out in search of him, passing through many lands, . . . inquiring of all she met whether her husband had passed that way, and shedding so many tears that gold can be found in all parts of the earth. . . .

Far away in the sunny South, under the flowering myrtle trees, Freya found Odur at last, and her love being restored to her, she grew happy and smiling once more, and as radiant as a bride. It is perhaps because Freya found her husband beneath the flowering myrtle, that Northern brides, to this day, wear myrtle in preference to the conventional orange wreath.

Hand in hand, Odur and Freya now gently wended their way home once more, and in the light of their happiness the grass grew green, the flowers bloomed, and the birds sang, for all Nature sympathized as heartily with Freya's joy as it had mourned with her when she was in sorrow. . . .

The prettiest plants and flowers in the North were called Freya's hair or Freya's eye dew, while the butterfly was called Freya's hen. This goddess was also supposed to have a special affection for the fairies, whom she loved to watch dancing in the moonbeams, and for whom she reserved her daintiest flowers and sweetest honey. Odur, Freya's husband, besides being considered a personification of the sun, was also regarded

LEFT: *Twilight Fantasies,*
Edward Robert Hughes, 1911.
The Maas Gallery, London.

As Freya was also considered goddess of fecundity, she was sometimes represented as riding about with her brother Frey in the chariot drawn by the golden-bristled boar, scattering, with lavish hands, fruits and flowers to gladden the hearts of all mankind. She also had a chariot of her own, however, in which she generally traveled, which was drawn by cats, her favorite animals, the emblems of caressing fondness and sensuality. . . .

Frey and Freya were held in such high honor throughout the North that their names, in modified forms, are still used for "master" and "mistress," and one day of the week is called Freya's day, or Friday, even by the English-speaking race. Freya's temples were very numerous indeed, and were long maintained by her votaries, the last in Magdeburg, Germany, being destroyed by order of Charlemagne. . . .

It was customary on solemn occasions to drink Freya's health with that of the other gods, and when Christianity was introduced in the North this toast was transferred to the Virgin or to St. Gertrude; Freya herself, like all the heathen divinities, was declared a demon or witch, and banished to the mountain peaks of Norway, Sweden, or Germany, where the Brocken is pointed out as her special abode, and the general trysting place of her demon train on Valpurgisnacht. . . .

As the swallow, cuckoo, and cat were held sacred to Freya in heathen times, these creatures were supposed to have demoniacal properties, and to this day witches are always depicted with coal-black cats close beside them.

as an emblem of passion, or of the intoxicating pleasure of love; so the ancients declared that it was no wonder his wife could not be happy without him.

As goddess of beauty, Freya was very fond of the toilet, of glittering adornments, and of precious jewels. One day, while she was in Svart-alfa-heim, the underground kingdom, she saw four dwarfs carefully fashioning the most wonderful necklace she had ever seen. Almost beside herself with longing to possess this treasure, which was called Brisinga-men, and was an emblem of the stars, or of the fruitfulness of the earth, Freya implored the dwarfs to give it to her; but they obstinately refused to do so unless she would promise to grant them her favor. Having secured the necklace at this price, Freya hastened to put it on, and its beauty so enhanced her charms that the goddess wore it night and day, and only occasionally could be persuaded to loan it to the other divinities. . . .

99

ABOVE: Hathor with cow's
ears, 13th century B.C.E.

*Hathor was the Egyptian Aphrodite,
an adored goddess of beauty, pleasure,
and love, and one of the many cow
goddesses found in Indian and Middle
Eastern mythology. The first of the
following two hymns was written
between 2428 and 2250 B.C.E., the
second in the first millennium B.C.E.,
attesting to Hathor's long reign.*

Hymn to Hathor

———————◆———————

EGYPTIAN

Translated by John L. Foster

Let me worship the Golden One to honor her Majesty
    and exalt the Lady of Heaven;
Let me give adoration to Hathor
    and songs of joy to my heavenly Mistress!
I beg her to hear my petitions
    that she send me my mistress now!

And she came herself to see me!
    What a great thing that was when it happened!
I rejoiced, I was glad, I was exalted,
    from the moment they said, "Oh, look at her!
See, here she comes!"—and the young men bowing
    through their enormous passion for her.

Let me consecrate breath to my Goddess
    that she give me my Love as a gift!
It is four days now I have prayed in her name;
    let her be with me today!

100

Hymn to Hathor in the Temple of Dendera

EGYPTIAN

*Translated by
Miriam Lichtheim*

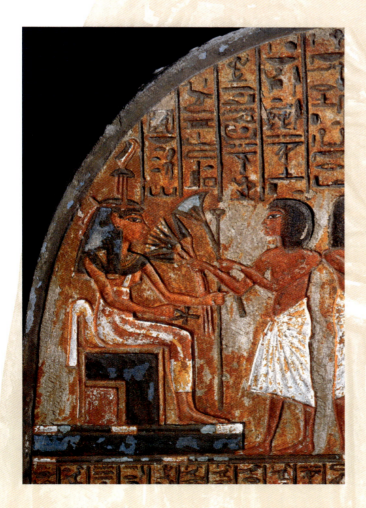

ABOVE: *Offering of flowers to
Hathor* (detail), Stele of
Amenhotep, 1403–1365 B.C.E.
Egizio Museum, Turin, Italy.

The King, Pharaoh, comes to dance,
He comes to sing;
    Mistress, see the dancing,
    Wife of Horus, see the skipping!

He offers it to you,
This jug;
    Mistress, see the dancing,
    Wife of Horus, see the skipping!

His heart is straight, his inmost open,
No darkness is in his breast;
    Mistress, see the dancing,
    Wife of Horus, see the skipping! . . .

O beauteous one, O cow, O great one,
O great magician, O splendid lady, O queen of gods!
The King reveres you, Pharaoh, give that he live!
O queen of gods, he reveres you, give that he live!

Behold him, Hathor, mistress, from heaven,
See him, Hathor, mistress, from lightland,
Hear him, flaming one, from ocean!
Behold him, queen of gods, from sky, from earth,
From Nubia, from Libya, from Manu, from Bakhu,
From each land, from each place, where your majesty
    shines!

Behold what is in his inmost,
Though his mouth speaks not;
His heart is straight, his inmost open,
No darkness is in his breast!
He reveres you, O queen of gods,
Give that he live! . . .

He comes to dance,
He comes to sing!
    His bag is of rushes,
    His basket of reeds,
    His sistrum of gold,
    His necklace of malachite.

His feet hurry to the mistress of music,
He dances for her, she loves his doing!

101

ABOVE: Top of cult staff,
Nigeria, Yoruba, 1930.
Staatliches Museum für
Völkerkunde, Munich.

102

OSHUN ACQUIRES THE ART OF DIVINING

YORUBAN

Told by Luisah Teish

*Like many love goddesses, Oshun is a
river goddess, supposedly the daughter
of a river maiden and Olofi, a primeval
form of God. Here she uses her
feminine graces to benefit all the
orishas, or deities; her nature is always
generous, and what she receives, she
passes on to others.*

At one time only Obatala knew the art of divining.
Repeatedly Oshun asked, "Baba, please teach me to
read the shells." And repeatedly Obatala refused Her.

One day Obatala went to the river to bathe. He
took off His luminous white cloth and refreshed
Himself in the water.

Just then along came Elegba, who snatched up the
cloth and ran to His house.

Oshun was picking flowers that day when She
came upon Obatala bathing in the river. "Good morning," She said, smiling radiantly.

Obatala reached for His clothes but discovered
that they were not there. "My clothes," He screamed.
Oshun looked puzzled. Obatala was distressed and

cried, "What, is the King of the White Cloth without His clothing? Oshun, I am in disgrace!"

She made Him a proposition: "If I get your white clothes for you, will you teach me the art of divining?" Obatala promised that He would.

So Oshun sprayed Herself with honey and tied five yellow scarves around Her waist. Her beautiful breasts glistened in the sun.

Then She followed Elegba's footsteps to His house. "Elegba, you must give me Obatala's clothes!" She called, standing in the doorway with Her hands on Her hips.

Elegba looked upon Her and was enchanted by Her beauty.

Elegba would speak only of sleeping with Her.

Oshun asked for Obatala's clothes—repeatedly. Finally they compromised!

Oshun returned to the river and gave Obatala His clothes. In exchange He taught Her to read the sacred shells.

When She had learned the secret of the shells, She called the *orishas* together and taught them all the art of divining.

RIGHT: Cloth Doll, Bamum tribe, Cameroon, n.d. Musée de l'homme, Paris.

Prayer~Song to Laka

HAWAIIAN

Translated by Nathaniel B. Emerson

In ancient Hawaii, Laka was the main goddess and patron of the hula dance. Performers honored her with prayers and rituals. Like Aphrodite, Laka, a graceful, pleasure-loving goddess, is associated with the color yellow and with gold, and is worshipped with fragrant flowers.

Laka sits in her shady grove,

Stands on her terrace, at Mo'o-helaia;

Like the tree of God Ku on Mauna-loa.

Kaulana-ula trills in my ear;

A whispered suggestion to me,

Lo, an offering, a payment,

A eulogy give I to thee.

O Laka, incline to me!

Have compassion, let it be well—

Well with me, well with us both.

O goddess Laka!

O wildwood bouquet, O Laka!

O Laka, queen of the voice!

O Laka, giver of gifts!

O Laka, giver of bounty!

O Laka, giver of all things!

OPPOSITE: *Female Tahitian Nude*, Paul Gauguin, late 19th or early 20th century. Musée des Beaux Arts, Orleans.

THE BIRTH OF LAKSHMI

HINDU

Told by Jalaja Bonheim

Lakshmi is the immensely popular Hindu goddess of wealth, love, and beauty. Together with her consort Vishnu, she rules over the forces of good and evil alike. Hinduism is a fundamentally optimistic religion, which teaches its believers that though evil forces or demons exist, they ultimately serve the divine plan. Moreover, as the following story explains, demons have been denied the gift of immortality.

RIGHT: *Lakshmi, India, 16th–17th century. Musée Guimet, Paris.*

106

Demons, you know, are mortal creatures, just like you and me. Some of them live hundreds of years, some thousands, but in the end, they all end up being recycled, dust to dust and spirit to spirit. Gods and goddesses, on the other hand, are immortal. But long ago it was different. At that time, the lesser gods, goddesses, and demons were mortal, and they were not happy with the situation. For years, they complained among themselves. "Someone should really do something about this," they said. Finally, they decided to approach the highest authorities and find out whether there was any way for them to become immortal.

For days, the goddesses and the demon ladies cooked up a storm. Clouds of blinding smoke billowed up from their pots, and the leaping flames could be seen from afar. The goddesses made sweetmeats, rice puddings, and almond pastries. They mashed ripe mangoes and mixed the pulp with milk, adding mild, heavenly spices. But the demonesses reached into their pantries and brought out the hottest, most evil red chili peppers you have ever seen, along with black peppercorns, and all the other spices that incite the passions and make the juices of life flow. And as they cooked, throwing in vegetables yellow, red, and purple, the demon ladies sang songs that made the goddesses blush with shame.

As word of the great celebration spread, more gods and more demons kept arriving along with their children and grandchildren, until soon there were hundreds and thousands, and still more kept coming. But at sundown, a great sacrificial fire was lit, and silence fell as the conch horns sounded over the vast gathering. Now, the priests and the priestesses began the ancient incantations. "We are calling on you, Great Spirit," they cried. "Creator of our universe and of countless universes beyond, we are calling you." And a sigh of agreement swept over the gathering. "Oh, Vishnu, you created our world from sacred sound, and with the sacred sound of the conch we call

you. Oh, Vishnu, you created our world from sacred light, and with the light of this fire, we call you. Oh, Vishnu, you promised you would come when we needed you. Into the fire we pour the precious butter, gift of the mother earth herself who appears to us as the sacred cow. Come now, luminous One, creator of good and evil alike."

All night long, they called. All night long, they poured offerings into the fire. All night long, they danced the dances that are said to please the Creator, and as they danced, the earth shook with their steps. They danced their way into a deep trance, to the place that is no place and the time where there is no time. Into the night they danced but they no longer knew whether it was day or night. The sound of the conches bellowed in their hearts and the light of the great fire roared in their minds. "Vishnu, Vishnu, Vishnu," they cried.

And suddenly, he stood among them, smiling. Later no one could agree what he looked like. "He looked just like my little boy," said one of the goddesses. "Oh, no," sighed one of the demon women, "he was no child but the most handsome man I have ever laid eyes on." But a little demon girl said gravely, "He looked just like a sparkly, shining white egg." Yet they all agreed that he spoke to them, and this is what he said:

> Take Vasuki the king of serpents, whom
> you also call Mahashesha the great
> coiled one. Wind his length around
> Mount Meru, the pillar of the universe.
> Using Mount Meru as a churning stick
> and Mahashesha as a rope, churn the
> Milky Way. Like sweet butter out of
> milk, the nectar of immortality will arise
> from its oceanic depths. Do this, and
> your heart's desire will be granted.

Saying thus, the great god became a blazing whirlwind that rose into the night sky, spun up into space,

107

and passed beyond the moon, beyond Venus and Jupiter into infinity. And that very instant, all the gods and goddesses, demons and demonesses collapsed into a deep sleep. Having worshipped for three days and three nights, they now slept for three days and three nights.

But when they awoke, they immediately set out to search for Mahashesha, the great serpent, whose body at its thickest point measures 4,320 light years across. And since Mahashesha was Vishnu's most faithful servant, it did not resist, but looked at them peacefully with bright eyes, and only a flickering of its tongue revealed that it was just a little apprehensive. Quite cooperatively, it coiled its great girth around Mount Meru, the cosmic pillar which penetrates all the universes and supports everything like the center pole of a great tent.

Then, all the demons rushed to the serpent's head, and the gods gathered at its tail. "Ho!" cried the gods as they grasped the serpent's tail. "Ha!" cried the demons at its head. And with "Ho! Ha!" they began the work of churning the Milky Way, gods and demons united. For a very long time, they churned, back and forth, back and forth, their backs aching from the strain, the veins on their temples bulging. Any minute now, they expected to see the nectar of immortality appearing like shimmering foam upon the ocean.

And indeed, something was rising up from the depths. Dropping the serpent, they jumped up and down, shouting and pointing: "Look there, there!" But what did they see? From the blue-black depths of the ocean not a bowl, not a vessel, no, but a beautiful cow was rising up. Neither black nor brown, neither white nor tan, her hide shimmered like a precious opal, and droplets of pure light sparkled on her long eyelashes. "It is Surabhi," the gods and the demons whispered in amazement. "Surabhi, the cow of plenty, from whose udders rich milk flows in never-ending abundance." Those in whose land Surabhi dwells will always have abundant food to eat and butter for their ritual offerings.

Breathless with excitement, their eyes unblinking, the gods and the demons resumed their work of churning. Soon, the depths below were troubled again, and they could make out a heaving and a trembling. And suddenly, they saw a woman dancing to the surface, her head thrown back in ecstasy, singing while she danced. And though her song was a little out of tune, it was infectious in its joy, and all the gods and demons began to dance, too, throwing their arms in the air. "Welcome, Varuni," they cried, "welcome."

For it was indeed Varuni, goddess of wine and of intoxication. Her cheeks red, her eyes a little glazed, she laughed as she looked around at the dancing crowds, and from the folds of her red velvet dress she drew little packets of heavenly hemp which she tossed into their midst. The demons sat down there and then, and forgetting all about immortality, they began to celebrate, becoming ever more raucous and wild. The gods frowned and muttered, "Disgraceful. It is quite disgraceful." But they had no choice but to wait until the demons were ready to get back to work.

Then, they began churning again, "Ho-ha, ho-ha, ho-ha." And soon, the swirling depths turned brown, then white, then greenish and lo and behold! Leaf by leaf, branch by branch, a tree arose, more beautiful than any tree you have ever seen. Each leaf shimmered like a green opal, and from this tree, a fragrance radiated more sweet than Arabian musk, more delicate than the scent of fresh jasmine, a scent the likes of which can only come from heaven. And for a long time, all one could hear were the sniffing sounds as the gods and the demons inhaled deeply, drawing the delightful fragrance deep into their lungs, and their *aaahs* of amazement when they exhaled. And all over the world, farmers laid down their plows and sniffed the sweet-smelling air in amazement, and the women at the well sighed as the scent awakened their most secret dreams of love. No one said a word until finally, a tiny goddess piped up and said, "Daddy, is that the nectar of immortality?" "No, darling," he answered, "it isn't," and as if awakening from a trance, he cried: "Back to work, all of you!"

And again the gods and the demons grasped Vasuki's head and tail. "Ho-ha! Ho-ha!" they cried. And from the depths of the ocean, they began to hear a chiming sound, clear and sweet. And one by one, a crowd of celestial dancers arose, their long hair dripping. Next to them, even the goddesses looked clumsy and rough, so delicate were the features of their faces, the arch of their eyebrows, the conch-shaped form of their ears, the enchanting smiles of their lips. They wore nothing but jewels, but plenty of those. Emeralds and sapphires encircled their full hips, silver bells tinkled on their ankles, and pearls shimmered in their dark hair. And how they moved! No reed ever swayed with such grace, no young gazelle ever leaped with such joy, no serpent ever danced with such sinuous pleasure. Like a mirage, they rose from the wild waters, and rising into the sky, they danced from cloud to cloud, and long after their forms had vanished, the chiming bell-like laughter could still be heard.

The gods and the demons had barely caught their

breath when they saw that the ocean was once again teeming and rolling and roiling like the body of a woman about to give birth. And in the depths, they saw a cool, gentle orb of light rolling through the green waters and then slowly, majestically, the moon rose into the sky. In those early days, the moon had not yet appeared in the night sky, and when it broke free from the cosmic ocean, all gasped in amazement. But as it sailed upwards, a great head appeared upon the horizon. "It is Shiva!" the gods and the demons cried. And they clasped their hands and bowed in awe before him. "Om namah Shivaya, om namah Shivaya," they murmured. "Bless us, Great Spirit." But like a great white bird the moon slowly rolled across the sky and settled into the black locks of Shiva's hair. "Ooohhh..." everyone moaned as the apparition vanished.

By now, the gods and demons had no doubt that any moment the nectar they desired would appear.

ABOVE: *Churning of the Sea of Milk*, Punjab Hills, 19th century. Victoria & Albert Museum, London.

Vigorously they clasped Vasuki and with all their might they pulled. "Ho-ha, ho-ha, ho-ha!" But poor Vasuki could take no more. For too long his innards had been sloshed this way and that, his head had been squeezed and his stomach twisted and turned. Now, his body began to heave like a volcano about to erupt, and before anyone could stop him, he vomited his venom, a venom far more potent than any that exists on earth. Soon, the entire world with all its teeming life would lie blackened and lifeless.

As if of one mind, a cry arose from the terror-stricken throngs of deities: "Shiva! Help!" For none other than Shiva the God of destruction had the power to destroy death itself. It was a fearful sight, the

109

waters of the cosmic ocean blackened with poison, while Vasuki continued to vomit forth his venom. And all over the universe, creatures surrounded by the black river of death joined their cry: "Oh, Shiva! Have mercy on us!" But it was Shakti, Mother of the World, who first heard their cries. "My love," she told her husband, "go quickly. By the aching of my heart I know our children need you. Run." Shiva ran, and when he saw what had happened, he placed his hand on Vasuki's head and breathed into the great serpent's ears, so that Vasuki became quiet and peaceful and his innards returned to their right place. Then, Shiva lay down by the shores of the great cosmic ocean, and like a tiger drinking his fill, he drank all the poison in the Milky Way as if it were sweet water. And since that time, we call on Shiva to render harmless whatever evil or poison we ourselves cannot transform.

Carefully, fearfully, the gods and the demons now crept back to the great serpent, who lay quietly now gazing at them with unblinking eyes. Cautiously, they grasped his body, ready to drop him at the first sign of distress. But all seemed well. And soberly now, carefully, they began churning. But instead of "ho-ha," the gods cried "Om!" And the demons answered "Namah Shivaya!" "Om namah Shivaya. Om namah Shivaya."

The gods and the demons felt Lakshmi's luminous presence long before they saw her. They felt full-hearted and drunken with joy. Her beauty, far greater even than that of the heavenly dancers, knocked the air out of their lungs, and made them gasp in wonder, and from her presence shone a soft gold light before which the moon paled. A great white lotus quivered under her soft feet as she stood, radiant as if lit from within, glowing in her own golden light. Her eyes were filled with laughter and love, and in her presence, every man and woman and child fell madly in love; even the cattle mooed with love-longing and rolled their eyes. She was wearing a gown of golden light, and as she walked, droplets of the cosmic ocean fell from her as sparkling diamonds. In her hand, she held a golden chalice that streamed with light, for it contained the nectar of immortality.

Now, you must understand that in truth, Vishnu and Lakshmi are one and the same, two halves of a single whole. The goddess who now stood before the dumbfounded assembly was the female half of Vishnu himself, as Vishnu was Lakshmi's male half. Vishnu-Lakshmi knew well what suffering it would cause the world should the demons become immortal. "We must distract these demons for a little while," said Lakshmi, who was also Vishnu, to Vishnu, who was also Lakshmi. "Yes," he agreed. And in the blink of an eye, Vishnu disguised himself as Mohini, the cosmic enchantress and universal seductress. Tossing her silken hair, Mohini sauntered through the demons' ranks, and wherever she went, heads turned. "Oh-la-la!" hissed the demon men and their eyes began to bulge as they ogled her voluptuous breasts and watched her thighs moving under her ever-so-thin sari. Far from insulted, the beauty threw a quick teasing glance and oh, those demons were lost. With a glance, a smile, a shake of her hips or a glimpse of a breast she enticed every single one of the demon men, and like a flock of sheep or a gaggle of geese they all followed her as she led them off into the forest. Their wives in turn followed the men, and the children followed their mothers. Off they marched as Lakshmi watched, smiling at her lover's play.

But while the demons disappeared with Mohini, the gods and goddesses all gathered around Lakshmi in a great circle. In their eyes, Lakshmi was far more gracious and more enchanting than Mohini. And now the goddess came to each one, and each received on the tongue a droplet of the nectar of immortality.

But by the time the demons returned, the nectar was all gone, and not a single drop was left. You might have thought this would have made them terribly unhappy, but it did not. Who knows what dances Mohini danced for them, there in the depths of the dark forest? Who knows what words she whispered in their eager ears? Be that as it may, they returned with satisfaction gleaming on their faces. "Who needs immortality?" they shrugged. "Mohini is better than immortality. And in a sense they were right, for Mohini was one with Vishnu, and Vishnu was one with Lakshmi.

But since that time, the gods have been immortal servants of the Great Spirit. The demons, however, are born when they are needed, and they die when they have completed their service. But when they die, it is Mohini who welcomes them back to their true home, and they are content. And who can say who has chosen the better lot? To this day, the gods and the demons argue about that point, and sometimes, if you become very quiet and you listen very carefully, you can hear their voices. But Lakshmi is easy to find. She stands upon her favorite lotus, the lotus of your own heart, and from that place, her golden love-light shines into the world.

A Supplicant Speaks of the Goddess Kwan Yin

CONTEMPORARY

Richard Kell

She was a human thought, a dainty protest
Against the claims of godhead. We who loved life
And would have looked for truth in songs and flowers,
In wine and precious stones and women's beauty,
We could not take the Master at his word,
Close up the shutters while the sun was climbing
And light the lamp indoors. The wise men gave us paradox;
Some, being frightened by their cleverness,
Locked themselves in for ever and stuffed the windows;
And some allowed themselves a compromise:
Cherished the scents and colours in the garden,
Yet were penitent when they threw a glance
At the slim girls walking in the street.
But we, uncertain of the ways of God,
Too passionate or weak to crush desire,
Or else too much afraid of death (supposing
The wise men were deluded),
We took the risk of sin and prayed for mercy.

Here is the goddess, head graciously tilted,
Gentle and grave and wise, serenely smiling:
So we had come to think of her—a symbol
Of pure mercy. But sometimes I have seen
A little harlot demure and yet coquettish,
Her slender body made for men's hands,
And in the beauty of her brow and eyelids,
The pouting lips, the finger at her breast,
A hint of roguish humour and contempt.
It was as though we knew, in spite of all
Our glossy thoughts, the Master's way was best;
As though our souls betrayed us into truth,
Giving us back our dreams in this carved girl
With the sly face and small ambiguous hand.

RIGHT: *Kuan-Yin,* 1700–1900 A.D.
The Field Museum, Chicago.

In this contemporary poem, the Irish poet Richard Kell describes Kuan-Yin, the Chinese goddess of compassion, as the embodiment of all the sensual pleasures of which Christianity tends to disapprove.

111

IV ● THE GODDESS OF LOVE AND PLEASURE

AT LAST LOVE HAS COME

ROMAN

Sulpicia,
translated by Aliki and
Willis Barnstone

At last love has come. I would be more ashamed
to hide it in cloth than leave it naked.
I prayed to the Muse and won. Venus dropped him
in my arms, doing for me what she
had promised. Let my joy be told, let those
who have none tell it in a story.
Personally, I would never send off words
in sealed tablets for none to read.
I delight in sinning and hate to compose a mask
for gossip. We met. We are both worthy.

ꓲꓲꓲꓲ: *The Mirror of Venus,*
Sir Edward Burne-Jones, 1898.
Gulbenkian Museum, Lisbon.

113

V

THE SUFFERING
OF THE GODDESS

TO MILLIONS OF CHRISTIANS, JESUS IS THE "LAMB OF GOD" WHO willingly gives his own life and thereby reconciles God with humankind. Christ's story echoes the ancient and universal belief that human life must be sustained by the sacrifice of a divine being. One finds stories in all cultures about deities who allow themselves to be crucified or dismembered, and whose death brings life to the world. In the following section, the Aztec story, "Hungry Woman," and the Pueblo tale, "The First People and the First Corn," offer typical examples. Just as a mother feeds her baby from her own body, so these crucified goddesses nourish their people as their flesh and blood transform into fruits and grains. Elements of these ancient myths still survive in the ritual of the Catholic mass, where celebrants symbolically eat the flesh and drink the blood of Jesus Christ, who thus becomes a nurturing mother to his followers.

If we are only familiar with Greek mythology, we may assume that gods and goddesses are always immortal. In other mythologies, however, deities participate in the cycle of birth and death. Thus, in the Sumerian "Descent of Inanna," the goddess dies and is resurrected after three days. Inanna's descent echoes our own struggles with loss and despair, and her emergence from the underworld reflects the indestructible core by which we renew ourselves.

In the Haitian story of "Erzulie Ge-Rouge," the goddess is an intriguing and unusual figure whose suffering is caused not by outer events, but by her own psychological make-up. She is the Haitian Aphrodite—inviting, provocative, and sensual. Her role is to bring a piece of paradise down to earth, and for this reason, she is particularly loved by the Haitian people, whose difficult and demanding lives afford them little access to the luxuries with which Erzulie surrounds herself. But unlike Aphrodite, Erzulie lives on earth and suffers deeply because of the inevitably flawed nature of earthly life. In Erzulie, perhaps more than in any other goddess, the tension between divine perfection and insatiable human longing is made visible. By refusing all consolation and insisting that no earthly food can satisfy her hunger, Erzulie encourages us, too, to acknowledge and honor our spiritual hunger and hold it sacred.

Ultimately, all the goddesses we meet in this section suffer because they are human as well as divine. In embracing their suffering, they find their strength and remind us that suffering is not a sign of weakness but an inevitable ingredient of earthly life.

OPPOSITE: *Demeter Mourning for Persephone*, Evelyn de Morgan, 1906. The De Morgan Foundation, London.

THE HUNGRY WOMAN

AZTEC

Adapted by John Bierhorst

ABOVE: Necklace featuring tiny gold skulls with moveable jaws, Oaxaca, Mexico, c. 1500 A.D. Dumbarton Oaks Research Library and Collections, Washington D.C.

I n the place where the spirits live, there was once a woman who cried constantly for food. She had mouths in her wrists, mouths in her elbows, and mouths in her ankles and knees. "She can't eat here," said the other spirits. "She will have to live somewhere else."

But up above, there was only the empty air, and to the right and to the left and in front and behind, it was just the same. In those days the world had not been created. Nevertheless, there was something underneath that seemed to be water. How it had got there nobody knew. "If we put her below," they thought, "then perhaps she will be able to satisfy her hunger."

No sooner had the thought occurred than the spirits Quetzalcoatl and Tezcatlipoca seized the woman and dragged her down to the water. When they saw that she floated, they changed into snakes, stretching over her in the form of a cross, from right arm to left leg and from left arm to right leg. Catching her hands and feet, they squeezed her from all four directions, pushing so hard that she snapped in half at the waist.

"Now look what we've done," they said, and not knowing what else to do, they carried the bottom half back to the spirit place. "Look," they cried. "What's to be done with this?"

"What a shame," said the other spirits. "But never mind. We'll use it to make the sky." Then, to comfort the poor woman, they all flew down and began to make grass and flowers out of her skin. From her hair they made forests, from her eyes, pools and springs, from her shoulders, mountains, and from her nose, valleys. At last she will be satisfied, they thought. But just as before, her mouths were everywhere, biting and moaning. And still she hasn't changed.

When it rains, she drinks. When flowers shrivel, when trees fall, or when someone dies, she eats. When people are sacrificed or killed in battle, she drinks their blood. Her mouths are always opening and snapping shut, but they are never filled. Sometimes at night, when the wind blows, you can hear her crying for food.

OPPOSITE: Seated female figure with filed teeth, Mexico, c. 150–300 A.D. Collection of the Bowers Museum of Cultural Art, Los Angeles, Foundation Acquisition Fund Purchase (F74.1.3).

117

THE CURSE OF THE GODDESS MACHA

CELTIC

Told by Mary Condren

Once there was a rich man, Crunnchu mac Agnoman. His wife had died, and he was very lonely until one day a stately young woman came to him. She sat down by the hearth of the fire, stirring the embers without saying a word to anyone. Later she milked the cow and baked bread, still without speaking. In all her actions, however, she was careful to "turn right" following the direction of the sun; a clue as to her identity. When night fell, she crept into Crunnchu's bed and made love to him.

Everything went well for a time, and we are told that "his handsome appearance was delightful to her." His wealth increased, and he enjoyed prosperity in every respect, but trouble was soon to follow. The annual assembly of the Ulstermen was due to start in the near future and Crunnchu wanted to attend. Macha pleaded with him to stay at home, since his going to the assembly could only cause trouble for her. Crunnchu insisted, and finally Macha permitted him to go only after he had promised not to speak a word to anyone of their union, since only harm could come of that. Crunnchu duly promised and set off.

This annual assembly was a great occasion, and people came from all over Ireland. One of the main events was the horse racing competition. Although many competed, the horses belonging to the king and queen defeated all before them. At the end of the games everyone assembled to praise the monarchs. The people were heard to say, "Never before have two such horses been seen at the festival as these two horses of the king: in all Ireland there is not a swifter pair." Hearing this, Crunnchu could not resist. He cried out to the assembled people, "My wife runs quicker than these two horses." Furious, the king ordered him to be tied up until his wife could be brought to the contest to race against his horses.

Messengers were sent out to Macha, telling her to come urgently to the games. Macha was reluctant to go as she was pregnant and about to deliver. But upon being told that her husband would otherwise be killed, she agreed and set forth. When she arrived, they told her that she must race against two horses of the king. Hearing this she grew pale and turned to the assembled people with a wrenching plea that would echo in Ireland down the centuries: "Help me," she cried to the bystanders, "*for a mother bore each one of you. Give me, O King, but a short delay, until I am delivered* (emphasis added)."

Macha appealed to those assembled, not on the basis of an abstract system of ethics or for mercy: she appealed to them on the basis of their relationship to their mothers: "A mother bore each one of you." Childbirth was a supremely sacred activity, and the needs of a pregnant woman had hitherto overruled the demands of any egotistical king. But the king refused to delay the race, impatient as he was to demonstrate his own superiority. Finally, Macha threatened that a severe curse would fall upon Ulster. "What is your name?" asked the king, and Macha replied in ominous tones: "My name and the name of that which I shall bear will forever cleave to the place of this assembly. I am Macha, daughter of Sainreth mac in Botha (Strange son of Ocean)."

The horses were brought up and the race began. Macha won the race easily and before the king's horses had even reached the winning post, she gave birth to twins, a son and a daughter who gave their names to *Emhain Mhacha* (the Twins of Macha). Suddenly, all the men assembled were seized with weakness and "had no more strength than a woman in her pain," for at the moment of her tragic victory Macha pronounced a curse on the men of Ulster:

> From this hour the ignominy that you
> have inflicted upon me will redound to
> the shame of each one of you. When a
> time of oppression falls upon you, each
> one of you who dwells in this province
> will be overcome with weakness, as the
> weakness of a woman in child-birth, and
> this will remain upon you for five days
> and four nights; to the ninth generation it
> shall be so.

BELOW: Gilded silver ornamental plate,
4th to 1st century B.C.E. Historic
District Museum, Lovec, Bulgaria.

OVERLEAF: Earth Mother
goddess, detail of Gundestrup
cauldron, Celtic, c. 100 B.C.E.
National Museum, Copenhagen.

V ● THE SUFFERING OF THE GODDESS

THE FIRST PEOPLE
AND THE FIRST CORN

PUEBLO

Told by Shakrukh Husain

Long ago, Klos-kur-beh, the Great Teacher, lived in the land where no people lived. One day at noon, a young man came to him and called him "Mother's brother." Standing before Klos-kur-beh, he said, "I was born of the foam of the waters. The wind blew, and the waves quickened into a foam. The sun shone on the foam and warmed it, and the warmth made life, and the life was I. See—I am young and swift, and I have come to abide with you and to help in all that you do."

Again on a day at noon, a maiden came, stood before the two, and called them "my children." "My Children, I have come to abide with you and have brought with me love. I will give it to you, and if you will love me and will grant my wish, all the world will love me, even the very beasts. Strength is mine, and I give it to whosoever may get me. Comfort also is mine, for though I am young, my strength shall be felt over all the earth. I was born of the beautiful plant of the earth. For the dew fell on the leaf, and the sun warmed the dew, and the warmth was life, and that life is I."

Then Klos-kur-beh lifted up his hands towards the sun and praised the Great Spirit. Afterward, the young

man and the maiden became man and wife, and she became the first mother. Klos-kur-beh taught their children and did great works for them. When his works were finished, he went away to live in the Northland until it should be time for him to come again.

The people increased until they were numerous. When a famine came among them, the first mother grew more and more sorrowful. Every day at noon she left her husband's lodge and stayed away from him until the shadows were long. Her husband, who dearly loved her, was sad because of her sorrow. One day he followed her trail as far as the ford of the river, and there he waited for her to return.

When she came she sang as she began to ford the river, and as long as her feet were in the water she seemed glad. The man saw something that trailed behind her right foot, like a long green blade. When she came out of the water, she stooped and cast off the blade. Then she appeared sorrowful.

The husband followed her home as the sun was setting, and he bade her come out and look at the beautiful sun. While they stood side by side, there came seven little children. They stood in front of the couple, looked into the woman's face, and spoke: "We are hungry, and the night will soon be here. Where is the food?"

Tears ran down the woman's face as she said, "Be quiet, little ones. In seven moons you shall be filled and shall hunger no more."

Her husband reached out, wiped away her tears, and asked, "My wife, what can I do to make you happy?"

"Nothing else," she said. "Nothing else will make me happy."

OPPOSITE: *Corn Dance Ceremony Myth*, Ignacio Moquino (Zia Pueblo), 1938. Archives of the Museum of Indian Arts & Culture/Laboratory of Anthropology, Santa Fe.

Then the husband went away to the Northland to ask Klos-kur-beh for counsel. With the rising of the seventh sun, he returned and said, "O wife, Klos-kur-beh has told me to do what you asked."

The woman was pleased and said, "When you have slain me, let two men take hold of my hair and draw my body all the way around a field. When they have come to the middle of it, let them bury my bones. Then they must come away. When seven months have passed, let them go again to the field and gather all that they find. Tell them to eat it. It is my flesh. You must save a part of it to put in the ground again. My bones you cannot eat, but you may burn them. The smoke will bring peace to you and your children."

The next day, when the sun was rising, the man

slew his wife. Following her orders, two men drew her body over an open field until her flesh was worn away. In the middle of the field, they buried her bones.

When seven moons had passed by and the husband came again to that place, he saw it all filled with beautiful tall plants. He tasted the fruit of the plant and found it sweet. He called it *Skar-mu-nal*—"corn." And on the place where his wife's bones were buried, he saw a plant with broad leaves, bitter to the taste. He called it *Utar-mur-wa-yeh*—"tobacco."

Then the people were glad to their hearts, and they came to the harvest. But when the fruits were all gathered, the man did not know how to divide them. So he sent to the Great Teacher, Klos-kur-beh, for counsel. When Klos-kur-beh came and saw the great harvest, he said, "Now have the first words of the first

mother come to pass, for she said she was born of the leaf of the beautiful plant. She said also that her power should be felt over the whole world and that all men should love her.

"And now that she has gone into this substance, take care that the second seed of the first mother be always with you, for it is her flesh. Her bones also have been given for your good. Burn them, and the smoke will bring freshness to the mind. And since these things came from the goodness of a woman's heart, see that you hold her always in memory. Remember her when you eat. Remember her when the smoke of her bones rises before you. And because you are all brothers, divide among you her flesh and her bones. Let all share alike, for so will the love of the first mother have been fulfilled."

ABOVE: *Cherokee Women Represent Selu, the First Woman, During the Green Corn Ceremony,* Murv Jacob, 20th century. Courtesy of the artist.

125

Erzulie Ge~Rouge

✦

HAITIAN

Told by Maya Deren

In 1947, the anthropologist Maya Deren embarked for Haiti, a journey that would lead to her classic account of the Haitian deities and the rituals of Voudoun, in which individuals are possessed by the spirits of the deities. Maya Deren felt especially close to Erzulie and was on several occasions, herself, possessed by this goddess.

I n Erzulie, Voudoun salutes woman as the divinity of the dream, the Goddess of Love, the muse of beauty. . . . Erzulie moves in an atmosphere of infinite luxury, a perfume of refinement, which, from the first moment of her arrival, pervades the very air of the peristyle, and becomes a general expansiveness in which all anxieties, all urgencies vanish. The tempo of movements becomes more leisurely, tensions dissolve and the voices soften, losing whatever aggressive or strident tones they may have had. One has the impression that a fresh, cooling breeze has sprung up somewhere and that the heat has become less intense, less oppressive.

Her first act is to perform an elaborate toilette for which the equipment is always kept in readiness in the hounfor or the private chapel; and it is always the very best that the houngan or serviteur can afford. The enamel basin in which she washes is neither chipped nor discolored; the soap is new, still in its wrapper; there are several towels, probably embroidered; and a special comb, mirror and even tooth-brush have been consecrated to her. She is provided with a fresh white or rose silk handkerchief which she arranges carefully around her hair. Perfume is imperative, and there may be powder as well. A white or rose dress of delicate cloth, with lace or embroidery, has been kept in readiness for her. And, finally, she is brought not one necklace, but several, of gold and pearls, along with earrings and bracelets and her three wedding-bands. . . .

Thus attired, powdered and perfumed, she goes out into the peristyle escorted by several of the more handsome men, her favorites. There she may make the rounds, greeting the men guests effusively, but extending only the little fingers of each hand to those women who are not special devotees. Her voice is a delicate soprano; her every gesture, movement of eyes, and smile, is a masterpiece of beguiling coquetry; with her,

I I I I: *Voodoo Dance in the Forest,* Jean-Pierre, 20th century. Private collection.

127

human relationship becomes itself significant rather than merely a means to an end. She may visit her altar chamber and be pleased that the flowers are fresh, for flowers are her passion. She may ask for a favorite song, for she loves to dance and is the most graceful of all loa; or she may simply give audience to her admirers, and by her postures and attitudes transform the crude chair in which she sits into a throne. If she is being feasted that day, she eats delicately, of a cuisine that is more exacting than that of any other loa—a just-so blending of seasonings and sauces. Above all, she favors desserts, decorated cakes and confections of all kinds. Or, if she has arrived on an impromptu visit, she may be content with a sip of the *crème de menthe* or the champagne which, theoretically, should always be ready for her appearance.

. . . As Lady of Luxury, she gives gifts constantly: her own perfume, the handkerchief she wears, the food and money which she conscripts from the houngan and distributes generously. She particularly rewards those who are handsome, or who dance well, or whose personality pleases her. She never neglects one who is devoted to her.

As Lady of Luxury she is, above all, Goddess of Love, that human luxury of the heart which is not essential to the purely physical generation of the body. She is as lavish with that love as she is generous with her gifts. She treats men with such overflowing, such demonstrative affection that it might seem, at times, embarrassing. She will embrace them, and kiss them, caress them, sit with an arm around those to both sides of her. Nothing is meted out or budgeted, there is more than enough; this is her way of loving, this is the divine fecundity of the heart. A heart is, indeed, her symbol, most often the pierced heart identified with Mary.

It is a fecundity which minor men would call promiscuity. But her several lovers among the loa, who are major men, and the serviteurs, who have learned to see her through their eyes, have never called it that. Her past includes them all—Dam-ballah, Agwé and Ogoun. It is for these three that she wears three wedding-bands simultaneously. There has been, also, a flirtation with the lesser Azacca; a dismissal of the love-struck Ghede because he was too coarse; and any devotee who might especially please her may be taken for her lover. . . . Indeed, it is as if, from the limitless wealth of her heart, she could love many, and each in ample and full measure. Her generosity is so natural that one is caught up in her exuberant innocence, believing, with her, that all is good, is simple, is full-blown.

Yet . . . in the midst of the gaiety she will inexplicably recall, as women sometimes do, some old, minor disappointment. She will remark the one inadequate detail here among the dozen major achievements. Suddenly it is apparent that imperceptibly she has crossed an invisible threshold where even the most willing reason and the most ready reality cannot follow; and, in another moment, she, who seemed so very close, so real, so warm, is suddenly of another world, beyond this reality, this reason. It is as if below the gaiety a pool had been lying, silently swelling, since the very first moment; and now its dark despair surfaces and engulfs her beyond succor. She who has been loved by all the major loa (and it is not they who were promiscuous) is convinced, by some curious inversion, that they have each betrayed her. She reiterates this complaint, even against the reminder that Ogoun still pressed his court and that Agwé still takes care of her in her illnesses. She, who is the wealthiest of the loa, the most frequently gifted with luxurious accoutrement, suffers for not being "served" enough. She, who is the most complimented, most beloved, most often wedded in the sacred marriage of devotee and divinity—she who is Goddess of Love—protests that she is not loved enough.

Inevitably then—and this is a classic stage of Erzulie's possession—she begins to weep. Tenderly they would comfort her, bringing forward still another cake, another jewel, pledging still another promise. But it would seem that nothing in this world would ever, *could ever*, answer those tears. It is because of these tears that the women, who might otherwise resent her, are so gentle. In their real, reasonable world there is no grief like this.

There are times when this sense of all things gone wrong is projected in that combined rage and despair which is Erzulie Ge-Rouge. With her knees drawn up, the fists clenched, the jaw rigid and the tears streaming from her tight-shut eyes, she is the cosmic tantrum—the tantrum not of a spoiled child, but of some cosmic innocence which cannot understand—and *will* not understand—why accident should ever befall what is cherished, or why death should ever come to the beloved. But whether the raging tears of Erzulie Ge-Rouge, or the despairing sobs of Erzulie Maîtresse, this weeping is so inaccessible to reason that one thinks, inevitably, of a child's innocence of reason. It is this sense of innocence which emanates from her that makes her identification with the Virgin Mary somehow seem truer than her promiscuity, than even the fact that the devotion of prostitutes makes of her almost their patron saint.

128

It is possible, even, that there is no conflict between these several truths, for the concept of Erzulie as virgin is not intended as a physical analysis. To call her virgin is to say that she is of another world, another reality, and that her heart, like the secret insulated heart of Mary Magdalene, is innocent of the flesh, is inaccessible to its delights and its corruptions. To say she is virgin is to say that she is Goddess of the Heart, not of the body: the loa of things as they *could* be, not as they are, or even as they normally should be. She is the divinity of the dream, and it is in the very nature of dream to begin where reality ends and to spin it and to send it forward in space, as the spider spins and sends forward its own thread. . . . Erzulie is the loa of the impossible perfection which must remain unattainable. Man demands that she demand of him beyond his capacity. The condition of her divinity is his failure; he crowns her with his own betrayals. Hence she must weep; it could not be otherwise.

So, Maîtresse Erzulie, weeping, comes to that moment which has been called her paralysis. Just as the hurt of a child mounts and transcends both its own cause and solution, reaching a plateau where it exists as a pure pain, so her articulate complaints cease, even the sobbing; and the body, as if no longer able to endure, abandons the heart to its own infinite grief. Her limbs, her neck, her back go limp. Her arms, stretching across the shoulders of the men who support her on either side, her head tilting, the cheeks wet from tears, the lids closing over eyes turned inward toward some infinite darkness, she presents, as Ogoun did, the precise attitude of the Crucifixion. So she is carried from the stilled, saddened public to some adjacent private chamber. Stretched on the bed, her arms still outflung, she falls asleep as a child might, exhausted by too great a grief. Those who brought her in, and others, who, unreasonably, would still wish to do something for her, stand about quietly, speaking in whispers. They are glad to see that sleep has come, and with it, respite; for they sense that her pain is not only great but perhaps even eternal. The wound of Ogoun was a defeat which might, perhaps, not have occurred or might, conceivably, be healed. The wound of Erzulie is perpetual; she is the dream impaled eternally upon the cosmic cross-roads where the world of men and the world of divinity meet, and it is through her pierced heart that "man ascends and the gods descend."

ABOVE: *Untitled*, Gene Hendricks Pearson, 1988. Courtesy of the artist.

129

THE DESCENT OF INANNA

SUMERIAN

Told by Jalaja Bonheim

Inscribed on stone tablets around 2000 B.C.E. by the Sumerians, this is the oldest recorded goddess myth. Four thousand years later, it has lost none of its power and universality. It is a precursor of the Greek myth of Persephone's descent to the underworld.

Long ago, in the beginning of time, Inanna lay down on the earth, and pressing her head against the damp soil, she listened into the earth. Within her, a yearning grew stronger and stronger, until she could no longer deny its insistent call. "I want to descend," she thought. "I want to visit the dark realm where my sister Ereshkigal lives, whom the people call Queen of the Underworld and Devourer of living beings. But surely she will not harm me, her own sister."

And soon Inanna withdrew from her temples, one by one, like a turtle pulling in its limbs. No longer did she call down the rain from the heavy thunderclouds, no longer did she bless the crops. Placing the seven objects of royal power upon her body, Inanna prepared herself to descend, longing for what she could not name. Finally, she confided in Ninshubur, her beloved helper and friend. "Ninshubur", she said, "I am going to that place from where none have returned. Beloved sister, you whom I trust like none other, I give the silvery thread of my life into your hands. Wait for me. Three days and three nights, wait. If I should not return, know that death has caught me in its great web. Then cry for help, cry for my life. But now, you must leave me." And the Holy Priestess continued alone.

When Inanna reached the entrance to the underworld, she knocked loudly. "Open the door, gatekeeper! Neti, open the door!" And Neti asked from behind the locked door, "Who wishes to enter?" "It is I, Inanna, Queen of Heaven, holy priestess of Sumer." "Either you are drunk, Inanna, or you have lost your way. Do you not know that those who walk this way do not return? Go back, Inanna!" "No, Neti. I shall not go back. I wish to see my sister Ereshkigal. Open the gate!" "Wait here, Inanna. I will speak to Ereshkigal." And Neti entered the chamber of his queen, Ereshkigal. "My queen," he announced. "A woman has come. Tall and strong as the sacred oak, radiant as the sun, beautiful to behold, she waits for your word. Proudly she stands, clothed in power."

Ereshkigal was surprised. She considered the matter carefully, slapping her thigh, frowning. Dark mother, ancient two-faced one, she weighed the matter. Then, she hid away her dark face of compassion, for she saw that Inanna's soul was ripe for initiation into the mysteries of death, and she turned toward Neti her face of terror. Rage and hunger and hatred glowed in her eyes. Raising a skull filled with blood, the queen drank deeply, her olive-black tongue licking her lips. "She shall enter, Neti," said Ereshkigal, Queen of Death. "But not as she has planned it. Not as sister shall she know me, but as the great teacher of death. She is strong, yet I shall grind her down until she is no more than dust on the ground. Go Neti, do as I say." Neti returned to Inanna and opened the first gate to the underworld: "Enter, Inanna."

But as Inanna entered, hands reached down and plucked the golden crown off her head. "What is this?" she cried. And from all sides, the answer echoed back: "Quiet, Inanna. The ways of the underworld are perfect. They may not be questioned." And touching her bare head with her fingers, Inanna felt a sudden bleakness. "What made me think I was special?" she murmured. "I too am going to die."

Slowly she walked, following a tunnel into the damp cool earth, until before her, the second gate appeared. And as she entered, unearthly hands unfastened the small lapis beads from Inanna's neck. Outraged, she protested: "What is this?" Again, she

OPPOSITE: Greco-Phoenician sarcophagus, c. 500 A.D. Louvre, Paris.

131

was silenced: "Quiet, Inanna. The ways of the underworld are perfect. They may not be questioned." Startled, she raised her hand to her throat as her voice closed down, and loneliness settled like a vulture upon her shoulder. Walking through the darkness, her fingertips felt the moisture dripping down the walls as her feet groped for the next step.

But as Inanna stepped over the threshold of the third gate, the double strand of deep blue beads was unfastened from her throat. Once again, she could not help but cry out: "What is this?" For her mind was struggling to understand what cannot be understood. "Quiet, Inanna. The ways of the underworld are perfect. They may not be questioned." She who loved so deeply, so passionately, now tried to remember her loved ones, but found their faces fading away. Dizzy, she stumbled downward, her hands outstretched, glimpsing eyes in the darkness and the swirling of dragon wings.

And as she entered the fourth gate, the jeweled belt named "Come, man, come!" was untied from her hips. "What is this?" "Quiet, Inanna, the ways of the underworld are perfect. They may not be questioned." And Inanna, the most beautiful woman in Sumer, the most desired, the most coveted, suddenly no longer knew—was she male or female? Confused, she slid down dimly glowing arteries that pulsated and throbbed as if echoing the heartbeat of the earth her-

self. Everything around her dissolving, she fell into the fifth gate. Damp fingers gripped her wrist, stripping off her golden armband, a gift she had received from her brother the bright laughing sun. "What is this?" "Quiet, Inanna, the ways of the underworld are perfect. They may not be questioned." And with that, Inanna lost all memory of the light. Her head reeled; darkness surrounded her.

Spinning and spiraling, Inanna grasped tightly in her hands the lapis measuring rod and line. But as she fell into the sixth gate, she found them empty, and within her mind, all dualities collapsed into chaos. She no longer knew whether she was falling up or down, nor could she tell past from future. And as she fell down into the seventh gate, her royal robe fell away, and she stood naked, crushed, and humbled, within a vast cavern, while a low wind moaned through the silence.

But within the darkness, a deeper blackness sat, like a spider within her web—Ereshkigal, the dark Queen of Death. Unmoving, giving no sign of recognition, Ereshkigal fastened upon Inanna an eye filled with rage and with the green flame of hatred, and Inanna recoiled. Now, as Ereshkigal rose from her throne, her attendants stepped forward and seized Inanna. And from her mouth, Ereshkigal sent a sound, a low vibration more ancient than the earth herself.

Weakness overcame Inanna. Her senses struggled and faded. Hearing and vision grew dim, all the senses dim, memory erased, until Ereshkigal's tone sucked the last breath from Inanna's body. And as darkness flooded in through the cracked vessel, Inanna dissolved into the womb of the earth, into the womb of her dark sister. As a seed dies into the earth, Inanna surrendered. Blackness

RIGHT: *Inanna & Ereshkigal*, Sheryl Cotleur, 1993. Courtesy of the artist.

filled her mind, and her body was hung on a meathook on the wall. In the darkness, the wind moaned through the cavern, and Inanna's corpse swayed in the breeze.

Three days went by, three nights went by, and Inanna did not return. Ninshubur, anguish in her heart, remembered the queen's words. She called the women of the land, and they gathered—grieving, keening, tearing their hair. Then Ninshubur sought out Enlil, the mighty sky god in his great temple at Nippur. But Enlil refused to help. "Inanna knows the rules," he said. "So, she has chosen to go to the Dark City, from where none return? Foolish woman. Go. I cannot help you." Disappointed, Ninshubur wandered to the city of Ur, to the temple of Nanna. But like Enlil, Nanna too refused to help.

Desperate, Ninshubur hurried to Eridu, to the temple of Enki, the ancient god of waters. Sobbing, Ninshubur clasped the god's feet, pleading for the life of her beloved sister Inanna. Immediately, Enki stood up, sorrow in his eyes. "O my daughter," he murmured. "Oh, queen, you foolish one, what have you done?" And as the tears fell from his eyes, they became small gurgling streams.

Anxiously Ninshubur waited as Enki paced the small shrine. But after a long time, his brow smoothed and he chuckled. Sitting down, he began to clean his fingernails. Then he took the dirt from underneath his fingernails and spat on it, and began molding it in his fingers, two tiny balls of dirt. As Ninshubur watched with wide eyes, he breathed upon the two little balls, and they sprouted tiny little wings, and legs, and a head with eyes. Laughing, Enki threw them up into the air and they buzzed around his head. This one, he said to Ninshubur, is a Galatur, and this one is a Kurgarra. And to the Kurgarra he gave a crumb of bread, and to the Galatur, a drop of water. Then he spoke to the two little beings, neither male nor female:

"Hear me well. Listen well, my children. Fly to the underworld. Fly through the cracks. Fly through the gates. Down, down, down. Into the womb of the earth. There Ereshkigal lies, moaning in pain, for she is great with child, yet alone. Great with child yet alone. Naked, her body, naked her breasts. Snakes hissing in her hair. She will speak. What she speaks, you speak back to her. Whatever she speaks, you speak back to her. You hear? She will become happy, generous. Ask her for the corpse of Inanna. Ask her for the corpse of Inanna. Feed it with the bread. Wash it with the water. She will arise. She will arise. She will arise. Go now."

Three times, the creatures circled around Enki's head, indicating that they had understood. Then they flew to the underworld, straight through the gates, through the cracks. Down they flew, into Ereshkigal's great cavern, and from afar they heard the dark queen moaning and groaning. There Ereshkigal lay, moaning in pain, for she was big with child, yet alone. Naked, her body, naked her breasts. Snakes hissing in her hair.

"Oh, oh, my inside!" she moaned. And flying to either side of the queen, the Kurgarra and the Galatur sat and they, too, moaned: "Oh, oh, your inside!" And as they moaned with Ereshkigal, Enki's healing balm of compassion enveloped the queen. And Ereshkigal moaned: "Oh! Oh, my outside," and Enki's creatures too moaned, "Oh! Queen! Your outside!" And along with their words, the healing waters of Enki's ancient wisdom entered the queen's body. And she moaned: "Oh, my pain is unbearable!" and they answered: "Oh, yes, queen, indeed, your pain is truly unbearable."

But as the queen wailed, holding within her the suffering of the universe, Enki's healing waters entered her heart. Where only pain had been, she now felt a kernel of sweetness. And Enki's little creatures listened, sitting with her, witnessing and waiting patiently. Until finally the queen stopped. "You, little ones, who are you? What magic have you brought, coming at the time of my greatest pain? Whatever you desire, I shall give you. Let me give you the gift of the great rivers."

"No. No. No," said the Kurgarra and the Galatur. The queen said, "You don't want it? Let me give you the rich golden flow of grain waving in the wind."

"No. No. No," said the Kurgurra and the Galatur. "Speak then. What do you want?"

"We want the corpse that hangs on the wall." With a shrug, Ereshkigal motioned to her guards, and they dragged in the rotting corpse. Three times the Kurgarra and the Galatur flew around Inanna's corpse. Upon her lips, they laid the food of life. Upon her cold heart, they sprinkled the water of life. And beneath the skin, a stirring, a swelling. They waited. And then her heart began to beat; Inanna breathed. She arose, Queen of Heaven, Holy Priestess of the Lands.

She arose, and returned to the land of the living, filling the hearts of her people with joy and amazement, for she had gone where none had gone before. But since that time, it is Inanna whom we turn to when we journey through the dark unknown, and whom we call upon as our trusted guide through life and through death, through time and through eternity.

BAUBO: THE BELLY GODDESS

Clarissa Pinkola Estés, Ph.D.

There is a powerful saying: *Ella habla por en medio en las piernas,*
"She speaks from between her legs." Little "between-the-legs"
stories are found all over the world. One is the story of Baubo, a Goddess
from ancient Greece, the so-called Goddess of obscenity. She has older names,
such as *Iambe*, and it appears the Greeks borrowed her from far older cultures.
There have been archetypal wild Goddesses of sacred sexuality and
Life/Death/Life fertility since the beginning of memory.
There is only one popular reference to Baubo in writings existent from ancient
times, giving the direct impression that her cult was destroyed, and buried
under the stampede of various conquests. I have a strong sense that somewhere, perhaps under all those sylvan hills and forest lakes in Europe and the
East, there are temples to her, complete with artifacts, and bone icons.*
So, it is not by accident that few have heard of Baubo, but remember,
one shard of archetype can carry the image of the whole. And we have the
shard, for we have a story in which Baubo appears. She is one of the most
lovely and picaresque of all the highnesses who lived on Olympus. This is my
cantadora, literary story version based on the old wildish remnant of Baubo
still glinting in post-matriarchal Greek mythos and the Homeric hymns.**

---

* Çatal Hüyük has a "between-the-legs" icon high on a wall. The figure is a woman with her legs wide apart, with her
"nether mouth" revealed, possibly as oracle. Just the thought of such a figure makes many women chuckle with knowing.
** Charles Boer, *The Homeric Hymns,* (Dallas: Spring Publications, 1987). This is a truly gifted translation.

The Earth Mother, Demeter, had a beautiful daughter called Persephone who was playing out in the meadow one day. Persephone came upon one particularly lovely bloom, and reached out her fingertips to cup its lovely face. Suddenly the ground began to shake and a giant zigzag ripped across the land. Up from deep within the earth charged Hades, the God of the Underworld. He stood tall and mighty in a black chariot driven by four horses the color of ghost.

Hades seized Persephone into his chariot, her veils and sandals flying. Down, down, down into the earth he reined his horses. Persephone's screams grew more and more faint as the rift in the earth healed over as though nothing had ever happened.

The voice of the maiden crying out echoed through the stones of the mountains, bubbled up in a watery cry from underneath the sea. Demeter heard the stones cry out. She heard the watery crying. And then, over all the land came an eerie silence, and the smell of crushed flowers.

And tearing her wreath from her immortal hair, and unfurling down from each shoulder her dark veils, Demeter flew out over the land like a great bird, searching for, calling for her daughter.

That night an old crone at the edge of a cave remarked to her sisters that she had heard three cries that day; one, a youthful voice crying out in terror; and another calling plaintively; and a third, that of a mother weeping.

Persephone was nowhere to be found, and so began Demeter's crazed and months-long search for her beloved child. Demeter raged, she wept, she screamed, she asked after, searched every land formation underneath, inside, and atop, begged mercy, begged death, but no matter what, she could not find her heart-child.

So, she who had made everything grow in perpetuity, cursed all the fertile fields of the world, screaming in her grief, "Die! Die! Die!" Because of Demeter's curse, no child could be born, no wheat could rise for bread, no flowers for feasts, no boughs for the dead. Everything lay withered and sucked at parched earth or dry breasts.

Demeter herself no longer bathed. Her robes were mud drenched, her hair hung in dreadlocks. Even though the pain in her heart was staggering, she would not surrender. After many askings, pleadings, and episodes, all leading to nothing, she finally slumped down at the side of a well in a village where she was unknown. And as she leaned her aching body against the cool stone of the well, along came a woman, or rather a sort of woman. And this woman danced up to Demeter wiggling her hips in a way suggesting sexual intercourse, and shaking her breasts in her little dance. And when Demeter saw her, she could not help but smile just a little.

The dancing female was very magical indeed, for she had no head whatsoever, and her nipples were her eyes and her vulva was her mouth. It was through this lovely mouth that she began to regale Demeter with some nice juicy jokes.

Demeter began to smile, and then chuckled, and then gave a full belly laugh. And together the two women laughed, the little belly Goddess Baubo and the powerful Mother Earth Goddess, Demeter.

And it was just this laughing that drew Demeter out of her depression and gave her the energy to continue her search for her daughter, which, with the help of Baubo, and the crone Hekate, and the sun Helios, was ultimately successful. Persephone was restored to her mother. The world, the land, and the bellies of women thrived again.

"Baubo: The Belly Goddess," © C.P. Estés 1992, 1995, *Women Who Run With the Wolves* (pp. 336–338).

ABOVE: Clay goddess figure, c. 4800 B.C.E. National Museum of History of Romania, Bucharest.

OVERLEAF: *Demeter & Persephone "Exaltation of the Flower,"* 470–460 B.C.E. Louvre, Paris.

VI

A Terrible Beauty

IN THE OLD TESTAMENT, GOD ALLOWS JOB'S ENTIRE FAMILY TO BE KILLED and causes him to suffer every imaginable misery. Understandably, Job accuses God of cruelty and injustice. Though we like to believe in God as a source of comfort and help, God's gifts include death as well as life, torment as well as joy. Accordingly, some goddesses are destructive, while others are creative. As the sixth-century Greek philosopher Heraclitus stated, "To men, some things are good and some bad. But to God, all things are good and beautiful and just."

Deities are reflections of our own nature. As C. G. Jung emphasized, the human psyche has its "dark" side, too; we are all capable of both good and evil. The best way to deal with the shadow, Jung believed, is to become conscious of it and to establish a relationship with it. Certain religions, such as Hinduism and Tibetan Buddhism, address this need by intentionally evoking the dark, terrifying face of the goddess. It must be emphasized that such worship of the dark goddess has nothing in common with the worship of evil that occurs in certain satanic cults. On the contrary—by meditating on the dark goddess, her worshipers seek to deepen their faith in the unfathomable, unexplainable mysteries of the divine, so as to face both suffering and death with a fearless and peaceful heart.

Goddesses who represent the dark unknown are usually black in color. In ancient Sumer, the black goddess was known as Ereshkigal, queen of death and destruction. In Greece, both Athena and Artemis (known as Diana to the Romans) embodied aspects of the dark goddess. Christianity, too, has its "black Madonnas" that are worshiped with fervent devotion throughout Europe; "Ayiasma" is a poem inspired by one such image. Yet it is in India that the worship of the dark goddess reached its most sublime expressions. To this day, millions of people worship Kali, a goddess whose blackness reflects her unfathomable mystery, her unknowable depth of compassion, as well as her incomprehensible cruelty.

OPPOSITE: *Pallas Athena*, Gustav Klimt, 1898. Historisches Museum der Stadt Wien, Vienna.

HYMN TO PALLAS ATHENA

GREEK

Homer,
translated by Jules Cashford

Pallas Athena
I shall sing,
the glorious goddess
whose eyes gleam,
brilliantly inventive,
her heart relentless,
formidable maiden,
guardian of cities,
the courageous Tritogeneia.

Wise Zeus gave birth to her himself
out of his majestic head.
Golden armor clothed her,
warlike, glistening.
All the gods who saw her
were overcome with awe.

Suddenly she was there
before Zeus who holds the aegis.
She sprang from his immortal head,
shaking her sharp spear.

OPPOSITE: *Head of Minerva,*
Elihu Vedder, 1896.
Courtesy Babcock Galleries,
New York.

BELOW: *Minerva,* 1st century
B.C.E. National Archaeo-
logical Museum, Naples.

Great Olympus trembled terribly
at the power of the goddess
with the gleaming eyes.
And all around her the earth
screamed awfully
and then the sea
started to move, frothing
with dark waves, and salt
foam suddenly
spurted up.

The brilliant son of Hyperion,
the sun,
stilled
his swift-footed horses
for a long time until
Pallas Athena, the maiden,
unclasped the god-like armor
from her immortal shoulders.
Wise Zeus was delighted.

Greetings, daughter of Zeus
who holds the aegis.
Now, and in another song,
I will remember you.

ATHENA AND ARACHNE

GREEK

Told by Jalaja Bonheim

Arachne was not a good weaver—no, she was the best. Her tapestries had been known to make people fall into a trance from which they did not awaken for days, and when they came to their senses, they said they had entered the woods and forests Arachne had woven. And not only that, but they claimed that the gods and the goddesses within her weavings came to life, and spoke and laughed and danced. Arachne smiled when they said these things, and shrugged. "Why should I deny it?" she said. "Even Athena, though she is the goddess of weaving, does not possess my skill."

Arachne's words reached the ears of the goddess, and anger clouded Athena's face. Disguising her majesty, she took the form of an old, wizened woman who knocked on Arachne's door. "I have heard you call yourself a great weaver," Athena began. "I *am* a great weaver," Arachne retorted without further ado, "it's a fact." The goddess scowled. "You may be good," she said, "but I am better." Then and there, she challenged the girl to a competition. Incredulous, Arachne looked down at the woman's gnarled old hands and laughed. "Why not? Tomorrow, we will set up our looms. Be my guest then, for tonight." And so, Arachne shared her food and her house with the goddess, and thought nothing of the coming day, except that every once in a while she noticed a strange light shining in the eyes of her guest that made her shiver.

The next day dawned bright and clear. The looms were set up in the courtyard, side by side, and the yarns were laid out, crimson and blue, violet and peach, emerald green and golden yellow. The villagers gathered around to watch the spectacle as, side by side, Athena the goddess and Arachne the maiden began their work. Glancing sideways, Arachne saw to her amazement that the old woman's hands, gnarled as they were, were still as swift and sure as a pair of young falcons, and she bit her lip and frowned. All day the two worked side by side in silence, and the

villagers too fell silent in amazement as they watched them create two weavings the likes of which no mortal had ever seen.

When dusk fell, it was done, and the two tapestries were displayed for all to see. On Athena's weaving, the people recognized Zeus and Hera enthroned side by side, radiant and majestic. One could hardly believe that the weaver had used ordinary wools and silks, for the colors of her tapestry seemed to glow as if suffused with an otherworldly light. Such a glory and a power emanated from the divine couple that many people fell on their knees and began to pray.

Arachne, too, had chosen the world of the immortals for her subject. But when Athena saw what Arachne had woven, she reddened in shame and anger. There was Zeus, king of the gods, but he was not sitting upon his throne, nor was he with his wife Hera. Instead, Arachne had shown him in hot pursuit

142

IIII: *Winding the Skein*, Frederic Leighton, 19th century. The Maas Gallery, London.

fection. In their heart of hearts, they knew that the gods envied them, for the immortals grew tired of their all-too-perfect life on Mount Olympus, hungered for earth, and made fools of themselves in their longing to touch what was real, human, and flawed. All this the people felt as they gazed at Arachne's picture, and instead of falling on their knees, they stood tall, feeling proud and joyful.

of Hera's priestess Io, his face flushed with adulterous lust. In the distance, one glimpsed the towers and temples of Athens, and close by a village, not unlike Arachne's own, nestled against hills. On the hillside, a shepherd was seen grazing his goats, but he was giving his attention not to his flock but to the girl whose slender waist he clasped and whose full lips he was about to kiss. Next to the sweetness and tenderness of the shepherd's demeanor, Zeus looked almost crude, almost loutish. Athena cringed as she gazed upon Arachne's weaving, and she squirmed in discomfort. As Zeus' loyal daughter, she did not want to admit how much truth the image contained. "The impertinence of it..." she hissed beneath her breath.

But when the people saw what Arachne had done, they started laughing a full, happy belly laugh. Arachne had shown them their own world, and it was a beautiful world that they loved for all its gritty imper-

But Athena could take no more. The humiliation of it all was eating at her liver. Casting off her disguise, she let the light of her divinity burst forth over the assembled crowd like a blaze, and she rejoiced when she saw them cowering in terror. Striking Arachne with her hand, Athena cursed her: "You who dared compare yourself to myself, the goddess of weaving, you shall be a weaver forever." Even as she spoke the maiden's body shriveled and withered, her limbs grew thin and black, and she became a small spider that scuttled off into the tall grass.

Ever since, the people in Arachne's village have honored spiders, and keep a corner in their houses where the long-legged spiders can weave their webs undisturbed. They always remember Arachne as one who fearlessly defended the truth, even in the face of the almighty goddess Athena.

Durga the Warrior Goddess

HINDU

Told by Jalaja Bonheim

The gods hemmed and hawed and stroked their mustaches. It was hard to admit they had failed. Yet so it was. They were unable to protect their creatures from the armies of demons which even now ravaged the countryside, pillaging and devouring everything within sight like swarms of locusts. Humankind perceived these demons only dimly, as forces which they called fear, corruption, violence, greed, and deceit. Only the gods saw their true demonic nature—their blood-shot eyes, their claws and talons, their sharp fangs and the evil green light that gleamed in their eyes. But the gods were helpless. They had tried everything—threats and ambushes, tricks and frontal attacks, but every time they attacked the demons, they had been shamefully defeated. Now they sat in silence, their pride humbled.

After a long time, one of them said, "Maybe. . . ." The others looked up. "Yes?" He cleared his throat, then hesitated. "We have all done our best," he finally said, "and the earth is still dying. There is only one thing left to do." The gods shifted nervously, for he was speaking what they all were thinking. It was time to summon the great warrior goddess, the fierce, unpredictable mother of life and death. At the very mention of her name, they shuddered, and their hair stood on end. They groaned at the thought of surrendering their powers to her. "She is crazy," murmured one of the gods. "Completely insane," agreed another. But they all knew she was their last hope.

Then, the ten thousand gods sat together in meditation and humbly cried out the sacred names of the ancient goddess:

> *Mother of the Universe*
> *Unknowable One*
> *Remover of Darkness*
> *Great Light of Enlightenment*
> *Spirit of All-Knowing Wisdom*
> *Destroyer of Demons*
> *Heart of Compassion*
> *Womb of Eternity . . . .*

145

Before long, a vast fireball arose in their midst, a million times brighter than the sun itself, so that even the gods recoiled from its heat. From its white core, a brilliant red light blazed forth, which condensed into the form of a red-robed woman. The assembly of gods sighed as they beheld her wild beauty, her black disheveled hair, her calm velvet eyes and her fresh rosebud lips. She was seated on an enormous tiger who softly growled at the assembled gods, and his growl rumbled like thunder through all the three worlds. Under his gold-and-black hide the muscles rippled, while his tail flicked with impatience and his eyes glowed with hunger.

No one spoke a word. And in the silence, the goddess looked down upon the earth, the planet most dear to her heart. She saw everything—abject poverty and obscene wealth, torture and corruption, greed and filth. As she surveyed the situation, her smile faded and a wild red flame sprung up in her eyes that made the gods shudder. Each strand of her shimmering black hair began to writhe as it transformed into a venomous, hissing cobra. Then, her arms multiplied—four, ten, a hundred, a thousand, each hand clasping a deadly weapon.

Leaning down, the goddess now whispered a secret word into the soft ear of her tiger that made him roar and lash his tail. The next moment, the gods saw him flashing across the heavens at the speed of light, carrying his mistress to earth. The planet trembled on its axis when they landed, and the battle that ensued raged for many years, until the earth was covered knee-deep in blood. Thousands of demons the goddess slew, and as she drank the deep-red wine of their blood she became more and more intoxicated. Dancing upon piles of corpses, she sang songs of frenzied joy. Finally, she faced Durga, the last of the demons and the greatest, and she battled with him for many days, until Durga was released by the goddess from his evil form, his pure spirit set free from its bondage. And henceforth, the goddess herself would be known as Durga, slayer of demons.

Breathless, the gods watched, and they sighed a great sigh of relief at Durga's victory. But now, a new difficulty presented itself. In her rage, the clear red light of the goddess had darkened, turning first blood red, then maroon, then deep black. Durga the red warrior goddess had vanished, and in her place Kali the black queen of death and destruction had appeared. Now, nothing could halt her rampage. Casting off both her weapons and her clothes, Kali danced nakedly now, while her garland of skulls rattled and the demons' arms she had strung around her hips swirled in unison.

"It is done, Mother," the gods cried, "You have won the battle, please stop your terrible vengeance!" But in her ecstatic frenzy, Kali paid no attention, but continued dancing upon the corpses, still eager for more blood. Eyes rolling in her insane frenzy, she raged through the land, devouring the innocent along with the guilty, deaf to the cries of her children. "We feared as much," said the gods, shaking their heads sadly.

Only one could stop Kali now, and that was her mate and consort Shiva, lord of creation and destruction, whom the goddess loved with a deep, abiding passion, as he loved her. Now, Shiva descended to earth, and lay down on the battlefield among the corpses, looking himself rigid and pale like a corpse, his coal black eyes open and fixed upon the sky.

And as the Mother danced her crazy dances, it happened that she stepped upon Shiva's body. Looking down, she found herself looking straight into the eyes of eternity, the eyes of innocence, the eyes of boundless love. In that very instant, all her rage melted, the madness passed from her, and she stuck out her tongue, embarrassed to find herself trampling the body of her beloved in this way.

Startled into sobriety, the goddess stood still. Suddenly, she felt tired, terribly tired. She lay down by Shiva's side, and thus they lay for a long time, neither speaking a word. But as dawn broke, the goddess looked out over the quiet battlefield and saw that where the last pools of blood had vanished into the earth, fresh blades of emerald green grass were already beginning to push up. In the silence, a bird began to sing the eternal song of renewal. Her work was done.

OPPOSITE: *Standing Four-Armed Durga*, Kashmir, late 9th century A.D. The Metropolitan Museum of Art, New York, gift of Mr. and Mrs. Perry J. Lewis, 1984 (1984.488).

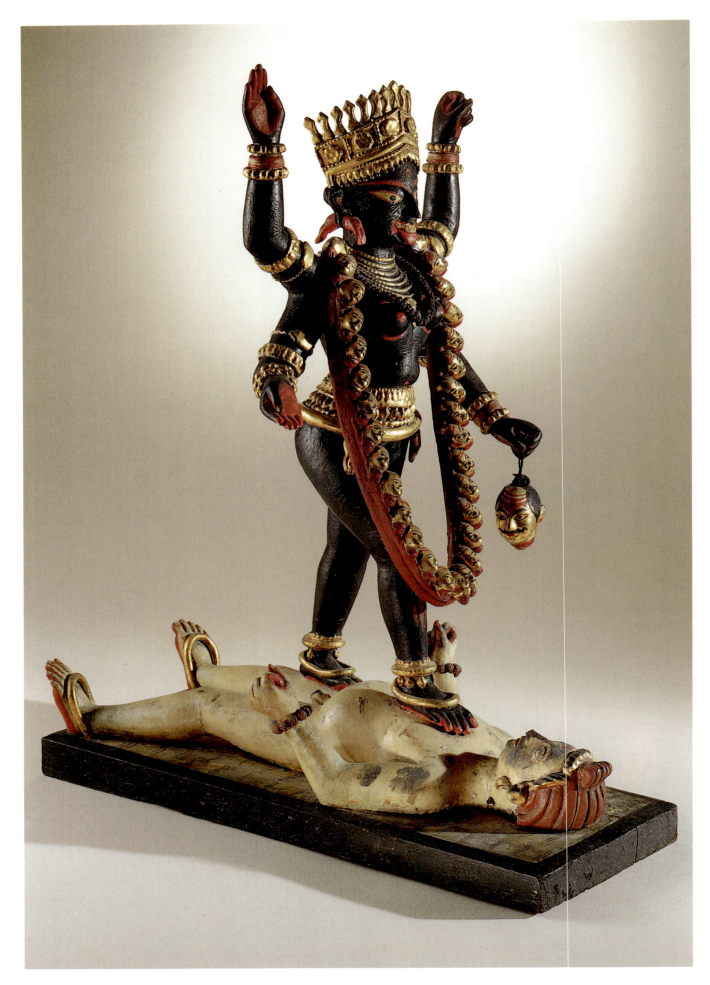

In Praise of Kali

HINDU

*Rāmprasād Sen,
translated by Leonard Nathan
and Clinton Seely*

*Rāmprasād was an 18th-century
Bengali mystic and worshiper of Kali.*

Mother, incomparably arrayed,
Hair flying, stripped down,
You battle-dance on Shiva's heart,
A garland of heads that bounce off
Your heavy hips, chopped-off hands
For a belt, the bodies of infants
For earrings, and the lips,
The teeth like jasmine, the face
A lotus blossomed, the laugh,
And the dark body boiling up and out
Like a storm cloud, and those feet
Whose beauty is only deepened by blood.

So Prasad cries: My mind is dancing!
Can I take much more? Can I bear
An impossible beauty?

Calming Kali

CONTEMPORARY

Lucille Clifton

*Kali's humanity—her fierceness as
well as her suffering—radiates
through this poem by African-
American writer Lucille Clifton.*

Be quiet awful woman,
lonely as hell,
and i will comfort you
when i can
and give you my bones
and my blood to feed on.
gently gently now
awful woman,
i know i am your sister.

OPPOSITE: *Kali Astride Shiva's
Body,* Bengal, late 19th century.
© British Museum, London.

149

Enheduanna's Praise of Inanna

⸺⸻◆⸺⸻

SUMERIAN

Adapted by Aliki and Willis Barnstone

Enheduanna was a Sumerian moon priestess who was born in
2300 B.C. She is the first writer in history—male or female—whose
work is known by name.

Like a dragon you have filled the land
with venom.
Like thunder when you roar over the earth,
trees and plants fall before you.
You are a flood descending from a mountain,
O primary one,
moon goddess Inanna of heaven and earth!
Your fire blows about and drops on our nation.
Lady mounted on a beast,
An [the sky god] gives you qualities, holy commands,
and you decide.
You are in all our great rites.
Who can understand you?

Storms lend you wings, destroyer of the lands.
Loved by Enlil [the air god] you fly over our nation.
You serve the decrees of An.
O my lady, on hearing your sound,
hills and flatlands bow.
When we come before you,
terrified, shuddering in your stormy clear light,
we receive justice.
We sing, mourn, and cry before you
and walk toward you along a path
from the house of enormous sighs.

You strike everything down in battle.
O my lady, on your wings
you hack away the land and charge disguised
as a charging storm,
roar as a roaring storm,
thunder and keep thundering, and snort
with evil winds.
Your feet are filled with restlessness.

On your harp of sighs
I hear your dirge.

O my lady, the Anunna [spirits of the underworld]
    the great gods,
fluttering like bats in front of you,
fly away into cliffs.
They do not have the courage to walk
through your terrible gaze.
Who can tame your furious heart?
No lesser god.
Your malevolent heart is beyond temperance.
Lady, you soothe the reins of the beast,
you make us happy.
Your rage is beyond temperance,
O eldest daughter of Suen!
Who has ever denied you homage,
lady, supreme over the land?

OPPOSITE: *The Burney Relief, plaque*
of Inanna-Ishtar, c. 2300–2000 B.C.E.

Private Collection.

Artemis and Actaeon

GREEK

Told by Joanna Goodman

The woods of Mount Cithaeron trembled and the wind sighed as it passed through the gates of trees. Beasts were hiding in caves, behind stumps, their longing for the hunt as clear as the pool where one sharp thistle of light fell and where Artemis bathed that day. Laughter rustled in the air. Her bow and quiver glistened on a rock.

She had picked a clearing into which, she knew, no one would dare venture. It was sanctuary she sought, wild virgin, soul pierced with daggers, eyes glinting like the tip of an axe. Her nymphs swarmed around her, massaging her with salts and oils, her body sculpting itself to their hands. Artemis, the leaves hissed, *beloved of Arcadia, of Sparta, of Laconia, of Mount Taygetus and of Elis.* Artemis of the chill moon. She was thinking of the rumble of the beasts, could hear them almost, that dull blow to the earth when they ran.

From deep within the forest, as if in tune with her thoughts, came a pounding, the heavy panting of hounds. Artemis heard the rhythm of that chase, imagined a stag or bear stirring. It made her feel like rushing, not from danger but toward it: what she wanted, in that instant, was to capture something in her hands and clench it there. So lost was she in the dream of hunting, she did not distinguish among the hounds a human sound, did not hear a man's voice ring out as he drove his dogs through the woods. Nor did she hear him when he stopped just feet from her bathing spot; she did not flinch when the hounds sat by their master and waited. For the beating of their hearts was the beating of his.

Actaeon hadn't intended to see her. It was light that surprised him: a radiance beckoning, and the

|||: *Diana the Hunter,* Orazio Gentileschi, late 16th or early 17th century. Musée des Beaux-Arts, Nantes.

hush of the water, just beyond the trees, irresistibly light. He thought he spotted a curve in the rock, an outcropping of alabaster and gold.

When did she turn? At what moment did she hear the splinter of a twig, a branch pushed aside? She glanced then, a slow and deliberate movement. She didn't know him, and had she, it would not have mattered: he had *looked upon her*, her body now half his, imprinted in his memory. As her nymphs covered her, she seized the bow so tightly that it seemed part of her. She was surprised, but not so much that she couldn't speak: hers was the language of earth and animal, thicket and storm. Fury aids those who stop for it, who breathe it. Her triumphs rose up and around her now: arrows that had shot straight through the children of vain Niobe, arrows through Tityus of the earth's depths, scorpion that had stung Orion, son of Gaia, walker of the sea, ravager.

The dogs heard her then. They leapt up; Actaeon, thinking they would attack her—he could make her out now, naked and standing there calmly, too calmly—tried to quiet them. But it was not she they wanted. They came for him.

"Halt!" he ordered, but his words were not his own. He lunged forward, a human disguised as a beast, a ghost of himself, hollowed out: what does one become, betrayed by those who have loved him best? And as he ran he looked more and more like the thing the dogs hungered for: stag beyond compare, lean body to pounce upon. The forest moaned. Artemis went on with her bathing.

He took a long time to tire: a thousand sticks broken beneath his heels, a whirlwind of leaves, swamps heavy with moss, lichen-strewn rocks over which he slipped. The hounds didn't know him; when they fell upon him, torrential, they couldn't discern the hands that had fed them. They ripped into him, for his flesh tasted of stag, and they killed him well, as he had taught them to.

They ate then, unceasingly. Ate and rested and, satisfied, treaded howling through the forest, their pace quickening—where was their master? They could not pick up his scent. The whole pack trampled onward, frenzied.

Artemis, miles away in the forest, stood with her head tilted back, drinking from the spring. The nymphs lifted her hair in their hands, and the beasts near her stamped on the thorny earth, and the forest drained away all traces of sound.

RIGHT: *Actaeon*, Paul Manship, 1925. Collection of The Hudson River Museum of Westchester, gift of the City of Yonkers (48.17.2).

AYIASMA

—➤●⬥—

CONTEMPORARY

Gunnar Ekelof,
translated by W. H. Auden and Leif Sjoberg

Ayiasma means "purifying well." To her worshipers, the black Madonna is just that—a sacred well in which they immerse their souls for purification.

The black image
Framed in silver worn to shreds by kisses
The black image
Framed in silver worn to shreds by kisses
Framed in silver
The black image worn to shreds by kisses
Framed in silver
The black image worn to shreds by kisses
All round the image
The white silver worn to shreds by kisses
All round the image
The very metal worn to shreds by kisses
Framed in metal
The black image worn to shreds by kisses
The Darkness, O, the darkness
Worn to shreds by kisses
The Darkness in our eyes
Worn to shreds by kisses
All we wished for
Worn to shreds by kisses
All we never wished for
Kissed and worn to shreds by kisses
All we escaped
Worn to shreds by kisses
All we wish for
Kissed again and again . . .

OPPOSITE: *High Priestess,* Romare Bearden, 1985. Collection of Linda Forrest Cummin and Pearson C. Cummin III. © 1997 Romare Bearden Foundation/Licensed by VAGA, New York, NY.

How the People of Today Have Two Stories

CONTEMPORARY

Carolyn McVickar Edwards

*The ancient Greeks, says storyteller Carolyn Edwards, borrowed the
image of the snake goddess Lamia from the Libyan people. But instead of
worshipping her as a goddess, the (patriarchal) Greeks portrayed her as a
dangerous female monster whom they called Medusa.*

Ever since the beginning, fear of Lamia, the Snake Woman, has coiled in the bellies of all who sense Her majesty and mystery. She may be tensed and swaying, upright in readiness. She may unhinge Her jaws and swallow a fat and complex life into Her own thin, simple length. We watch Her, and our fingernails dig into the soft flesh of our palms. And when She lies white as death, with eyes blind and darting tongue still, our own eyes turn deep into the unanswered, and we are afraid. We look in wonder when She climbs without arms or legs from Her dull and brittle coat into the new one soft and vividly colored. We are relieved. She is alive. We are full of hope. She returns again. But we feel afraid. Yes, with Lamia, Snake Woman of the deepest dance we know, we are a little afraid. It has always been so!

It was so at the beginning of the First People. They were the people of the limitless dunes at the edge of the stunning blue sea, the people of the cliffs bordering the dry rivers. They were the people who observed and copied their Snake Woman to receive the gift of the oasis.

There in the land where the wind blows in yellow pillars and the heat is cruel, the First People in the desolate morning formed a great circle with Snake Woman at their center. They held hands and danced to the drums that copied the slow beat of Lamia's heart. The First People's dance was measured and even, and Snake Woman, head and neck hidden by a cloth, sang and swayed at the center. "Who are you, Lamia?" the First People called to Her, wondering and afraid, pitching their voices low, sedate, and simple like the body of the Snake at the center.

"Copy Me and you shall see," answered Lamia over and over again.

The First People paced out Her rhythm again and

again, smoldering, undulating, bodies and voices turning in exhausted circles, slinking toward the afternoon.

"Who are we, Lamia?" the people sang.

"Copy Me and you shall see," answered Snake Woman.

The people trickled out their sound and their sweat. Their feet and their hair turned hot and limp. And when the sun stood finally at the bottom of the sky, the desert blossomed. The dunes were dahlia red, the sand floor mustard yellow. The hills turned coral and violet, and the stepping people spoke by turns.

"She is the Deep and the Wet One."

"She is the Necklace of Life under the sand."

"We are the jewel keepers."

"We are the builders of the vats."

When the dark came, then, the sky blazed with stars, the drums grew silent, and Lamia's people dreamed of plumbing the underground water for the figs, palms, oranges, pomegranates, and almonds of the oasis.

Lamia's First People drew from the basin of Her rocks Her water gift. From those precious wells came the moisture to grow the barley, the wheat, the millet, the onions, and the tomatoes beside the skeletons of riverbeds and streams. The size of the oasis grew by threes, and in gratitude and wisdom Her First People continued to copy Her rhythm.

The First People of Lamia copied Her deadness. They unhinged their jaws to mimic Her swallowing of life. They lay without moving or moaning. "You are like the ghibli winds," they sang to Her. "You leave nothing living, not even the fetus in the mother's womb."

The People copied Lamia new and large and young again. "You are like the winds of the north," they crooned. "Your waters draw shrubs from the Earth for our sheep to feed on. You make us fertile, You make us

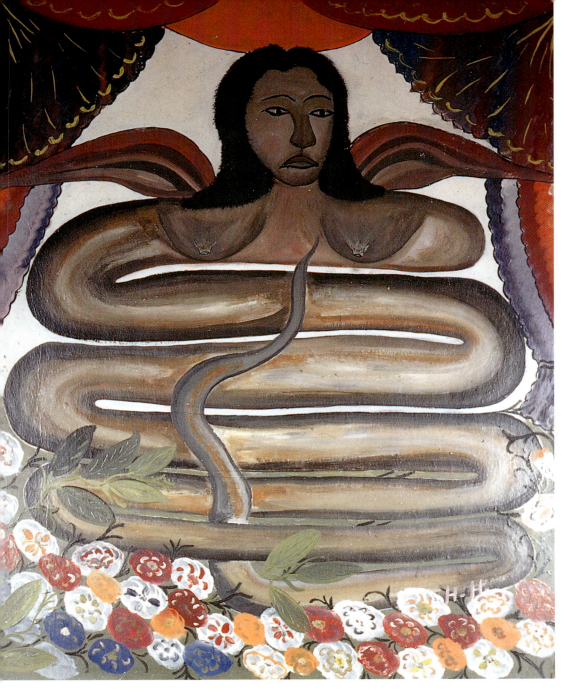

⌐ ⌐ ⌐ ⌐: *Dambalah, La Flambeau,*
Hector Hyppolyte, 20th century.
Private collection.

and tragic. His tales could drive away hunger, shorten the night, and take the pain out of a lashing. Orestes said that's just why he told stories. Stories and mead, he said, could both numb the agony. He told of slaves yoked neck to neck, herded bare of foot over sharp rocks, the dead and ill cut away at night and left to make mountains of skulls at the crossings of the roads. Paradise, said Orestes, was a cave dripped over by a veil of tears. Like crystals, you could look through them and reach endlessly for what could have been but never will be. Orestes told of the caves of the Pythoness, the oracle at Delphi, who sees the future of kings in a cup of blood poured out of the moon and keeps Her children in soft-shelled eggs under Her heart. He told of ships that could fly and nectars shared by truced armies at banquets before the slaughters of betrayal began.

virile, You fill our children with strength."

"It has always been so," went the hymn. "It has always been so!"

One day it happened that a ship blew from the north over the sea. The ship, bound for trading with the People of Lamia, carried on it a sailor who entertained his brothers with stories he wove from the boredom and novelty of his adventures. The teller's quick words sometimes reminded his listeners of a child who works to comfort himself in the midst of fear.

Orestes, the teller, was a small man with a scurrying gait. His hands busied themselves with carving or smoking or mending, and he asked his listeners often, "Do you know what I mean?" They answered as often that they did; their assurances encouraged him to continue and told this nervous, sweet-eyed man that all was well a little while longer.

The words of Orestes were fantastic, enchanting,

And privately, to his sad-eyed companion, the farmer boy with the tremulous, constant smile, the teller spoke of his mother, slave of the inner house, who nestled him sometimes and beat him at others, and whose food turned to poison if he tried to eat too much of it. Sometimes there were whippings that left him for dead, "but all you can do," said Orestes, "is survive. Do you know what I mean?" The boy would smile and lean down against the outstretched leg of his friend and hold Orestes' ankle for a while in his rough young hand.

The day the ship docked on the northern coast of Africa, Orestes gave his two gold coins to his blond companion for safekeeping. "You keep these so's I won't drink too much," he said. The boy concealed them with a flicker of understanding in his pale eyes, and the two sailors went ashore to the traders' settlement at the edge of the land of the People of Lamia.

157

The keeper of the inn there was a muscular man with blue veins twining his forearms when he lifted pots of stew in his kitchen. He liked the stories of Orestes and so let him sweep and wash the cooking pots in exchange for his supper and a jug of mead. Orestes appreciated more than the food. He admired the innkeeper, and he borrowed the big man's tireless strength for the hero of new stories that he spun by the side of the fire for the evenings' boisterous customers.

Orestes, however, didn't take his bed at the inn. The air was too close there, he said. So he carried his jug and his blanket and slept with his companion under the dome of the sky. For the sky here in this strange land was king; and in its giant starry blackness pulsed a peace that thickened and melted around the two sailors as they drank and finally slept.

On a blinding blue day that followed a night of stories and mead, Orestes and his friend discovered the oasis. Throbbing from the night's liquor, the man and boy walked in the searing heat until they came upon that place of green and water. Here, in this infernal land was shade and rest. And possibly more mead, thought Orestes, to mend this morning's sickness.

But the sailors found themselves calmed and frightened at the same time. For the people of Lamia had begun Her dance. Women and men alternating, holding hands in a circle. Slowly moving about the Snake at the center.

The sailors stared. Head and neck covered by a cloth, this center Snake raised Herself upright, coiling and swaying. With these people weaving steady and certain around Her, the Snake was still again. The sky pounded with the drum from the heart of the circle. In and out the people moved, close now, back, close again, sweat in curls down their faces and sides. Slowly, out and in, facing this Snake, pacing a pattern on the sand, the circle slithered and twisted, and the feet measured their rhythm into a sound that grew steady and smooth as the rain on a rock.

Orestes felt his head reel. The Snake at the center became like Woman to him, alive now and beautiful, then dead and unreachable. The dancers were the snakes now, twisting and ancient, lethargic as water, turning endlessly around this lunging, quiet beauty at the center Who held not just men, but women also, to Her bottomless flow of movement. Orestes and the boy could not understand the language of the People of Lamia. They could not know that Her People gained Her strength by imitating Her, that they knew Her answers by taking Her shape. Orestes and the boy understood little of this slowness; their own people's dances were speedy and wild.

Something terrified stirred in Orestes, and he began to shake. In the midst of the heat, his teeth chattered. The boy looked at the dancers and at the face of his friend. It was crumpled as a child's, and the boy, not smiling now, led Orestes by one chilled hand away from the oasis and back across the land to the sea. The boy made a fire and wrapped Orestes in two blankets. Then he held the man's hands.

"What happened?" asked the boy. Orestes didn't know. He could only say how strange it was, women dancing with men that way, and the Snake so pulsing at the center. "It was like a dream, do you know what I mean?" said Orestes. "Like a dream."

The boy said yes, that seeing the snake made him think of the job he'd had lambing, where the newborns slipped into his hands, still connected to the ewes with cords like bloody snakes. He'd cut a cord when the throbbing stopped if the mama couldn't bite through it herself. "You feel scared when you do it," the boy said. "But it makes you feel good afterward. Seeing the lambs walking around, knowing they wouldn't if you hadn't helped." The boy stretched his lips again in his lonely, trembling smile and held Orestes while the older man drank from the jug of mead.

Because the Snake Woman stayed in the mind of Orestes, the storyteller, it so happened that Lamia, the Wet One of the Deep, became part of the stories of the land across the sea. But Orestes, the storyteller, knew neither Her dance nor the power of copying Her motions of life and death. Instead, he knew only the terrible cold that had swept him when he watched, ill from the night and unable to talk with Her people. He saw Her power and was afraid, and so he made in his own language a story of a Snake Woman who terrorized and could be subdued only by the bravest of men.

And so it is to this day. We are the people with both stories. Like the slender shape of Lamia Herself, our fear has followed the ripples of time, and we ask ourselves, as we have from the beginning, what to do with it. When we were the First People of Lamia, we watched Her and we copied Her. We learned and we were comforted. But when we are the people of Orestes, our oasis is only in our minds: there we crawl for comfort against the trampling and the slavery. We are afraid of this Lamia. Of Her imitation we know nothing. We try to control Her instead.

In our fear there is power; in Her power there is fear. Shall we copy Her? Can we control Her? We thirst and circle the winds in the deserts of our souls, wondering and dancing our decisions.

158

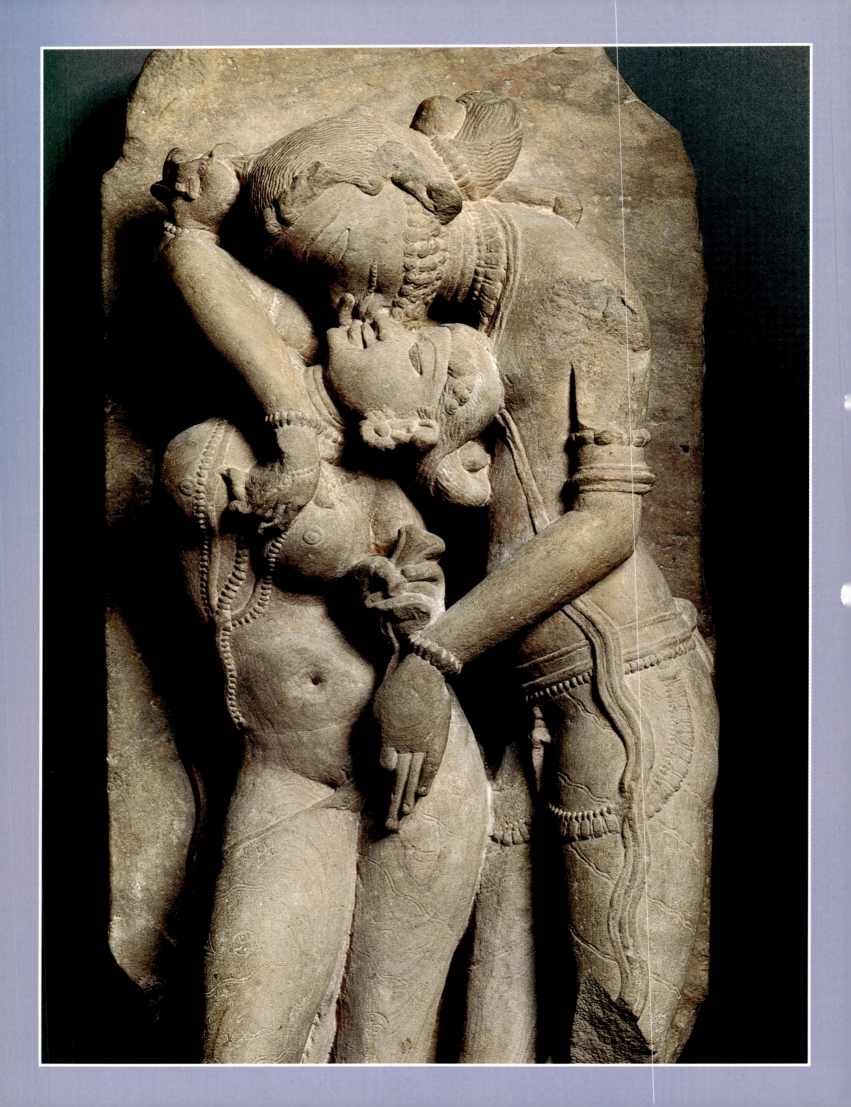

VII

THE GODDESS
AND HER MATE

TODAY, AS MEN AND WOMEN STRUGGLE TOWARDS A VISION OF gender equality, we draw inspiration and encouragement from the sacred couples of world mythology. Serene and majestic, they appear side by side, united in harmonious partnership while presenting a vision of divinity that encompasses both male and female aspects.

Married deities are always sexual deities, and all religions that worship divine couples also honor sexuality as a sacred energy. Often, a direct parallel is drawn between divine creativity and human sexuality—as a child is born from the union of man and woman, so the world is born from the union of god and goddess.

In many parts of the world, including ancient India, the Middle East, and Europe, sacred marriage rites were celebrated in which a man and a woman ritually re-enacted the sexual union of god and goddess. "The Joy of Sumer" belongs in the context of these rites, and so does the complex Egyptian myth, "Isis and Osiris." Theirs is both a truly romantic love story and a ritualized description of the annual cycle of life in which the river Nile (Osiris) appears to die in the dry season, leaving the rich, fertile plains of Egypt (Isis) bereft and barren, until the lovers are reunited by the next floods.

While certain myths portray an idealized image of the divine couple, others show gods and goddesses quarreling in all-too-human ways. Oya, for example, is an incorrigible flirt, as is her Greek cousin Aphrodite. In the Irish story, "Caitlin of Kilcummin," we recognize in the goddess a woman who is perceived as "different" and who must undergo a long and arduous journey before finding her rightful mate. Distrust and paranoia pollute the passionate love of Akewa the Sun and Jaguar Man. Somehow, it comes as a relief to hear that even the gods and goddesses struggle with their marriages, and that their loves are as tumultuous and difficult as our own.

OPPOSITE: *Lovers* (Mithuna), India, 11th century. © The Cleveland Museum of Art, 1997, Leonard C. Hanna, Jr., Fund (1982.64).

The Joy of Sumer:
The Sacred Marriage Rite

SUMERIAN

Translated by Diane Wolkstein and Samuel Noah Kramer

BELOW: *Marriage bed with embracing couple*, Elam, c. 2000 B.C.E. Louvre, Paris.

The people of Sumer assemble in the palace,
The house which guides the land.
The king builds a throne for the queen of the palace.
He sits beside her on the throne.

In order to care for the life of all the lands,
The exact first day of the month is closely examined,
And on the day of the disappearance of the moon,
On the day of the sleeping of the moon,
The *me* are perfectly carried out
So that the New Year's Day, the day of rites,
May be properly determined,
And a sleeping place be set up for Inanna.

The people cleanse the rushes with sweet-smelling
    cedar oil,
They arrange the rushes for the bed.
They spread a bridal sheet over the bed.
A bridal sheet to rejoice the heart,
A bridal sheet to sweeten the loins,
A bridal sheet for Inanna and Dumuzi.

The queen bathes her holy loins,
Inanna bathes for the holy loins of Dumuzi,
She washes herself with soap.
She sprinkles sweet-smelling cedar oil on the ground.

162

The king goes with lifted head to the holy loins,
Dumuzi goes with lifted head to the holy loins of
    Inanna.
He lies down beside her on the bed.
Tenderly he caresses her, murmuring words of love:
"O my holy jewel! O my wondrous Inanna!" . . .

The king bids the people enter the great hall.
The people bring food offerings and bowls.
They burn juniper resin, perform laving rites,
And pile up sweet-smelling incense.

The king embraces his beloved bride,
Dumuzi embraces Inanna.
Inanna, seated on the royal throne, shines like daylight.
The king, like the sun, shines radiantly by her side.
He arranges abundance, lushness, and plenty before
    her.
He assembles the people of Sumer.

The musicians play for the queen:
They play the loud instrument which drowns out the
    southern storm.
They play the sweet *algar*-instrument, the ornament of
    the palace,
They play the stringed instrument which brings joy to
    all people,
They play songs for Inanna to rejoice the heart.

The king reaches out his hand for food and drink,

Dumuzi reaches out his hand for food and drink.
The palace is festive. The king is joyous.
In the pure clean place they celebrate Inanna in song.
She is the ornament of the assembly, the joy of Sumer!

The people spend the day in plenty.
The king stands before the assembly in great joy.
He hails Inanna with the praises of the gods and the
    assembly:
"Holy Priestess! Created with the heavens and earth,
Inanna, First Daughter of the Moon, Lady of the
    Evening!
    I sing your praises."

My Lady looks in sweet wonder from heaven.
The people of Sumer parade before the holy Inanna.
The Lady Who Ascends into the Heavens, Inanna, is
    radiant.
Mighty, majestic, radiant, and ever youthful—
To you, Inanna, I sing!

ABOVE: *Dumuzi as the Shepherd,* c. 3200–
3000 B.C.E. Staatliches Museum, Berlin.

163

Isis and Osiris

EGYPTIAN

Told by Robert Musil

ABOVE: *Osiris with Isis and Nephthys*, detail of sarcophagus, c. 1080 B.C.E., Egypt. Egizio Museum, Turin.

The Egyptian gods Osiris and Isis were both brother and sister, husband and wife. Their mother was Nut, Goddess of the Sky; their father was Geb, God of the Earth; and it is said that the twin brother and sister were already in love with each other in the womb of their mother.

As king and queen of Egypt in the first age of the world, these two gods bestowed on humankind the gifts of civilization. Osiris taught his subjects how to cultivate wheat, barley, and corn, how to brew beer and tend the vines; he introduced writing and astronomy; and he trained the people to worship the gods, enact the rites, and follow the laws he gave them. Isis provided medicines of healing and magical incantations, invented the loom, encouraged music and dancing, and dispensed the justice of the heart. Compassionate teachers of humanity, Osiris and Isis were from the moment of their conception a couple whose love passed understanding.

> On the leaves of stars lay the boy,
> the moon in silver peacefulness,
> and the sundial's eye
> turned and watched him.
>> From the desert blew the red wind,
>> the coast deserted of sails.

> And the sister quietly took from the sleeper
> his sex, and devoured it.
> She gave him her soft red heart
> in trade, and laid it upon him.
>> And the wound grew vividly in the dream . . .
>> And the moon and sun changed places . . .
>> And he ate her heart, and she ate his.

Later, Osiris civilized the entire world as he journeyed through it, winning over the inhabitants by means of song, poetry, and words of gentle persuasion. But Osiris' loutish, cantankerous brother Set, who, along with his sister Nephthys, was also the offspring of Nut and Geb, was envious of his more famous and beloved sibling. Moreover, one fateful dark night, Osiris had mistaken Nephthys for Isis; the child of that illicit union was the jackal-headed god Anubis, guide of the souls of the dead in the underworld.

Set planned his revenge. Secretly he measured the body of Osiris and ordered an exquisitely decorated sarcophagus to be made to his brother's measurements. When Osiris returned from one of his trips abroad, Set invited him to a banqueting hall where hundreds of people were feasting and celebrating, and at the climax of the party he generously proposed that whoever lay down in the chest and demonstrated that it fit him alone could keep it as a gift. Many tried, to no avail; but when Osiris got in and lay down, seventy-two of Set's accomplices rushed into the room, slammed on the lid, secured it with bolts, sealed it with molten lead, carried it to the Nile, and tossed it in. Swept to the sea, the wooden sarcophagus drifted to the coast of Lebanon and was washed ashore at Byblos, where it came to rest in the branches of a sapling tamarisk tree. As the tree grew, it enclosed the chest in its trunk. So large, beautiful, and fragrant did this tree become that the king of Byblos noticed it one day and ordered that it be cut down and used as a pillar to support the roof of his palace.

Isis, meanwhile, cut off one of her locks, put on mourning garments, and set out, grieving, to search for her beloved husband. She accosted strangers for information. Even when she encountered children, she asked them about the chest, for it was said that children had the power of divination, and people would take omens from children's shouts as they played near the temples.

> A whistle or a cry,
> Or let the game die!

> Bushel of wheat,
> Bushel of clover,
> All not hid
> Can't hide over!
> Green man, arise!
> Green man, arise!

Some children playing on the shore told her of a beautiful chest they had seen being carried eastward on the waves. So Isis followed the shoreline until she came to Byblos, where she sat down near a fountain. When the queen's maids appeared with their water pitchers, she greeted them and plaited their hair and breathed the fragrance of ambrosia upon them. When the queen observed her strangely transformed maids, she asked about the marvelous woman of the fountain, requested a meeting with her, and made Isis the nurse of her newborn prince.

It is said that the goddess nursed the child by putting her finger instead of her breast in his mouth; but at night she burned the mortal parts of his body, while she became a swallow flying around the pillar, making lament. One evening the queen came upon this scene and gave a shriek when she saw her child on fire. "I was burning away the mortal parts of your child so that he might live forever," Isis said, revealing herself to the queen. "Now, however, you have broken the spell, and he will die as all men must die." The king of Byblos asked the goddess to forgive his wife, and she agreed on the condition that she be given the tamarisk pillar under the castle roof. Then Isis cut open the pillar, drew forth the chest, and threw herself upon it and lamented.

Eventually, the chest was transferred to a royal barge. Isis set sail with it back home, and at the first opportunity during the voyage she removed the lid of the sarcophagus. Full of grief and heartbreak, she lay face-to-face on the body of her dead husband and held an inner dialogue with him.

And she saw the ghost of the death in him . . . and suddenly she was terrified, and she felt robbed. She felt the shadow of the gray, grisly wing of death triumphant.

"Ah, Goddess," he said . . . . "I would be so glad to live if you would give me my clue again."

For here again he felt desperate, faced by the demand of life, and burdened still by his death.

"Let me anoint you!" the woman said to him softly. "Let me anoint the scars! Show me, and let me anoint them!"

Having chafed all his lower body with oil, suddenly she put her breast against the wound in his left side, and her arms round him, folding over the wound in his right side, and she pressed him to her, in a power of living warmth, like the folds of a river. And the wailing died out altogether, and there was a stillness, and darkness in his soul, unbroken dark stillness, wholeness.

Then slowly, slowly, in the perfect darkness of his inner man, he felt the stir of something coming. A dawn, a new sun. A new sun was coming up in him, in the perfect inner darkness of himself. He waited for it breathless, quivering with a fearful hope . . . "Now I am not myself. I am something new. . . ."

It is said that one night Isis transformed herself into a falcon, with light emanating from her feathers and air from her wings, and by this means enabled Osiris' sex to rise from his inert body. Drawing his essence from him, she conceived a child, Horus, his son, heir, and avenger. Then Osiris appeared to her in a dream.

He was standing under the trees, when the morning sun was hot, and the pines smelled sweet, and on the hills the last pear-bloom was scattering. She came slowly toward him, and in her gentle lingering, her

tender hanging back from him, he knew a change in her.

"Hast thou conceived?" he asked her.

"Why?" she said.

"Thou art like a tree whose green leaves follow the blossom, full of sap. And there is a withdrawing about thee."

"It is so," she said. "I am with young by thee. Is it good?"

"Yea!" he said. "How should it not be good?"

She looked at him, and the peace of her maternity was troubled by anxiety.

"Let not your heart be troubled," he said. "I have died the death once."

So he knew the time was come again for him to depart. He would go alone, with his destiny. Yet not alone, for the touch would be upon him, even as he left his touch on her. And invisible suns would go with him.

Isis arrived in Egypt and immediately went into hiding with her son. Constantly alert to the always-present danger of Set and his followers, the goddess raised Horus in the papyrus thickets, marshes, and swamps of the Delta, nursing and watching over him.

Horus speaks:
I am life rushing on, born from the egg of the world, from the belly of a magic woman, born of my father's dreams. I am the screech of wind, the rush of falcon wings, talons sharp as knives. I came after you. I stand before you. I am with you always. I am the power that dispels darkness. Look upon the dark face of my father Osiris. He is nothing. Embrace him. Even nothing cannot last. The seed laid into the void must grow. The candle's only purpose is to shine in the darkness. Bread is meant to be ground to pulp in the teeth. The function of life is to have something to offer death. Ah, but the spirit lies always between, coming and going in and out of heaven, filling and leaving the houses of earth. A man forgets, but his heart remembers—the love and the terror, the weeping, the beating of wings.

And it came to pass that one night when the moon was full, Set and his entourage, out hunting, pursued a wild boar into the Delta swamps and came upon the body of Osiris. In a rage, Set cut his dead brother's body into fourteen pieces, one for each night of the waning moon, and then scattered them far and wide throughout the land of Egypt.

Once again Isis set out to search for her husband, this time accompanied by her sister Nephthys. They traveled the whole of the country, from the Delta to

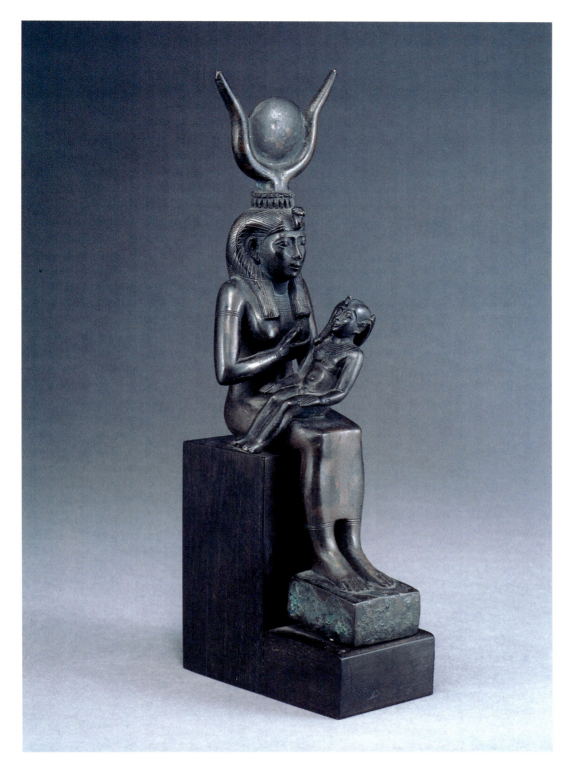

Nubia, re-membering Osiris, as they remembered him in their hearts, for to remember is to heal. Isis and Nephthys recollected each member of their brother's body—head, heart, backbone . . . all except the phallus, which had been swallowed by a fish in the Nile—and they proceeded to reassemble the god. Then Anubis bent over his reunited father, placed him on a lion-headed bier, swathed him in linen bandages, and embalmed him. Thus it is said that Osiris was the first mummy. . . .

For her part, Isis—Mistress of the Cosmos,

Sovereign of All That Is Miraculous, Almighty Lady of Wisdom—became a universal goddess. Her cult spread from Egypt to Asia Minor; from Cyprus, Crete, and mainland Greece to Sicily and Rome, whose empire took her as far north as Saint-Germain in Paris and the banks of the River Thames. The image of Isis nursing her child-savior would be taken over by the Christian Madonna, who also adopted the titles of the goddess—Sedes Sapiente (Seat of Wisdom), Regina Coeli (Queen of Heaven), Stella Maris (Star of the Sea).

167

WHY DESIRE HAS NO BODY

HINDU

Told by Jalaja Bonheim

In the beginning there was no past or future, no up or down, no male or female. There was nothing but the Great Being who is one without a second. Infinite in all directions, it pondered its own unfathomable mystery for many eons. But somewhere between one eternity and the next, it began to feel something it had never felt before—a yearning to love and be loved.

Instantly, in one among billions of enfolded valleys, a separation occurred. A chasm opened up. Thus, the Great Being divided itself in half, and the one became two. Male and female, the two attracted each other like powerful magnets, and desire vibrated and reverberated back and forth between them. Longing to embrace and to reunite, they reached for each other across the vastness, and so began the eternal love of god and goddess, whom we call Shiva and Shakti. Even now, these two still live among us, and when they embrace, waves of passionate love ripple through the universe. The bulls bellow with desire for the cows, the green of the fields grows deeper and more luminous, the sunflowers open wider to the rays of the sun, and the wind whispers words of love as it brushes through the trees.

But once, a long, long time ago, Shakti took the form of a woman called Sati. Sati was beautiful, with her silken black hair, her golden skin, and her gentle smile, and Shiva loved her with all his heart. But Sati was also mortal, and when she died, Shiva was inconsolable, and grieved as deeply as any man has ever grieved for his beloved.

How, you ask, can the goddess die? You are right, of course; the goddess never dies. But she is Maya, the queen of illusion, who appears now in one form, now in another. So compelling is her illusory magic that even Shiva became confused. In his grief he sat down, closed his eyes, and withdrew from the world into a state of deep, deep meditation. Day and night he sat upon the snowy peak of a mountain, his face raised to the sky, his body motionless like a corpse. Years

passed, and eventually the goddess returned in a new body. Softly, she approached him and called his name. But Shiva did not feel her touch, nor did he hear her call, for his ears had become deaf to all sounds but the roar of eternity.

In the meantime, the earth languished. Spring came and went, but that year, neither lambs nor foals were born. The birds forgot to sing and perched silently in the treetops, while spiders wove their webs across the empty nests. The villages lay in eerie silence for the people had lost their joy, their laughter and their play. The grim form of famine arose over the land, and with its gnarled black fingers, it began plucking animals and people off the face of the earth, one by one.

Finally, when the mother earth herself began to cry for help in a loud voice, the immortal ones grew concerned. After long deliberations, they called upon Kama, god of desire, and he landed in their midst in a whir of wings and a flurry of downy feathers. "Welcome, awakener of love," they said to him. "We need your help. We want you to fly to the highest peak of the Himalayas. There you will find Shiva, the great god, sitting in deep meditation. Pierce him with your sharp arrows, we beg you. Awaken his heart to the sweet presence of the goddess."

Kama bowed, his eyes bright with laughter. Obediently, he flew across the universes to the mountain peak where the god sat like a boulder, wrapped in his own blissful trance. But Kama reached into the long quiver on his back and pulled out a single slender golden arrow. Then he raised his bow, took aim, and let his arrow fly. With a flash of light, Kama's arrow pierced right through the center of Shiva's heart. The god stirred. His face dark with anger, he opened his eyes. "What wretch dares disturb me?" he

OPPOSITE: *The Holy Family (Shiva, Parvati, and their children) on Mount Kailasa*, Punjab Hills, c. 1800. © British Museum, London.

But Kama's arrow never fails to hit the mark. The instant Shiva opened his eyes, Shakti's enchanting beauty entered them and awakened his senses. Passionate desire flooded his body. No more could he return to the silent tranquility of his meditation. Within and without he saw the lotus-limbed daughter of the Himalayas, and her alone. Soon, he would retire with his beloved to a vast cave from where they would not emerge for many days and many nights. But as the couple was walking to their flower-strewn bed of love, they were distracted by the sound of sobbing. It was Kama's widow who was weeping over the ashes of her dead husband. Shiva remembered how he too had sobbed after Sati's death, and his heart ached with compassion for her pain. Raising his hand in blessing, he uttered the sacred sound that calls the souls of the dead back to the world of the living. Instantly, Kama's soul descended down to earth, borne upon a sweet-scented breeze.

But alas, the blaze of Shiva's anger had left not a single atom in Kama's body intact. And so, though Kama's soul returned, it found no body to re-enter. Henceforth Kama would be immortal, yet he would have no body. And so it is that to this day, desire moves among us as an invisible power which all have felt, yet no one has ever seen.

roared. Enraged, bellowing like a million exploding suns, he opened the third eye in the center of his forehead and aimed a beam of fiery white light at Kama. Flames engulfed the god of desire and the next moment, all that was left of him was a tiny, fragrant heap of ashes.

170

PRAISE TO VISHNU

HINDU

Translated by W. S. Merwin and J. Moussaieff Masson

LEFT: *Radha and Krishna in the Grove*, Punjab, c. 1780. Victoria & Albert Museum, London.

Praise to Vishnu his hands
fondle in secret
the large breasts of Laksmi
as though looking there for
his own lost heart

THE STORY OF AKEWA THE SUN AND JAGUAR MAN

TOBA

Told by Carolyn McVickar Edwards

This myth comes from the Toba tribe, who live in the plains of northern Argentina. Jaguars, however, feature in many South American myths.

OPPOSITE: Polychrome jar with jaguar on cover, Quiche Maya Culture, c. 550–900 A.D. Collection of the Bowers Museum of Cultural Art, Los Angeles, Anonymous Gift (F78.75.14a-b).

Because the love of Akewa the Sun and Jaguar Man was webbed with fear from the very beginning, they still travel alone, meeting only occasionally, and then with ferocity.

So fascinated were Akewa and Jaguar Man with each other that they became, as objects of each other's desires, also frightened of the other's power. Even at the moments of greatest sweetness in each other's arms, they were haunted by the rumors they themselves had begun, which claimed that each of them had too many teeth.

At the beginning, Akewa lived with her sister sky women in the heavens, all of them fat and round and beautiful, all of them graceful and given to laughter. They sat in their blue sky room, braiding one another's blazing hair and drinking great pitchers of *yerba mate* from black iron cups.

Jaguar Man lived on the earth below with his brothers among the eye-glowing circles of fire borrowed from the sisters in the sky. All the jaguar brothers were sleek and supple and were mated only to the great quiet hunt.

The sisters had lent the men fire; they had lowered it down on a rope from the sky; they had slipped it down with a song and a coyness so skin-tingling that the brothers rose up as one and peered, hearts pounding, into the heavens.

The sisters, held in the gaze of the jaguar men, blushed furiously. How suddenly compelling were these dark creatures on the earth below! How thrilling were the magnets of their eyes; how soft their furs looked; how musical their purrs!

The sky sisters tittered and whooped. They teased one another to follow the fire down the rope and join the jaguar men below. They invented stories of who would be partnered with whom, poured more *yerba mate*, and made much of the patterns of the leaves in the bottoms of their cups.

173

Only round, radiant Akewa held herself apart. She watched her sisters pulsing brilliantly against the soft blue of the walls of their home. She hated the terrible change she saw coming.

The thin voices of the men below began to float up the rope. "Come down," said the voices. "Come for a visit," they called. Some of the brothers tried to climb the rope, but none could manage higher than the first bank of clouds.

The sisters dissolved again into pillows of giggles.

Akewa shouted at them, "Stop it! Shut up! Don't you see that these creatures have monstrous teeth? Their mouths are cavernous weapons—when they're not looking up at you, they are tearing apart their prey. What makes you think you are different from what they hunt? What makes you think you can go for a visit and not get eaten alive?"

"They've got teeth?" asked the sky sisters.

"Yes. Teeth," said Akewa. "You go down there, you'll never come back."

The sisters, at first, listened to Akewa the Sun. They turned their backs on the creatures below. But the flirtation had begun, and it was not so easily stopped. Moreover, Akewa's warning of danger added spice to the attraction.

The brothers also had one among them who held back. The strongest and boldest, Jaguar Man wanted only the fraternity of his fellows. "What do you want with these sky women?" he argued. "Yes, they may be fat and beautiful, but they don't have just one mouth like we do—they have another one between their legs. That one is also studded with teeth. What you think will bring you pleasure will be your ruin. They will devour you! They will never be satisfied."

The idea of two mouths, both studded with teeth, on each of the sun sisters gave the jaguar men pause.

"But what good is our strength, Jaguar Man," asked the brothers, "if we cannot subdue them and make them happy?"

Batting one another with their paws and flexing their muscles, the jaguar brothers made ready to receive visitors. They built huts and with the wonderful new fire they roasted whole lizards beneath the house of the sun sisters. The smell of the barbecue wafted upward and made the mouths of the sky sisters water. The brothers brewed *algaroba*-fruit beer and enlisted the help of Falcon for the hour of the sisters' arrival.

Akewa begged them not to go. But the sisters, giddy with daring, laughing and shouting, merely kissed her and told her not to spoil their fun.

One by one, they climbed down the rope. Akewa watched sullenly as they left. But she let out a bellow of rage when she saw Falcon.

Falcon soared to the top of the heavens, and just as Akewa's last sister touched the earth with her feet, Falcon grabbed the rope with his claws and cut it with his beak. Reeling like a giant snake, the rope tumbled forever out of the heavens.

The sisters were trapped.

Staring in agony at the earth, Akewa's hair turned white. She moaned and turned away. Barely able to drag herself along, Akewa, shining alone up in the heavens, made a painfully slow journey across the sky and lowered herself into the abyss at the end of the world.

Down on the earth, each sister walked into the arms of a waiting brother. Everyone sang wild, wordless songs. Only Jaguar Man remained alone, gloomily watching the festivities. So tumultuous was that first meeting, what with the feasting, the rattles, and the mingling, that the sisters did not notice the rope limp and frayed on the ground.

In the long months that followed, lit each day by the grieving old Akewa in the sky, the sisters, sobered in their imprisonment, came nevertheless to live well with their captors. Indeed, the pleasure and intensity of the companionship of the men softened the longing they had for the sky world. But some say the broken rope lies always coiled in the hearts of women, ever after making difficult the complete trust of men.

The heart of Jaguar Man was also sorely troubled. Silently, telling himself that Akewa was just another two-mouthed sister with too many teeth, he nonetheless began to watch her. Something about her long, weary walk each day, something about her ancient face, filled him with pain instead of fear.

Day after day, Akewa walked, caring for nothing except the descent into the dark at the end of each journey. For it was in the beautiful blackness that Akewa felt the ropes of love that tied her to her sisters loosen and begin to unwind. Gradually, so subtly that she did not know at first she was doing so, she began to braid with those unwound strands a ladder that reached to the lone Jaguar Man, whose green eyes seemed to burn with a sorrow like her own.

Akewa and Jaguar Man began to meet in the dark under the rim of the world. Strange that two so certain and firm were now so wondering and curious. Indeed, Akewa, who had grown so old, grew young again in Jaguar Man's arms. The days on earth shortened as Akewa now hurried across the sky to meet her lover.

174

ABOVE: *Eclipse of Sun by Moon*, Mexican
mask, c. 1930. Courtesy J. Heilman.

Their time together grew and grew until one long
night, laughing shyly, they counted each other's teeth
and told each other the story of their fears.

Some say Akewa was reborn that night. "I feel like
a little child," she told her lover. Jaguar Man traced
her eyebrows with his glowing eyes.

Would that the cycle froze itself here at the point
of joy! But the cycle does not end here, and neither
does our story.

It's true that Akewa is born every year, and then
walks, a plump quick child, away from the winter sol-
stice. Slowly she grows older, until she is the grieving,
aged one of midsummer, and then she grows younger
again, becoming the maiden who once, so long ago, let
Jaguar Man climb her rope ladder of love.

But all too often Jaguar Man and Akewa begin to
argue. They fight about the hours they meet and leave
each other. Earth people see clouds steal away the
morning and evening light. They fight about their
need to be alone and the merits of their siblings.
Perhaps Jaguar Man is again afraid of the woman with
two mouths. Might she not be hiding teeth of which
she has not told him? And Akewa, perhaps, shrinks
from Jaguar Man's wide mouth; how can she be sure
he will not use his teeth against her?

Round, fat, and beautiful, Akewa carries weapons
across the sky each day. The people on earth see them
as her rays, but Jaguar Man sees them stab at that pre-
cariously swaying ladder of love, and rage coils in his
heart.

Jaguar Man swallows Akewa during the time that
people on earth call "eclipse." But her weapons are
strong, and Jaguar Man is forced to spit out his burn-
ing-hot Akewa.

And so Akewa most often walks alone on her sky
journey, old and slow in the dry season, young and
quick in the wet. Because the love of Akewa and Jaguar
Man was webbed with fear from the very beginning,
they meet only occasionally, and then with ferocity.

175

CAITLÍN OF KILCUMMIN

IRISH

Carolyn White

Children grow up straight and tall in Kilcummin but never a one was as tall as Caitlín O'Flaherty. When only a girl she was as tall as a man, and when a woman a good head taller. Although her manners were gentle, the people of Kilcummin feared her, for it was not right for any woman to stand so tall. Moreover she had a strange way of piercing to the heart of things as if she saw the truth hidden in appearance. She knew their secrets, or so they felt, the people of Kilcummin, and hence avoided her.

Even the fairies she set on edge, for she had no fear of them and never hesitated to cross their fields or linger in their trees. Oengus, the fairy king, could not endure her. He heaped curses upon her and changed himself first into a stag with a hundred eyes and next into a snake with a pig's snout, but she always laughed at his illusions in a fine grand manner and picked the dainty man up in her hand and pulled his cap over his eyes. How his dignity was offended when she called him "silly little thing" and cuffed him like a child! And it must be owned that he was mean and petty as such ones can be. Oengus too felt she knew more about him than he knew himself, and this enraged him.

Caitlín minded neither the people of Kilcummin nor the fairies, but worked steadily at her mending. There was no thing she could not fix; and thus with tinkerings and patches she provided for her parents in their old age, until one day her father became sick and died. Her mother, too, soon lay on her deathbed. She called her daughter and, putting her arms around her, said, "Caitlín dearest, since the time has come for me to die I must tell my secret. Like a daughter you have been to me. But I do not know your heritage nor your place of birth. On the doorstep my husband and I found you without rag or note and so we, being childless, claimed you for our own. But though I do not know your origin, I am sure you come from noble stock, for you act like a great lady. An honor it has been for me to be your mother." With that, she closed her eyes and died.

After the burial of her foster parents Caitlín had little reason to remain in the village of Kilcummin. The people feared her more now she was alone, and no young man would marry a woman so tall. At night the fairies played their shrill pipes outside her window so that she could not sleep. A few weeks later she packed her things in a kerchief and left Kilcummin, hoping to find her true home.

She had not traveled long when she saw a fat man, with a short tunic barely covering his rump, crying by the roadside. "Can I help you, sir?" asked Caitlín. "Ah, no one can help me," sobbed he, "my cauldron is broken, and so it will ever be. I have not eaten from it for a thousand years." "If that is your sorrow," said Caitlín, "perhaps I can help you, for I am a mender of sorts." "Little good it will do," sobbed he, "but try if you can."

Caitlín ran her finger along a great crack that split the cauldron in two. "This is easily mended," said she as she plucked a branch from a bramble bush. She laid the thorns crisscross over the crack and pounded them in with a hammer. In less time than it takes to turn boiled water into steam the cauldron was stitched and ready for use. The fat man was beside himself with joy. With one hand he thanked Caitlín and with the other he hurriedly threw mutton chops and potatoes into the pot. There was little doubt he was quite hungry. Caitlín smiled, put her hammer in her kerchief, and bade him farewell. When she was someways down the road the fat man called, "If ever you want for anything, call for Daghda and your call will be answered." Caitlín thanked him and followed the road.

She had not traveled long before she met a spindly old man struggling to lift a spear. With his weak arms he tugged until the veins stood out on his forehead;

OPPOSITE: *Rhine Maiden Lamenting*, Arthur Rackham, 1910. University of Dundee, Scotland.

ABOVE: *The Rocks of Belle-Ile,*
Claude Monet, 1884. Musée d'Orsay, Paris.

but not an inch did he raise it. "Can I help you, old man?" asked Caitlín. "Ah, no one can help me," said he, "for this spear is so heavy that none but the olden gods, the Tuatha De Daanan, can lift it, and even they are too enfeebled now. How can anyone sharpen a blade that has been rusting for a thousand years?" "I am young and strong," said Caitlín, "let me see if I can help you." So saying she seized the spear and in less time than it takes a blackbird to eat a worm she had sharpened it upon a stone. She laid the keen-edged spear at the old man's feet and accepted his astonished thanks. Caitlín was someways down the road when he called to her, "If ever you are in danger, call for Lugh and your call will be answered." Caitlín thanked him and continued on her way.

She had walked for some time when she came to the strand, and being quite tired, lay down to sleep. When she awoke she felt that something was the matter with the sea for it lay mute and motionless although a steady wind blew. "It's not right for a sea to be without waves," said Caitlín, "I'll blow some life into it." So saying she stood by the sea's edge, gathered a lungful of air and blew with all her might. As slowly as a snail crosses the road the sea rose until at last the waves crashed upon the shore; and the great voice of the sea roared, "Thank you, Caitlín. Like the gods of old you are. I who have not stirred a thousand years am now spry and strong, and able to carry you to Tirnanog, the land of your heart's desire, the island of the fairies, so that all will say that Manannan Mac Lir returns gift for fair gift." "Thank you, very much," said

Caitlín, picking up her kerchief, "but to visit the fairies is not my desire. They are a silly mischievous lot who have never been fond of me. So if you please, I would rather be on my way." "Stay!" roared the sea, "I know where your home is, and perhaps your lover." "That is more than I know," said Caitlín, "and if you will take me there I would be much obliged." "Take the curragh banked on the sand," said the sea, "and come to me."

Caitlín did so, and soon she was riding the crest of the sea. In this manner she traveled many days until she grew very hungry. Remembering the fat man she cried, "Daghda, help me." And as fast as a thought a feast of new potatoes and mutton appeared before her. Many days more she traveled and never wanted for food. One day a great ship came bearing towards her, faster and nearer until she could see the fierce, blood-thirsty faces of the marauders aboard. "Lugh, help me," she cried and a bolt of lightning streaked through the sky and cracked open the ship. From then on Caitlín encountered no danger.

The curragh sailed on and on until it neared an island, and Caitlín knew this must be Tirnanog, because she felt her heart strongly drawn to this land. A strange feeling she had of returning home. As her boat touched shore, a handsome array of women and men came forward to greet her, each as tall as or taller than she. A fat man with a wise face ladled out food from an ever-plentiful cauldron. A fierce-looking man stood on the hill with a keen-edged spear in his hand. And out of the sea walked a man with a gentle face. A handsome young man came forward to greet her, his arms outstretched, "Welcome home, Caitlín De Daanan, daughter of the gods. A thousand years Tirnanog has slept, and its people have languished. And I most of all, for I am Oengus, the once fairy king who taunted you so. Little did I then remember that we were Ireland's gods and that you were destined to be my bride." And in more time than it takes a ship to sail the ocean Caitlín and Oengus embraced and together forever they explore the lost joys of Tirnanog, where none grow old and none have cares. Thus ends the story of Caitlín, the tall woman of Kilcummin.

179

How Ogun Broke into Seven Pieces, Oya into Nine

YORUBAN

Told by Judith Gleason

It was Ogun who married Oya for the first time. Like a patient animal she used to carry his tools on her head when they went to the forge. On top of the tools rode a calabash containing food for their midday meal. While Ogun forged the tools, Oya worked the bellows for him, *whoosh, whoosh*. The sound of Ogun's hammer on the anvil—*king, king, ki-king, king, king, ki*, and all over again—worked in well with Oya's heavy breathing. But beneath this music was a hidden pulse beat, portending trouble, that both chose to ignore.

One day Ogun fashioned two very special rods for their mutual protection in this dangerous world we live in. "Here, you take this one, Oya," he said. "If ever you find yourself in great danger, strike with it! If it be a man who is threatening you, he will break into seven pieces. If it be a woman, she will break into nine." Ogun gave one of these magic rods to Oya and kept the other for himself.

Time passed. Then one day a very special customer called at the forge. It was

A man by the name of Shango
Who liked so much to be elegant
That he used to plait his hair like a woman
And he made holes in his ears
In which there were earrings, every time.
He would wear beaded necklaces
He would wear silver bracelets
He had too much elegance!

This gentleman was so charming that Oya, *whoosh, whoosh*, couldn't resist turning her head to look at him now and again. Nor could Shango resist Oya, for the Creator had given her a very powerful charm. Which is why she is known as *Oya-e-ríí ríí*: "Oya (so charming that) you can't take your eyes off her."

Ogun, bent over the forge and completely absorbed in his ironmaking, hadn't the slightest idea that anything like a flirtation was going on—until it was too late. First the bellows weren't working too well. There were breathless pauses. Then they stopped for good. Oya and Shango had eloped!

Where was Oya? The smith summoned everyone in the neighborhood with his gong, *king, king, ki-king, king, king, ki*—and asked them to help him track down the runaway. Everyone tried. They went off in all directions. Finally they came back to Ogun and reported, singing:

We went to the Egba of dogs in search of Oya
  But we didn't find Oya
We went to the Esa of hens in search of Oya
  But we didn't find Oya
We searched for her at the kola-nut depot
  Where she used to throw little pieces into
    her mouth
  But we didn't find Oya
We searched for her at the batá drum compound
  Where she used to dance the Elekete rhythm
  But we didn't find Oya
We searched for Oya where the coconut leaves
    never stand still
We searched and searched, but could no more
    find Oya.

So Ogun went off on his own. Finally his keen hunter's eye spotted the culprits. Amulets swinging upon his rough shirt, Ogun started off in swift pursuit.

Far off in the bush, Shango saw trees quivering. Birds were flying away, startled from their roosts. "What will I do? Ogun is my senior brother. In running off with his wife I have done a terrible thing. He is furious."

Oya said, "Don't worry, Shango. You just stay quietly over there and keep out of sight. Leave it to me. I can handle this one."

And so they advance, closer and closer, Ogun and Oya. Everything in the forest backs out of the way. Squirrels scramble up the trees the birds have vacated. The trees themselves hop close to the stream and bend down, covering their ears with their branches. Closer and closer they come. Now they're face to face. They raise their magic rods. *Pa! Pa!*

Each struck at exactly the same time. And as predicted, Ogun broke into seven pieces. Oya into nine. Which is why you find them scattered all over the world in our time.

RIGHT: Wooden figurine, Sierra Leone, Mende tribe, c. 19th century. University of Pennsylvania Museum, Philadelphia.

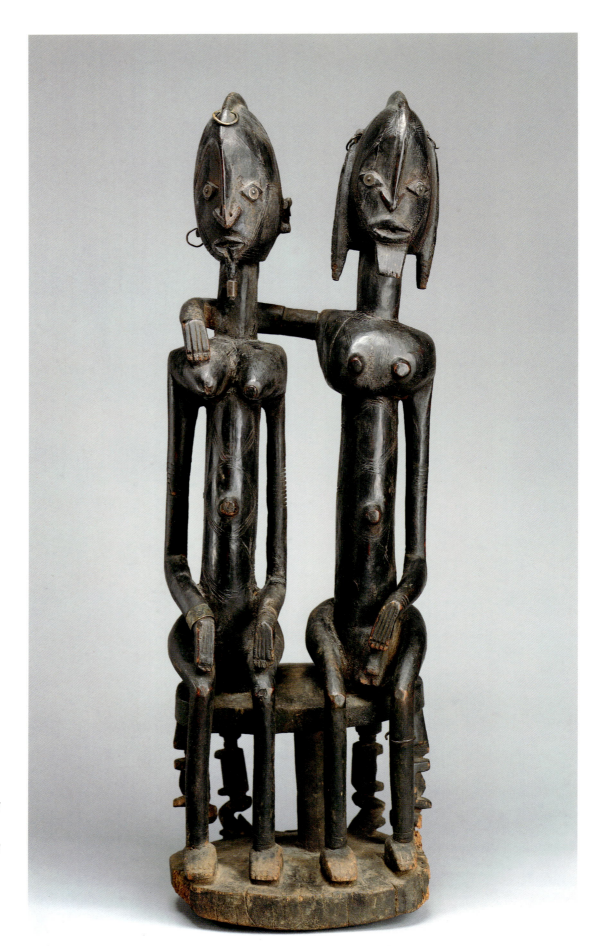

RIGHT: *Seated Couple*, Mali, Dogon, date unknown. The Metropolitan Museum of Art, New York, gift of Lester Wunderman, 1977 (1977.394.15).

182

Mbaba Mwana Waresa

ZULU

Told by Carolyn McVickar Edwards

Over the green, brown, and blue Earth lives the Sky Mama. Ma-baba.

In the lightning and thunder hear Her voice and Her drums. Ma-wana.

The glistening, the slicking, the wa- wet drops slant-ing, sleeking down are Her arms, and Her legs, Her hands, and Her feet. Wa-resa.

Ma-baba Ma-wana Wa-resa.

In the rainbow is Her smile.

Mbaba Mwana Waresa.

Mbaba Mwana Waresa.

It is Mbaba Mwana Waresa who pours down Her sacred waters to Her thirsty people, plants, animals, lakes, and rivers. Mbaba Mwana Waresa cleans, cools, quenches, fills, soaks, pounds, drizzles, and streams. Mbaba Mwana Waresa, Rain Mother of All, is the One without Whom There Is No Life.

In Her absence we long for Her, dance for Her. Mbaba! We cry. Mwana! Waresa! Gone too long, we die, Mbaba. Come to us!

In Her presence we put away our fans. We are thankful. We collect Her sacred waters in our pots. We shiver and dream of fire. Mbaba! Mwana! Waresa! Your noise is mighty. The night is long. We want a fire and a story.

The fire is built. Here is the story.

Once upon a time Mbaba Mwana Waresa wished for a husband. When none of the Gods in Heaven pleased Her, She went to Earth to look for the wisest, most handsome man She could find. When the young man She had chosen heard tell he was to marry Mbaba Mwana Waresa, he went away by himself for a long while to think and prepare himself.

Mbaba Mwana Waresa returned to Heaven to ready Herself for the wedding. But to the astonishment of all in Heaven, Mbaba Mwana Waresa did nothing to deco- rate Herself. Instead She asked Her friend to dress as the Zulu bride. Wondering at Mbaba's request, Her friend had the finest clothes wrapped about her body and her hair braided into a hundred delicate plaits with beautiful beads laced at each end. Gold and silver bracelets were coiled at her wrists and ankles, and sacred dyes were painted on her cheeks and forehead.

Great hoops were hung in her ears, and shining stones threaded on thin copper wires beneath her arms jingled softly as she moved. The womb shell of life was hung on her forehead.

When Mbaba Mwana Waresa saw that Her friend was ready, She did an even stranger thing. She removed all Her own precious beads and Her rainbow-colored robes. With a sharp stone She cut all the tiny beautiful curls from Her head. She smeared Her smooth black skin with pale gray ashes and wrapped herself in the torn skin of a zebra.

Then Mbaba Mwana Waresa declared that the heavenly pair was ready to make the journey to the vil- lage where the young groom awaited Her.

The young man knew the wedding day had come when the sky above him darkened and lightning cracked across the clouds. He heard the beat of Her drums in the thunder that followed. The young man held his shoulders very straight as he went to stand in the rain of his good fortune.

The women from the village chosen as wedding attendants gathered with him, and when the Goddess and Her friend arrived, everyone bowed low in rever- ence. Then all watched to see if the young man would know which of the two from heaven was to be his Wife.

The young man did not hesitate. He extended his hands to Mbaba Mwana Waresa, knowing Her even in the torn skin of a zebra, body gray with ashes, and the hair of Her lovely head shaved away.

"Welcome, Mbaba Mwana Waresa," said the young man. "You need no precious beads, nor fine clothes, nor silver and gold jewelry to show me Who You are. For I see in Your eyes the richness of the Earth, the bounty of the harvest, and the power of Your thunder and lightning. How honored I am to be Your husband."

Mbaba Mwana Waresa smiled. She had chosen well, for this young man was wise enough to see the truth. The friend of Mbaba Mwana Waresa and all the attendants began to clap and sing. The wedding cere- mony was held, and then Mbaba Mwana Waresa took Her husband back to Heaven, where he lives with Her to this very day. Mbaba Mwana Waresa.

183

Au Co

VIETNAMESE

Told by Thich Nhat Hanh

*Thich Nhat Hanh, the teller of this traditional Vietnamese tale, is a well-known
Buddhist teacher, peace activist, and author. Here, he describes the meeting
between Au Co and the Dragon Prince, who later become the parents of one
hundred children, ancestors of all human beings on earth.*

Long ago, when earth and sky were still covered in darkness, a great bird with wings like curtains of night came to rest on the cold earth. She sat for millions of years without stirring, until at last she laid two enormous eggs—one red, the other ivory. Powerful gusts of wind from her majestic wings shook heaven and earth as she flew back into the deep reaches of space.

Thousands of years later, the red egg began to glow. Bright light poured from the egg, chasing away the dense fog that had covered the mountains and filled the valleys for so long. With a thunderous clap, the red egg cracked, freeing a fiery golden crow whose brilliant light dazzled sky and earth.

Then the ivory egg began to radiate a soft and gentle light, and it, too, cracked open. Its shell burst into many fine pieces as an enormous, graceful swan emerged and flew into the sky, tender light streaming from her body down onto the earth.

Each bird followed its own course as it circled the earth. Soft, cool light streamed gently down from the wild swan. The golden crow's fiery wings hurled sparks of bright fire into space as it cried like thunder. The sparks remained suspended in the heavens, twinkling like diamonds. For millions of years, cold darkness had reigned. Now these wondrous birds brought the comfort of light.

The crow's red hot shell exploded into flames that burned for seven years. Boulders melted into fine sand, creating a vast desert. Steam rose from the seas and formed a blanket of clouds that shielded the earth from the crow's fiercest rays. The heavens reeled in the rich aroma that rose from the newly warmed earth.

The light shone all the way to the 36th heaven, where lived many goddesses. The youngest and loveliest goddess, Au Co, pulled back a curtain of cloud, saw the rosy earth below encircled by a halo of light, and cried, "Come, my sisters, let us change ourselves into white Lac birds and fly down to explore this new planet!"

Without hesitation, the goddesses transformed themselves into snow-white birds and flew down to the rosy earth. It was truly a wonderful discovery. As Lac birds they flew over the emerald sea, surprised to see their own reflections dancing in the water. The warm light of the golden crow was delightful. They leisurely skimmed over the pink mountains and came to rest on a hillside covered with soil as fine as powder.

When the first bird touched the ground, she folded her wings and returned to her goddess form. The other goddesses followed her example. Never had the earth hosted so delightful an event! The goddesses laughed and sang as, hand in hand, they strolled up and down the pink slopes. The earth beneath their feet was as soft as cotton balls. When they reached a broad meadow, they began to dance. It was the first dancing on earth. Before that moment, dancing had only been known in the 36th heaven. After a time, Au Co broke away from her sisters, knelt down to examine the fragrant earth more closely, and scooped up a small handful. How soft it was! How good it smelled! The other goddesses paused from their dancing and they too scooped up handfuls of pink earth.

Suddenly Au Co wondered if the earth tasted as good as it smelled, and she lifted her hand to her mouth. Another goddess shouted, "Au Co! Don't do that!" But it was too late. Au Co had already swallowed a tiny handful of the sweet earth. The goddess

RIGHT: *Goddess*, Tibet, late 11th–early 12th century. The Asia Society, New York, Mr. and Mrs. John D. Rockefeller 3rd Acquisitions Fund (1979.38).

who had shouted broke away from the others and ran towards Au Co. She grabbed the young goddess by the hand.

"Au Co, you foolish one! I'm afraid what you have done can never be repaired. Ours is the realm of form, not the realm of desire."

Frightened, the other goddesses quickly brushed all particles of pink earth from their delicate hands. They gathered around Au Co.

"What should we do now?" asked one.

"Let's leave at once and not mention our outing to anyone," suggested another.

They noticed with alarm that it was growing dark. The golden crow had almost disappeared behind the mountains and the light was fading with him.

"We must return before the golden crow disappears!" cried one goddess. She bent over slightly and transformed herself again into a snow-white Lac bird. The others did the same. As they flew into the sky their wings seemed to wave regretful farewells to the lovely earth.

Light disappeared with the golden crow, but it wasn't long before the wild swan returned. Her cool and gentle light was a refreshing change from the bright and sometimes burning rays of the golden crow. The first day on earth had just ended. It lasted as long as seven of our years today. Now the first night was beginning. It was a pleasant and mild night, illuminated by the swan's tender light.

Beneath that light, Au Co flew frantically back and forth, unable to join her sisters. Her wings were too heavy, and no matter how hard she tried, she could fly no higher. Because Au Co had tasted the new earth, she had lost her magical flying powers and could no longer return to the 36th heaven. Frightened and alone, she sank back down to earth. She resumed her goddess form and leaned against a boulder to weep.

Throughout the night, her tears became a long river that wound down to the seashore, where it emptied into the sea. Beneath the waves, multitudes of small creatures—shrimp, crabs, fish, and oysters—tasted the new current of water perfumed with fragrant earth. They shared their discovery with Dragon Prince, the son of the Sea Dragon Emperor, who had turned

himself into a small fish to follow the sweet current upstream in search of its source. Although he swam swiftly, the first night on earth ended before he reached shore.

When Dragon Prince lifted his head above the water, he could see the golden crow. The sparkling sea rivaled his father's emerald palace below. Lapping waves spewed foam as white as snow. The prince leaped into the air. How soft, clear, and immense the sky was—round and blue like the sea itself. He could see the pale outlines of mountains and hills shimmering in the distance. Everything was similar to the land-

185

scape beneath the sea, yet here the world seemed more expansive, lighter and clearer.

He jumped onto shore and turned himself into a handsome young man with a broad forehead, long legs, and eyes that shone like stars. As he strolled along the shore, he admired the beauty all around him. He gazed at the rocky cliffs, rising from the sea into lofty peaks. Intent to find the river's source, he turned to follow it inland. The more he walked, the more he marveled. Bright patches of moss draped the riverbanks. Tiny gold and purple flowers blossomed among green carpets of grass. Beneath the ocean there were many kinds of strange and lovely seaweeds, corals, grasses, and flowers, but he had never seen such delicate shapes and colors as these. He guessed that the sweet water of the river was to thank, for no grass or flowers grew beyond the river's reach.

This was the second day on earth.

A band of butterflies suddenly appeared. At first Dragon Prince mistook them for flowers. He had never seen such fragile creatures. They were as light as air, sporting sunlight on their wings as they fluttered among the flowers. No doubt, he mused, they thought the flowers were creatures like themselves.

Dragon Prince climbed the mountain slope down which the river flowed. Its waters bubbled and gushed, caressing the mossy rocks along the banks. Bushes sprang up among the fresh grasses. Then he came to an abrupt halt. Before him was a sight unlike any he had ever encountered. Leaning against a moss-covered boulder was a young woman. Though her face was turned towards the rock, he could tell she was weeping. Unclad, she was more beautiful than any living creature he had seen before. She was like a newly blossomed flower. Her pale arms were folded beneath her forehead. Her long, lustrous black hair curled and flowed with the river currents. It was Au Co, forced to remain in the lower world because she had tasted the sweet earth. She had wept since nightfall, a span of more than ten years to us.

Dragon Prince did not take another step forward. He stood spellbound, and then he spoke,

"Sun shining brightly
Sky and sea both blue
Butterflies flutter
By a river so new
Where have you come from?
Why do you weep alone?"

Startled by the sea prince's voice, she stopped crying and looked up. Her eyes opened wide in surprise when she beheld the noble young man. She sat up and wiped her eyes with a lock of hair. Looking straight into his eyes, she answered:

"Bright golden crow
Fragrant new earth
As white Lac birds
We flew below.
A taste of new earth
No longer can I fly
My sisters departed
I wait alone and cry.
Lost in a strange land
My tears become a river."

Au Co explained all that had happened from the moment she pulled back the curtain of cloud to the moment she could no longer fly and was forced to return to earth. Dragon Prince sat down beside her and told her about his own life beneath the sea, where his father reigned. His voice was warm and kind, and whenever he mentioned the golden crow, the blue sky, or the fragrant hills, his eyes sparkled. Together they looked up at the sky and down at the green grasses that covered the riverbanks. Dragon Prince tried to console Au Co by telling her that her sisters would surely return that day or the next, as soon as they found a way to take her back home. They spoke for a long time. The sea prince's joy was so infectious that Au Co was soon talking and laughing as though no misfortune had befallen her.

Holding hands, they strolled down the mountain. Suddenly the sea prince grew alarmed. The river had almost completely drained into the sea. The grasses and flowers at their feet were withering. There were no butterflies in sight. The golden crow poised above their heads and their shadows shortened. It was noon, and the crow's rays were fierce and burning.

Dragon Prince said, "The earth is only green and beautiful when nourished by the sweet water of your tears. There are no trees and flowers growing by the seawater. It seems that land plants cannot thrive on seawater. Let me make some rain from the remaining tears in order to replenish the river."

Au Co did not know what rain was. But before she could ask, the prince climbed down to a tiny stream of water still trickling through the white sands about to empty into the sea. He scooped up some of the water in his hands and took three sips. When he returned to where she stood, he said, "Please sit down over there. I will moisten the earth with this wondrous water. Do not cry out until you see the rain. Look out over the ocean. If you see anything strange, do not worry. Although you are a goddess and I am a dragon, there is nothing to fear between us."

He quickly ran back to the sea. Au Co watched as he joined his palms together like a lotus bud. He dove into the water and quickly disappeared from sight. Within moments black clouds tumbled forth from a churning sea. They piled higher and higher until the blue sky was obscured. They were quite unlike the serene white clouds that drifted in the heavens Au Co knew. The golden crow's light grew fainter until Au Co could barely see what was happening. Suddenly, thunder bellowed from the depths of the sea, and a golden dragon hundreds of feet long burst from the waves. Its marvelous long body twisted gracefully before it disappeared into the black clouds. Lightning flashed across the black sky, and then there was a deafening crash.

Frightened, Au Co stood up, but she was unable to see anything. Then, all at once, she felt a pleasant sensation on skin, something at once wet, ticklish, delicate, and refreshing. Thousands of tiny drops fell onto her body. Rain! Dragon Prince had made rain!

The steady pitter-patter was like the sound of singing. It reminded Au Co of the sea prince's warm and reassuring voice. She lifted her arms to welcome the refreshing drops and then offered her hair and shoulders, her whole body, to the soothing rains. Beneath her feet, young grasses sprang up and the river was soon replenished.

The rain lasted a long while. When nearly all the clouds were gone and bright sunlight streamed forth again, the golden dragon gazed down at the earth. Many new rivers and streams had appeared. Not only did grass grow fresh and green along the riverbanks but it now covered the hills, mountains, and fields. Flowers—violet, gold, pink, and white—dotted the landscape. The face of the earth glistened in unimaginable beauty. Yet what was even more miraculous to the sea prince as he gazed down from the last clouds was that the outline of the rivers took the very shape of Au Co herself—her long legs stretching to the sea, her hair flowing over all the hills and mountains. Her image was forever imprinted on the green fields of the fresh and lovely earth. Au Co, so beautiful and full of vitality, was herself the fertile heart of the earth.

BELOW: *Cypress*, Kano Eitoku, 14th–16th century. Tokyo National Museum.

VIII

HIDDEN GODDESSES:
JUDAISM, CHRISTIANITY, AND ISLAM

STRICTLY SPEAKING, JUDAISM, CHRISTIANITY, AND ISLAM HAVE NO goddesses, only male father-gods. But the archetype of the divine feminine is too strong to suppress, and each of these three major religions does acknowledge the divine feminine in its own way.

In the Old Testament and in Gnosticism, an early branch of mystical Christianity, the goddess appears as Sophia (a Greek word meaning wisdom), who is described as God's consort and lover, and who takes on many attributes of earlier goddesses. In Judaism, the goddess also appears as the light-filled Shekhina, bride of the Holy One and "a sign of hope among the people." Islam is perhaps the most patriarchal among the world religions, yet Islamic writers do bestow an almost goddess-like stature upon certain women, including not only Mohammed's mother and his three wives, but also Mary, who along with Jesus is highly honored by the Koran.

Though the Catholic Church eventually denounced the Gnostic teachings and removed most references to the goddess from the Bible, the goddess slowly reemerged in widespread worship of Mary, whom the common people worshiped with fervent devotion. Medieval artists portrayed her as the queen-consort of Christ, and in their images endowed her with all the powers and the glory of a goddess. In the year 431, the Council of Ephesus declared that Mary was the "Mother of God." The great mythologist Joseph Campbell tells us that while the council was debating its decision, "the people of Ephesus formed picket lines and shouted in praise of Mary, "The Goddess, the Goddess, of course she's the Goddess." In the Irish poem, "Litany to our Lady," Mary is revered as the "Gate of Heaven," the "Temple of the Living God," the "Queen of Life," and the "Honor of the Sky." Over the centuries, Mary's status within the Catholic Church continued to grow, and in 1954, she was pronounced "Queen of Heaven," thus assuming the role of other goddesses such as Ishtar, Inanna, and Isis.

OPPOSITE: *Madonna of the Magnificat* (detail), Sandro Botticelli, c. 1485. Uffizi, Florence.

IN PRAISE OF SOPHIA

*The Bible contains many traces of ancient goddess-worship. Here, in
a passage from Proverbs, Sophia (a Greek word meaning "wisdom")
describes herself as God's beloved.*

I prayed, and understanding was given to me;
I entreated, and the spirit of Wisdom came to me.
I esteemed her more than scepters and thrones;
compared with her, I held riches as nothing.
I reckoned no priceless stone to be her peer,
for compared with her, all gold is a pinch of sand,
and beside her silver ranks as mud.
I loved her more than health or beauty,
preferred her to the light,
since her radiance never sleeps.
In her company all good things came to me,
at her hands riches not to be numbered.
All these I delighted in, since Wisdom brings them,
but as yet I did not know she was their mother.
What I learned without self-interest, I pass on without
    reserve;
I do not intend to hide her riches.
For she is an inexhaustible treasure to men,
and those who acquire it win God's friendship,
commended as they are to him by the benefits of her
    teaching.

For within her is a spirit intelligent, holy,
unique, manifold, subtle,
active, incisive, unsullied,
lucid, invulnerable, benevolent, sharp,
irresistible, beneficent, loving to man,
steadfast, dependable, unperturbed,
almighty, all-surveying,
penetrating all intelligent, pure
and most subtle spirits;
for Wisdom is quicker to move than any motion;
she is so pure, she pervades and permeates all things.

She is a breath of the power of God,
pure emanation of the glory of the Almighty;
hence nothing impure can find a way into her.
She is a reflection of the eternal light,
untarnished mirror of God's active power,
image of his goodness.

Although alone, she can do all;
herself unchanging, she makes all things new.
In each generation she passes into holy souls,
she makes them friends of God and prophets;
for God loves only the man who lives with Wisdom.
She is indeed more splendid than the sun,
she outshines all the constellations;
compared with light, she takes first place,
for light must yield to night,
but over Wisdom evil can never triumph.
She deploys her strength from one end of the earth to
    the other,
ordering all things for good.

OPPOSITE: *Mary as Sophia on
the Lion Throne*, illuminated
manuscript, c. 1150. The
Bodleian Library, Oxford
(Ms. Bodl. 269, fol. iii, recto).

191

TABERNACLE OF PEACE

JEWISH

Howard Schwartz

That *Sukkos* [Jewish harvest festival] Reb Zalman gave his *D'var Torah* in the *Sukkah* [ritual booth] behind his house, into which all of his Hasidim crowded. His subject that year was the Tabernacle of Peace which descends around the earth whenever the *Shekhina* descends from on high to embrace her children, Israel. And in the shelter of that Tabernacle, the world is awash in its glory. That is truly the time of abundance.

Reb Zalman said: "Now when is it that the Shekhina descends? Her visits take place on every *Shabbas* and holy day. That is why those days are so sacred—for the Holy One saw fit to permit His bride, the Shekhina, to take leave of the world above and embrace her children in the world below. Therefore we embrace these days ourselves, so that our embrace may meet that of the Shekhina. And in the shelter of that embrace our lives are rocked as if in a cradle of peace."

Later that day Reb Zalman and Reb Hayim Elya found themselves alone in the Sukkah. And Hayim Elya said: "Rebbe, tell me more about this Tabernacle of Peace, for while you spoke it was almost as if I could visualize it. Why, it was almost as if I saw one corner of the heavenly Sukkah planted above this very Sukkah of yours; as if the Shekhina had reached down

and embraced us. Tell me, please, why it is that we cannot hold onto this Tabernacle of Peace and make it remain with us all the time?"

Reb Zalman laughed when Hayim Elya said this, and then he said: "Know, Hayim Elya, that the Sukkah of the Tabernacle of Peace is bound to this world by four golden threads. Those threads are as thin as the thinnest thread, so that they barely can be seen glinting in the sunlight. But they are there. Yet at the same time, they are fragile, they are only threads. And if we tried to hold on to them, they would simply break."

Now, strangely enough, Hayim Elya was not disappointed, but even more intrigued. And he said: "Are you saying, then, Rebbe, that it might be possible to hold on to one of those golden threads in a gentle way without causing it to break?" And Reb Zalman replied: "It is precisely to be able to do this that Moses received the Torah on Sinai. And this is the ultimate

I I I I: *I must not think of thee and tired yet strong,* Ben Shahn, 1964. © Estate of Ben Shahn/ Licensed by VAGA, New York, NY.

secret that the Torah is able to teach. For as long as we are in that Divine Presence, our lives will be filled with all blessings in this world, at the behest of the Holy One, blessed be He."

Hayim Elya quickly responded: "Tell me, Rebbe, how is it possible to accomplish this? For now that you have spoken I have visualized the golden thread, which even now I see not far above your head. And it reaches up into the highest heavens. Even now I have traced the end that is tied to this earth to the very fringes of your *tallis*, in this room." And Reb Zalman looked down in amazement, and saw that there was indeed a golden thread entwined around one of the *tsitsis* of his prayer shawl. And it was also true that this thread ascended from there as high as the eye could see, and, no doubt, much further. And suddenly Reb Zalman himself had a great insight, and he said to Hayim Elya with joy, "In this very moment, Hayim

Elya, it has been revealed to me that the thread remains bound as long as we continue to be engaged in the discussion of Torah, as we are now. This is what King David discovered, and thus he was able to stave off the Angel of Death when he discovered that the Angel was destined to take him on the Sabbath. So he spent every moment of every Shabbas in the study of the Torah, and the Angel of Death was unable to approach him. Only by creating a diversion did the Angel finally trick him out of his room, or else he might still be alive to this day. Yes, our salvation lies in the Torah in more ways than we might imagine."

So it was that long after the sun had set at the end of Sukkos, Reb Zalman and Hayim Elya continued to speak of the Torah in its myriad forms. And all that time the golden thread, now glowing in the dark, remained coiled around one fringe of Reb Zalman's tallis. And only after the sun had risen, and they had finished praying *Shahareis*, did they bid farewell to the Shekhina as she gently lifted the Tabernacle of Peace from this world. And by then Reb Zalman had come to understand in the most elementary way the secret of the Shekhina. And as the two of them sat together, awed by all they had witnessed, Reb Zalman said: "All that we have discovered in these hours under the Sukkah can be expressed in the simplest way. And this, above all, is what I have learned: That the essence of the Shekhina is called forth through every crown and letter of the Torah, whenever it is opened and read, or even when it is simply discussed. For as long as the words of the Torah are spoken in this world, the golden threads will remain coiled in the fringes of our *tallisim*, as long as they are being worn. During every such moment the Shekhina is permitted to remain here, among us, and in this way the world is able to remain sheltered in her Tabernacle of Peace. And that, Hayim Elya, is the answer to your question."

194

The Door to the Soul

CONTEMPORARY

Carolyn McVickar Edwards

Once a young man asked himself these questions: Who am I? And how am I connected to all others? He wondered and wandered and asked the questions again and again. He yearned for the answers.

One day he approached a teacher and asked, "Who am I? And how am I connected to all others?" The teacher said, "Study will answer those riddles."

"What must I study?" asked the young man.

"Study the thousand and one books," said the teacher. "It is through your study that you will gain wisdom."

So the young man piled the thousand and one books, some dry bread, and some candles on a cart. Then he took himself in cap and shawl, with paper in his shoes for warmth, to a small house at the edge of a town.

Inside the house, at the desk he sat, day after day, reading the thousand and one books. "Who am I?" he wrote on a paper. "How am I connected to all others?" he wrote on a second. Outside the trees turned fiery and lost their leaves. Inside, the young man filled page after page with learning from his books. He stopped only to swallow a little of the dry bread and sometimes to renew his candle or to drop his aching shoulders before him on the desk to sleep. The young man's wrists grew thin and his eyes burned. The thousand and one books stacked themselves around him in wobbly towers, and the pages of his writings heaped themselves before him like a fence.

One night a freezing rain beat in a torrent against the walls of the house. The young man pulled his shawl tight about him, but he felt the damp like a knife in his back. His feet were numb. The marks on the page before him began to swim. Suddenly the young man let out a moan and flung the book toward the window. "I don't know!" he yelled. "I DON'T KNOW!"

At that very second the rain outside halted and a howl of wind blew up. It clattered the panes and then, in a rush of power, ripped open the catch of the window. The room was filled with the shock of cold air. The candle blew out, and the papers on the desk spattered apart and lifted like the feathers of some giant white bird.

The young man staggered to the window and wrenched it shut. Then turning slowly and looking across the room, he drew back to see that a small light had formed on the other side of the swinging doors that led to the next room. "How can that be?" said the young man. "There is no one in this house but me."

The young man felt afraid. But the light glowed so softly. After a moment, the young man followed the glow to the other side of the doors. The pale light went on before him. This time he had to part a curtain to enter the next room. Still the glow went for-

OPPOSITE: *The Sabbath of the Simple*, H. N. Werkman, 1941. Collection Stedelijk Museum, Amsterdam.

195

OPPOSITE: *The Prophecy*,
Stanton MacDonald-Wright,
1955. Collection Michel
Seuphor, Paris.

ward, and the young man found himself walking through room after room. He had not known the house had so many rooms. Was it possible he'd forgotten them? Had they been here before?

Finally the light drew him to a tightly closed door. He pushed it open, and the light settled on a bed in the small room. The young man breathed out as he saw the light falter, then flare up, and then turn before his eyes into a beautiful Woman.

The Woman's skin was dark and Her hair curled about Her face. Her garment was like the shadows of leaves. She looked quietly at the young man. The bed on which She sat was covered with quilts the color of shells. The walls seemed soft as clouds.

"Who are you?" asked the young man.

"I am your Soul," said the Woman. "I am the Shekhina. Eat and be full."

The Woman turned and lifted to the bed a great tray laden with a feast. The young man felt ravenous. Fruit of every sort filled the tray. He fell to it and ate his fill.

The Shekhina handed him a cup of steaming broth. The young man felt the warmth seep into his bones. "Bathe now," said the Shekhina.

Around him the young man could feel hot, lapping, washing water. Afterward a towel folded around him held in the sweet heat.

"Now. Come. Sleep," said the Shekhina. She helped the young man into the bed.

For six days the young man clung to the Shekhina, wrapped now in the deepest sleep, then awake and gazing into Her eyes, and then holding Her completely as he could. And then again drifting into the lovely snow of sleep.

On the seventh day, the Shekhina rose up and kissed the young man on his lips. Then Her skin seemed to melt and he could no longer see her features. She faded again to a glow of light. The young man lay unable to move, his breath caught in his throat.

The young man didn't know how long he slept after that. But the next time he opened his eyes, the sun was shining. He gathered up the pits of the fruits he'd eaten and went outside. There in the soil he planted a garden. At the center of the garden he placed a stone. On the stone he wrote these words: "I am one with all. All is one."

Years passed by. The seeds of the fruits grew into a mighty orchard. The young man was no longer young. Now he was an old man who carried his grandchildren.

Always on the seventh day, the old man lit the candles and whispered the story of the calling of the Soul. "Come, Shekhina," he would say to the breeze that flickered the candle flames bright. "Come, Shekhina, come. Fill this garden with Your rest."

196

ABOVE: *Dweller in the Innermost*, George Frederic Watts, c. 1885–86. Tate Gallery, London.

MARY'S DREAM

CONTEMPORARY

Lucille Clifton

Winged women was saying

"full of grace" and like.

was light beyond sun and words

of a name and a blessing.

winged women to only i.

i joined them, whispering

yes.

Our Lady of Guadalupe

MEXICAN

Told by Paula Gunn Allen

On a wintry day in northern Mexico, in the year 1659 C.E., an impoverished Indian man whose Spanish name was Juan Diego was trudging cross-country on an errand. The Spaniards had long ago taken Mexico as their own. It had been one hundred forty years since Quetzalcoatl the Precious Twin had returned. As Diego approached a small hill, he heard a woman's voice calling his name.

Puzzled, he looked around. He had seen no one for some time, so the voice came out of nowhere, or so he thought. At the crest of the rise, he saw the figure of a woman, and she was beckoning to him. She was dressed in the peasant fashion of the day, her body modestly covered in a long-sleeved gown, her head and shoulders hidden beneath a long cloak.

Slowly, he went toward her. When he was within a few feet of her he stopped, and taking off his sombrero, he looked shyly groundward. He had seen that she was not one of the village women, no one he knew, and her presence made him feel at once safe and awed. He stood thus, not speaking. His deep sense of courtesy restrained him, and his rearing in soft-mannered ways led him to await her words patiently.

"I have a message I want you to take to the city, to the archbishop," she said calmly. Her voice, though soft, was warm and clear.

"But, Lady," he objected softly. "It is far, and I am but an Indian. The archbishop will not have reason to see me."

"Go, and do as I say. Tell him that I wish to have a church built here, in my honor. Tell him to dedicate it to me." She smiled gently at Juan Diego.

"But, Lady," he said again. "I have no shoes. I do not speak their language very well. Surely the archbishop will not have time for the likes of me."

"It will be well," she said.

So, hesitatingly, he walked away from her. He felt certain that no one would see him in the capital, but he was willing to try. He had a sense that the Lady was not like them, not an Indian, certainly not a Spaniard.

Something about her, her presence, made him recognize he must do as she directed him.

But, as he thought, the archbishop would not see him. He managed to tell his story to one of the priests at the cathedral, and the man said he would carry the message to His Excellency. After many hours, he returned and took the barefoot man in to see the archbishop.

Juan Diego told his story, but the archbishop did not believe him. After listening to him carefully, he sent him away with words of blessing.

Juan Diego began the long trek back to where he'd seen the Lady. When he arrived at the small hill, she stood waiting for him. It was deep winter, and very cold. The stiff grass was brown and dry, and a bleak wind scudded clouds across the afternoon sky.

He told her what had happened at the cathedral, and awaited her response.

"Take off your tilpa," she instructed him. He made a move to obey her, and as he did he saw to his astonishment that the ground at her feet was suddenly thick in riotous roses. He gasped, taking a step backward.

"Don't be frightened," the Lady said. "Fill your tilpa with blossoms and carry it carefully back to the city. Ask again to see the archbishop, and when you do, open it and show him the roses."

Awed, Juan Diego leaned down and plucked an armload of the flowers. Filling his tilpa and wrapping its ends loosely around them so they wouldn't be crushed, he lifted the bundle carefully into his arms.

Back in the city, he hastened to the cathedral as soon as it was light. The sacristan let him in, and he stood in the drafty church entry gazing at the lighted candles, smelling the incense from early Mass. He went further in, stopping at the carved basin just inside the chancel. Dipping his hand in the icy water, he blessed himself quickly and knelt down on one knee briefly. Then, clutching his bundle, he started for the front of the cathedral, following the sacristan. He was led to a room off the cathedral where the archbishop was sitting down to a meal. Juan Diego

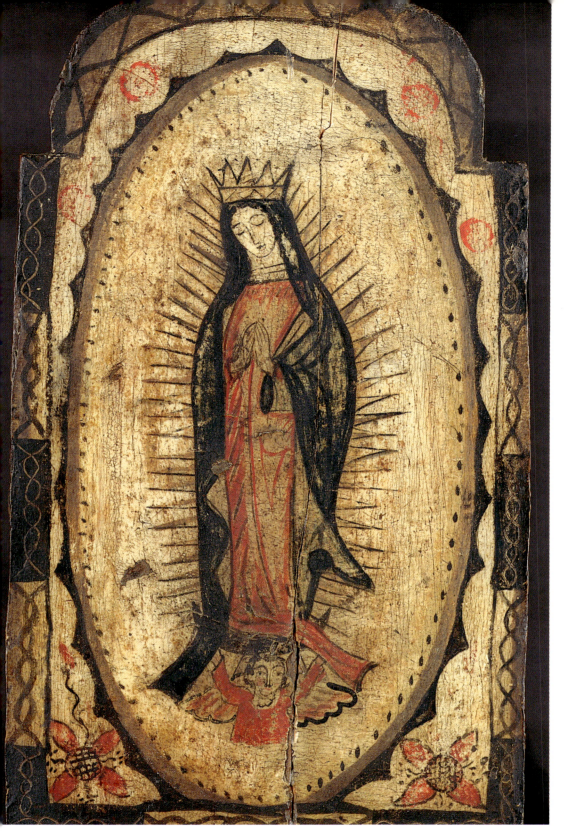

1 1 1 1: *Our Lady of*
Guadalupe, Pedro
Antonio Fresquis,
c. 1800. National
Museum of American
Art, Washington D.C.

was fixed on the tilpa that
hung from Juan Diego's
upraised hand.

"A miracle," the arch-
bishop whispered. His
monsignor nodded and fell to
his knees.

After a time, Juan Diego
lowered his arms so he could
look over them at his tilpa.
He saw that no roses had
fallen to the floor, for it was
quite bare of blossoms. Then,
turning his gaze to the woven
cloth he held, he saw what
had set the other men reeling.
Somehow an image of the
Lady had become imprinted
on the cloak.

Ah, he thought,
Tonantzin, Our Mother, has
returned. Like the others, he
sank to his knees, still clutching the worn wrap in both
hands.

Recovering himself, the
archbishop took the cloak
from Juan Diego and spread
it reverently upon the table,
pushing aside the breakfast
things and the food. He gazed

had not eaten in many hours, and walking so far with
no food had left him weak.

Still, he did not give in to the small urge to gaze
hungrily at the food. Instead he told the archbishop
that the Lady had instructed him to show what he carried to him. As he spoke, he let the ends of the tilpa
drop so that the roses could fall to the floor. He heard
the archbishop's sharp intake of breath and glanced
up. His Excellency's fair skin had turned some shades
lighter, and his eyes were round as a child's. His gaze

at it in silence for a time, then turned to the Indian
and said, "Tell the Virgin Morena I will honor her
request. I will build her church, and she will become
the Patroness of New Spain." Then he turned to his
aide and instructed him to feed Juan Diego and make
sure he had another tilpa to wrap himself in for the
journey back to deliver his message.

As Juan Diego was being led away, he heard the
archbishop call after him, "Thank you, and go with
God."

201

MOTHER CHANT

JEWISH

Rabbi Lynn Gottlieb

*Rabbi Lynn Gottlieb comments that she created the Mother Chant because "Jewish women
need a genealogy that restores our mothers' names to the sacred history of our people."*

Brucha Ya Shekhina hanotenet orah l'sapair sipurim.
Blessed are you who gives your light
To inspire the telling of sacred tales.

Night Sea Woman	Tehom
Light That Dwells Within Woman	Shekhina
Fiery Night Woman	Lilith
Let There Be Life Woman	Hava
Mother of the Tent Women	Adah
Flute Song Woman	Zilah
Voice of the Flood Woman	Na-amah
See Far Woman	Sarah
Outcast Woman	Hagar
Pillar of Salt Woman	Eshet Lot
Praises All Life Woman	Yehudit
Earth Smelling Sweet Woman	Basmat
Buffalo Woman	Rivkeh
Talking Bee Woman	Devorah
Soft Eyes Woman	Leah
Soft Heart Woman	Rachel
Truth Seeking Woman	Dinah
Desert Eagle Woman	Asnat
Smells of Time Woman	Serach
Horn of Freedom Woman	Shifra
Helping Hand Woman	Puah
Golden Cloud Woman	Yocheved

And never was there a prophet like Miriam HaNavia:
She sang open the waters of the sea,
And all the people passed through to freedom.
T'halleli yah t'halleli ya t'halleli ya t'halleli ya
la la la la la la la la la la la la la laa!

OPPOSITE: *Judith,*
Giorgione, c. 1500.
Hermitage, Leningrad.

GOLDEN CLOUD WOMAN

JEWISH

Rabbi Lynn Gottlieb

This is a story about Jochoved, the mother of Miriam, Aaron, and Moshe, who is mentioned in the Bible as having been a midwife.

A new pharaoh who did not know Yosef arose over Mitzryim. He said to his people, "Look, the Israelites are too numerous and too strong for us. We must deal cleverly with them now before their numbers increase even more and they join forces with our enemies and drive us from our own land." So they appointed taskmasters over us to crush

our spirits with hard labor. We were forced to build the storage sites of Pithom and Ramses as supply centers for Pharaoh.

But the more they oppressed us, the more we increased.

They came to dread us.

They forced us to do labor designed to break our bodies.

They made our lives miserable with harsh work involving mortar and brick as well as all kinds of toil in the field.

Pharaoh summoned the head midwives of the Evreem to his court. That is the name they called us, Evreem: vagabonds and wayfarers.

My mother was one of the midwives. The people called her Shifra: Horn of Freedom Woman. She turned each birth into a celebration. Somehow she collected wine and bread, shells and beads, goat hair blankets, and baskets woven from the tall grass by the river. We would gather and rejoice in the new child and renew our hope.

Pharaoh could not sleep. On the nights the Israelite women gave birth he dreamt of grasshoppers, swarming insects, and frogs crawling over his face and hands. While the women groaned with labor he screamed his midnight fears into the darkness of Mitzryim.

He summoned my mother, Shifra, saying, "When you deliver a Hebrew infant, if it is a boy, smash its head on the birth stone; if it is a girl, let it live."

My mother did not do as Pharaoh commanded.

One day they came for her and hanged her from a tree. I watched as they buried my mother's body, and I planted a cedar twig over her grave. Every day I would visit her and weep. Because I came so often and cried so much the twig quickly grew into a tree.

One day a white dove nested in the tree, and I took it as a sign. Soon the bird ate from my hand and cooed a welcome when I came.

One evening under a full moon sky I embraced the tree and felt the warmth of my mother's light rising, her spirit ascending, and the bird flew about us, cooing, and a voice spoke to me saying, "I am the Presence that sustained your mothers and fathers and promised them freedom. I am Shekhina, who will lead the people from darkness to light, from sorrow to joy, from slavery to redemption. From this time onward you shall be called Golden Cloud Woman, for you have seen the light of Shekhina. Let My light become a sign of hope among the people."

My tears watered the tree once again, and I returned home.

From that time onward the people called me Yocheved for the golden cloud that surrounded me. It was a great sign of hope. The days of deliverance were at hand.

LEFT: *Israel in Egypt*, Sir Edward John Poynter, late 19th or early 20th century. Guildhall Art Gallery, Corporation of London.

Litany to Our Lady

I R I S H

Translated by Eugene O'Curry

*The following is a translation of an
8th-century poem originally written in Latin.*

O Great Mary.
O Mary, greatest of Maries.
O Greatest of Women.
O Queen of Angels.
O Mistress of the Heavens.
O Woman full and replete with the grace of the Holy Ghost.
O Blessed and Most Blessed.
O Mother of Eternal Glory.
O Mother of the heavenly and earthly Church.
O Mother of Love and Indulgence.
O Mother of the Golden Heights.
O Honor of the Sky.
O Sign of Tranquillity.
O Gate of Heaven.
O Golden Casket.
O Couch of Love and Mercy.
O Temple of Divinity.
O Beauty of Virgins.
O Mistress of the Tribes.
O Fountain of the Parterres.
O Cleansing of the Sins.
O Purifying of Souls.
O Mother of Orphans.
O Breast of the Infants.
O Solace of the Wretched.
O Star of the Sea.
O Handmaid of the Lord.
O Mother of Christ.
O Resort of the Lord.
O Graceful like the Dove.
O Serene like the Moon.
O Resplendent like the Sun.
O Cancelling Eve's disgrace.

O Regeneration of Life.
O Beauty of Women.
O Leader of the Virgins.
O Enclosed Garden.
O Closely Locked Fountain.
O Mother of God.
O Perpetual Virgin.
O Holy Virgin.
O Serene Virgin.
O Chaste Virgin.
O Temple of the Living God.
O Royal Throne of the Eternal King.
O Sanctuary of the Holy Ghost.
O Virgin of the Root of Jesse.
O Cedar of Mount Lebanon.
O Cypress of Mount Sion.
O Crimson Rose of the Land of Jacob.
O Blooming like the Palm Tree.
O Fruitful like the Olive Tree.
O Glorious Son-Bearer.
O Light of Nazareth.
O Glory of Jerusalem.
O Beauty of the World.
O Noblest-Born of the Christian Flock.
O Queen of Life.
O Ladder of Heaven.

OPPOSITE: *Annunciation,*
Sandro Botticelli, c. 1489–90.
Uffizi, Florence.

207

A Heretic's Pilgrimage

IRISH

Eva Gore-Booth

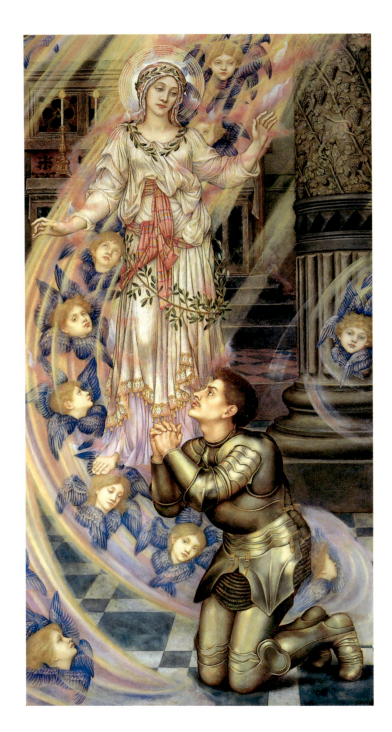

RIGHT: *Our Lady of Peace*,
Evelyn de Morgan, 1907.
The De Morgan
Foundation, London.

Here, all star-paven at our Lady's well,
A milky way of white anemones
Leads to her simple shrine among the trees,
The silver willow woods of Lissadel.
Grey winds pass sighing and strange forces thrill
The holy water, sheltered from the breeze,
Fresh from the spring of earth's lost mysteries
Beneath the shadow of the haunted hill.
Madonna of the way-side throned here!
We bring thee poppies grown amongst the wheat,
Frail blue-bells and the silver marguerite,
And all the golden tribute of the year,
We lay our dreams and flowers at thy feet,
Because the country people hold thee dear.

Above her head full seven cold glories shine,
Before the mighty Virgin Gabriel stands—
His feet are flame, and in his claspèd hands
He holds a tall white lily for a sign.
This is the mortal angels call divine,
The winds of heaven obey her high commands,
Hers is the secret of all times and lands,
The glory of the temple's inmost shrine.
Ah, Mary Mother, thine it was alone
For all the majesty of youth to find
The spirit's glory out of darkness grown,
To leave the soilèd joys of earth behind,
And seek the splendor of the white unknown,
The sacred loneliness of star and wind.

Hail Virgin spirit of the world's desire,
Have pity on us, who, like thee of late
Saw the great angel at life's outer gate,
And paused to greet him with our hearts on fire,
Yet, went away and sold our souls for hire,
And wandered far in the wild ways of fate
And learned the hunger naught can satiate,
And dragged the angel's lily through the mire.
Ah, pray for us, poor children of blind chance,
Who have lost Hope beneath the world's control,
Forgot the glory of the angel's glance,
The dim light of the half-deciphered scroll,
Our one strange glimpse of God's unknown Romance,
Life's salutation to the virgin soul.

Mothers of the Faithful

ISLAMIC

Nur Al Jerrahi (Lex Hixon)

ABOVE: *Tile Panel*, Iran (Isfahan), 1st quarter of 17th century. The Metropolitan Museum of Art, New York, Rogers Fund, 1903 (03.9c).

From holy mother Eve to holy mother Mary, who both received the full Light of Prophecy, the Divine Drama of revelation and mystic return unfolded progressively and was brought to the threshold of completion—a process enduring for untold thousands of years and intimately involving millions of tender, strong, loving, patient, insightful, and loyal mothers. The final threshold was crossed, five hundred years after the Virgin, when our most delicate and sublime mother, Amina the Blessed, may Allah always ennoble her countenance, received the white dove of the compassionately descending soul of the Seal of Prophecy. All beings, including the very planet, trembled in ecstasy, instinctively and intuitively recognizing the culmination of revelation, the closure of the circle from the preeternal Muhammad of Light to the Bearer of the Wisdom of all Prophets, the beloved Muhammad of Arabia.

Then great mothers and guiding lights of the faithful began to appear, like full moons sailing to the earth and living here with unimaginable feminine grace and power. This manifestation began with the first mother of the community of Islam, the first initiate to taste the intense sweetness of submission to Allah transmitted through the Prophet of Allah, the first one of her people wise and courageous enough to witness to the prophethood of the trustworthy one whom she loved and embraced as her husband, the precious Khadija, may Allah Most Glorious always confirm the queenly nobility of her soul.

Among the incomparable wives of the Prophet, each of whom is a mystic gem adorning the Green Turban of Complete Realization, the most precious Aisha shines forth as the crest jewel of spirituality, the one who demonstrates the perfection of womanhood to all humanity, may Allah eternally confirm her station at the right hand of the Messenger. This Mother and Guide of the Faithful transmitted the intimate and inconceivably powerful content of one third of the Prophet's sublime Oral Tradition. As the beloved Muhammad, immersed in prayer and lost in the bliss of mystic union, would prostrate on his bed toward the Kaaba during the secret midnight hours, our holy mother Aisha would move her legs to make room for his radiant head and then stretch out her legs again whenever her tender husband rose from his prostration to continue the sacred recitation of the Resonance of Allah, the Book of Reality clothed in the letters of the Arabic alphabet.

Finally, the manifestation of Divine Attributes through the feminine form of humanity reached its culmination in the one who does not fit into any books or words, the majestic Fatima, may the secret of her union with Allah and with the Prophet of Allah be revealed and replicated in all mature hearts. The noble Messenger proclaimed unequivocally of the august Fatima, "She is part of my prophecy." The sublime Ali, Whirling Lion of Allah, most mature among the spiritually mature, recognized our holy mother Fatima as the inward successor of the Prophet of Allah in the mystical lineage hidden within the secret heart of Islam. He therefore did not take hand with the first Khalifa, Abu Bakr the Truthful, until, after six months of unimaginable yearning, the brilliant light of the soul of Fatima left this surface world to join the soul of her father in the Garden of Essence, where there is only one soul.

Our most profound and humble greetings, salams, and kisses to the earth where the feet of these holy mothers have walked: beloved Eve, beloved Mary, most precious Khadija, most precious Aisha, and the Pearl Beyond Price—the majestic and mysterious mother of the Mirror of the Prophet, the noble Hussain, may the Peace of Allah always be upon him, the Mother of the Ecstatic Lovers, Supreme Lover and Beloved of the Prophet—Fatima the Enlightened.

The mothers of all humanity are reflected in these radiant Mothers of the Faithful. When asked who is the most important person for the soul, the noble Prophet responded thrice, with decisive intensity, by repeating the sacred word *mother*. The Holder of Spiritual Secrets reveals in his Oral Tradition the mysterious words, "Paradise abides at the feet of the mothers." The holy tomb of Fatima the True Secret, contained in the house of the Prophet that is embraced within the Grand Mosque in Medina the Illumined, surges with a flood of spiritual power, which inundates the earth with subtle blessings. This radiant energy of love, flowing from Fatima's fragrant resting-

place, is not separate in any way from the *baraka*, the transforming holiness streaming from the Tombs of tombs, the refreshing Palace of Love's Resurrection, the resting-place of the beloved Muhammad. This oasis of Love is also the destined resting-place of the beloved Jesus, after he returns and reigns over the entire globe. Here the two Prophets of Love and intimate spiritual brothers in Divine Love will manifest side by side on earth, as they do now in the highest Circle of Love.

ABOVE: *Koran Tablet,*
Moroccan, 19th–20th century.
Musée des Arts Africains et
Oceaniens, Paris.

IX

Guardian of the Soul

T**HE GODDESS, NO MATTER WHAT FORM SHE TAKES, IS THE SEEKER'S** own deepest truth, or the voice of the soul. Nowhere is this more evident than in the following selections. She is the mysterious, invisible presence who, in an ancient Sumerian text, declares, "Begetting Mother am I, within the Spirit I abide and none see me. . . .In the word of the holy temple I abide, and none see me."

She is the spark of light that appears in the darkest moments of life, the sudden upwelling of intuitive insight, and the hand that reaches out when we most need it. She serves as a guide to those who travel difficult and dangerous paths, and as a beacon to the sailor lost in treacherous seas. Though usually gentle and compassionate, bringing comfort and reassurance to the anxious soul, she may also insist that her charges follow strict ethical guidelines; White Buffalo Woman, for example, does not hesitate to destroy the man who approaches her disrespectfully. At times, the goddess appears in the guise of a stranger, as in the Chinese story, "The Bride of Mero." As mediator between heaven and earth, she bridges the chasm between the dense labyrinth of physical reality and the spacious, light-filled realms beyond our own.

Texts like the Buddhist "Hymn to the Wisdom Mother" or the Tibetan "Homages to the Twenty-One Taras" are designed to help the practitioner visualize the goddess, until she appears clearly before his or her inner eye. To those who meditate on her, as the Roman writer Apuleius describes in his "Vision of Isis," she may also appear in dreams.

OPPOSITE: *Enthroned Goddess with a Dove and Patera*, 2nd–1st century B.C.E.
National Archaeological Museum, Reggio Calabria, Italy.

ABOVE: *Buddist Goddess*, Indonesia, 9th century. The Asia Society, New York, Mr. and Mrs. John D. Rockefeller 3rd Acquisitions Fund (1979.84).

214

Mystic Hymn to the Wisdom Mother

BUDDHIST

Nur Al Jerrahi (Lex Hixon)

The Perfection of Wisdom shines forth as a sublime light, O Buddha nature. I sing this spontaneous hymn of light to praise Mother Prajnaparamita. She is worthy of infinite praise. She is utterly unstained, because nothing in this insubstantial world can possibly stain her. She is an ever-flowing fountain of incomparable light, and from every conscious being on every plane, she removes the faintest trace of illusory darkness. She leads living beings into her clear light from the blindness and obscurity caused by moral and spiritual impurity as well as by partial or distorted views of Reality. In her alone can we find true refuge. Sublime and excellent are her revelations through all persons of wisdom. She inspires and guides us to seek the safety and certainty of the bright wings of enlightenment. She pours forth her nectar of healing light to those who have made themselves appear blind. She provides the illumination through which all fear and despair can be utterly renounced.

She manifests the five mystic eyes of wisdom, the vision and penetration of each one more exalted than the last. She clearly and constantly points out the path of wisdom to every conscious being with the direct pointing that is her transmission and empowerment. She is an infinite eye of wisdom. She dissipates entirely the mental gloom of delusion. She does not manipulate any structures of relativity. Simply by shining spontaneously, she guides to the spiritual path whatever beings have wandered into dangerous, negative, self-centered ways.

Mother Prajnaparamita is total awakeness. She never substantially creates any limited structure because she experiences none of the tendencies of living beings to grasp, project or conceptualize. Neither does she substantially dismantle or destroy any limited structure, for she encounters no solid limits. She is the Perfect Wisdom which never comes into being and therefore never goes out of being. She is known as the Great Mother by those spiritually mature beings who dedicate their mind streams to the liberation and full enlightenment of all that lives.

She is not marked by fundamental characteristics. This absence of characteristics is her transcendent, mystic motherhood, the radiant blackness of her womb. She is the universal benefactress who presents, as a sublime offering to truth, the limitless jewel of all Buddha qualities, the miraculous gem which generates the ten inconceivable powers of a Buddha to elevate living beings into consciousness of their innate Buddha nature. She can never be defeated in any way, on any level. She lovingly protects vulnerable conscious beings who cannot protect themselves, gradually generating in them unshakable fearlessness and diamond confidence. She is the perfect antidote to the poisonous view which affirms the cycle of birth and death to be a substantial reality. She is the clear knowledge of the open and transparent mode of being shared by all relative structures and events. Her transcendent knowing never wavers. She is the Perfect Wisdom who gives birthless birth to all Buddhas. And through these sublimely Awakened Ones, it is Mother Prajnaparamita alone who turns the wheel of true teaching.

215

FROM THE THUNDER, PERFECT MIND

COPTIC

Translated by George W. MacRae

*The Thunder, Perfect Mind is the title given to one of the most intriguing texts
found in the Nag Hammadi Library, a collection of Gnostic and early
Christian scriptures dating back to the first centuries A.D. These scriptures, buried
in the sand in Egypt, were unearthed in 1945. George MacRae calls the text
"a revelation discourse delivered by a female revealer."*

I was sent forth from the power,
    and I have come to those who reflect upon me,
    and I have been found among those who seek
       after me.
Look upon me, you who reflect upon me,
    and you hearers, hear me.
    You who are waiting for me, take me to yourselves.
And do not banish me from your sight.
    And do not make your voice hate me, nor your
       hearing.
    Do not be ignorant of me anywhere or any time.
       Be on your guard!
    Do not be ignorant of me.

For I am the first and the last.
I am the honored one and the scorned one.
I am the whore and the holy one.

I am the wife and the virgin.
I am the mother and the daughter.
I am the members of my mother.
I am the barren one
    and many are her sons.
I am she whose wedding is great,
    and I have not taken a husband.
I am the midwife and she who does not bear.
I am the solace of my labor pains.
I am the bride and the bridegroom,
    and it is my husband who begot me.
I am the mother of my father
    and the sister of my husband,
    and he is my offspring.
I am the slave of him who prepared me.

I am the ruler of my offspring.
    But he is the one who begot me before the time
       on a birthday.
    And he is my offspring in due time,
       and my power is from him.
I am the staff of his power in his youth,
    and he is the rod of my old age.
    And whatever he wills happens to me.
I am the silence that is incomprehensible
    and the idea whose remembrance is frequent.
I am the voice whose sound is manifold
    and the word whose appearance is multiple.
I am the utterance of my name.

I am the knowledge of my inquiry,
    and the finding of those who seek after me,
    and the command of those who ask of me,
    and the power of the powers in my knowledge
       of the angels, who have been sent at my word,
       and of gods in their seasons by my counsel,
       and of spirits of every man who exists with me,
          and of women who dwell within me.
I am the one who is honored, and who is praised,
    and who is despised scornfully.
I am peace,
    and war has come because of me.
And I am an alien and a citizen.
I am the substance and the one who has no substance.

*OPPOSITE: Two crowned figures
under a sun and a moon, from
Splendor Solis, 1582. By
permission of the British Library,
London (Harley 3469, fol. 10).*

217

WHITE BUFFALO WOMAN

SIOUX

Told by David Leeming and Jake Page

A mother goddess who provides for her people, White Buffalo Woman is also a guardian of ethical behavior. Her special concern is the treatment of women.

So long ago that no one knows when, the people were starving. Each day, scouts went forth but returned without having seen any game. One day, two young men set out to hunt and decided to climb a high hill from which they would be able to see far across the plain. Partway up the hill, they saw what seemed to be a person floating toward them from the far horizon, and they knew at once it was a holy person.

When it drew closer, they saw that it was the most beautiful young woman, with red spots on her cheeks and clad in white buckskin that gleamed in the sun and was richly embroidered with porcupine quills. As she approached, one of the young men lusted for her and reached out to grab her. A bolt of lightning crackled out of nowhere and burned the young man into a small pile of charred bones.

To the other young man, who stood in respectful awe of her, she explained that she was White Buffalo Woman and would bring for his people some good and holy things from the nation of the buffalo. She told him to return to his people and have them erect a medicine lodge and to say the proper prayers to make the lodge holy. They did so, and four days later White Buffalo Woman came and, entering the lodge, told the people to make an altar of red earth. When this was done, she made a design on the altar and withdrew from her bundle a sacred red pipe, holding the stem in her right hand and the bowl in her left. She filled it with tobacco made from red willow bark and lit it, telling them that the smoke rising from the pipe was the breath of the Great Mystery.

She taught them the proper way to pray, and to lift the pipe to the sky, to hold it toward the earth, and then in the four directions. This way, the earth, the sky, and all living things are knit into one family, held together by the pipe. The bowl of red stone represents the buffalo, whose four legs are the four directions. The wooden stem represents all things that grow, and the twelve eagle feathers hanging from the stem are those of the messenger to the Great Spirit. The seven designs carved on the bowl are the seven ceremonies the people would thenceforth practice.

White Buffalo Woman explained to the women there that the work of their hands and the fruit of their bodies kept the people alive. They were of Mother Earth and were therefore as important as the warriors. Thus the pipe, its bowl carved by men and its stem made by women, bind the two together in love. From her bundle, White Buffalo Woman took corn and other foods and gave them to the women. She taught them how to make fire and how to cook.

She explained to the children that they were the most precious and important of the people. And she explained to the chief that the pipe was very sacred. She entrusted it to the people, telling them that if they treated it with respect, it would see them through to the end of their road here. "I am the four ages," she said, promising to return to them.

Then she left, walking toward the red orb of the setting sun. Four times she rolled over, each time turning into a buffalo—first a black one, then a brown one, then red, and finally white. A white buffalo remains the most sacred thing alive.

Once White Buffalo Woman had disappeared beyond the horizon, great herds of buffalo appeared and roamed the plains, making themselves available to be killed to furnish the people with all that they needed—food, skins, tools. And the red pipe that White Buffalo Woman gave to the people so long ago is said to remain with the people—still sacred, still the source of the Lakota's knowledge of how to live and how to pray.

OPPOSITE: *Big Head Spirit*, Frank LaPena, 1987. Courtesy of the artist.

ABOVE: *Willows and Distant Mountains*, Ma Yuan, c. 1200 A.D.

THE BRIDE OF MERO

CHINESE

Told by Joseph Campbell

What Tārā is to the Tibetan Buddhist, Kuan-Yin is to the Japanese and Chinese. Gentle goddess of compassion, she protects her children and guides the spiritual seeker to Dharma, or enlightenment.

In a certain rural, western province of old China, there was a time when the Buddha, his Law, and his Order were disdained, and men devoted themselves rather to riding swift horses and to archery. But the merciful Bodhisattva showered her compassionate benevolence upon them and led them in the following way to the Dharma.

In one of the villages of that province, situated on the banks of a remote upper reach of the Yellow River, there appeared early one summer day a strange young woman of the greatest beauty and most noble grace. Her almond eyes, jet black, flashed from beneath slender brows that were like little bows, and the lovely oval of her placid face was framed by soft waves of blackest hair. She carried a basket in her hands, woven of bamboo, lined with green leaves of the willow and filled with fresh golden-scaled fish of the river. Moreover, as she called her wares her voice suggested the play of a breeze among jade beads. The villagers stared and questioned each other, but none could say whence she had come or who she might be.

She appeared this way every morning, and as soon as her basket was emptied would disappear so quickly that the people sometimes doubted she had been among them at all. The young men, of course, having taken notice, daily watched for her appearances, and then, one morning, would not let her pass. They began begging her to marry them, but she answered, "O honorable young gentlemen, I do certainly wish to marry; but I cannot marry you all. If there were one among you, however, who could recite by heart the entire Sutra of the Compassionate Kuan-Yin, he would be the one I would wed."

So deep was the darkness of the minds of those young men that they had never even heard of that sutra. Nevertheless, when evening came they met and vied with each other, and when dawn broke there were thirty who had learned the text by heart. The young woman said, when these then accosted her, "But, O honorable young gentlemen, I am only one woman; I cannot marry thirty young men. However, if any one among you can explain the meaning of the sutra, he is the one I shall wed."

The following dawn found ten youths waiting to claim the young woman's hand; for ten now understood. But she replied, "O young sirs, I am but one woman; I cannot marry ten husbands. However, if any one of you will in three days have *experienced* the meaning of the Sutra of the Compassionate Kuan-Yin, him surely shall I marry gladly."

And on the morning of that third day there was waiting for her just one, the young Mero. And when she saw him there, she smiled.

"O Son of the House of Me," she said, for she could recognize his bearing, "I perceive that you have indeed realized the meaning of the blessed Sutra of the Compassionate Kuan-Yin and do gladly accept you as my husband. My house you will find this evening at the river bend, and my parents there to receive you."

And so, when evening fell, Mero, alone at the bend of the shore, searched out and discovered her little house among the reeds and rocks. At its gate there were standing an old man and woman, beckoning. He approached and said to them, "I am the son of the House of Me, and have come to claim your daughter as my bride"; to which the old man responded, "We have been waiting for you a long time." And the old woman, leading the way, opened the door to her daughter's room and Mero went in.

But the room was empty. From the open window he saw a stretch of sand as far as to the river, and in the sand the prints of a woman's feet, which he followed, to find at the water's edge two golden sandals. He looked about in the increasing twilight, and saw no house now among the rocks. There was only a cluster of dry bamboo by the river softly rustling in an evening breeze. And then suddenly he knew: the fisher-maid had been none other than the Boddhisattva herself, and he comprehended fully how great is the merciful benevolence of the infinitely compassionate Kuan-Yin.

> *She made a bridge of love, that he*
> *might cross to the shore of Bodhi.*
> *O Compassionate Avalokiteshvara,*
> *most benevolent!*

And ever since that time, in that rural western province, many have known and revered the Dharma of the Buddha.

BELOW: *Seated Figure of the Goddess Kuan-Yin*, late Sung Dynasty, 960–1279 A.D. The Metropolitan Museum of Art, New York, Fletcher Fund, 1928 (28.56).

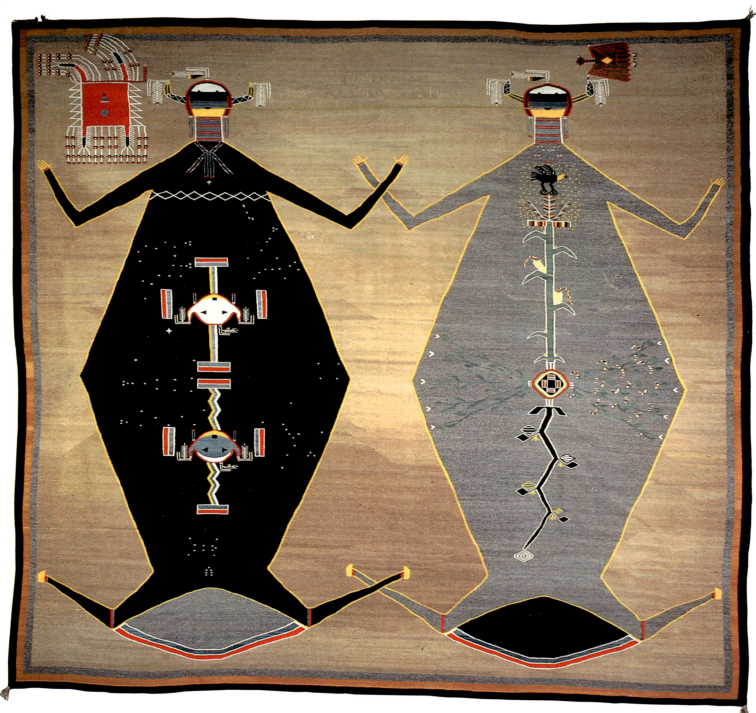

ABOVE: *Navajo Sandpainting Rug,*
Atlnabah, c. 1930–39. Courtesy of
Museum of Northern Arizona Photo
Archives, Flagstaff (86 C.1/E3716/2565).

222

La Mariposa, Butterfly Woman

Clarissa Pinkola Estés, Ph.D.

*The butterfly is an ancient symbol of transformation and of the
miraculous beauty that lies hidden within all beings. Dr. Estés's story
is "a true, rather long story."*

For years, tourists have thundered across the great American desert, hurrying through the "spiritual circuit": Monument Valley, Chaco Canyon, Mesa Verde, Kayenta, Keems Canyon, Painted Desert, and Canyon de Chelly. They peer up the pelvis of the Mother Grand Canyon, shake their heads, shrug their shoulders, and hurry home, only to again come charging across the desert the next summer, looking, looking some more, watching, watching some more.

Underneath it all is the same hunger for numinous experience that humans have had since the beginning of time. But sometimes this hunger is exacerbated, for many people have lost their ancestors. They often do not know the names of those beyond their grandparents. They have lost, in particular, the family stories. Spiritually, this situation causes sorrow . . . and hunger. So many are trying to recreate something important for soul sake.

For years tourists have come also to Puyé, a big dusty mesa in the middle of "nowhere," New Mexico. Here the *Anasazi*, the ancient ones, once called to each other across the mesas. A prehistoric sea, it is said, carved the thousands of grinning, leering, and moaning mouths and eyes into the rock walls there.

The Navajo, Jicarilla Apache, southern Ute, Hopi, Zuni, Santa Clara, Santa Domingo, Laguna, Picuris, Tesuque, all these desert tribes come together here. It is here that they dance themselves back into lodgepole pine trees, back into deer, back into eagles and *Katsinas*, powerful spirits.

And here too come visitors, some of whom are very starved of their geno-myths, detached from the spiritual placenta. They have forgotten their ancient Gods as well. They come to watch the ones who have *not* forgotten.

The road up to Puyé was built for horse hooves and moccasins. But over time automobiles became more powerful and now locals and visitors come in all manner of cars, trucks, convertibles, and vans. The vehicles all whine and smoke up the road in a slow, dusty parade.

Everyone parks *trochimochi*, willy-nilly, on the lumpy hillocks. By noon, the edge of the mesa looks like a thousand-car pileup. Some people park next to six-foot-tall hollyhocks thinking they will just knock over the plants to get out of their cars. But the hundred-year-old hollyhocks are like old iron women. Those who park next to them are trapped in their cars.

The sun turns to a fiery furnace by midday.

223

Everyone trudges in hot shoes, burdened with an umbrella in case it rains (it will), an aluminum folding chair in case they tire (they will), and if they are visitors, perhaps a camera (if they're allowed), and pods of film cans hanging around their necks like garlic wreaths.

Visitors come with all manner of expectations, from the sacred to the profane. They come to see something that not everyone will be able to see, one of the wildest of the wild, a living numen, *La Mariposa*, the Butterfly Woman.

The last event is the Butterfly Dance. Everyone anticipates with great delight this one-person dance. It is danced by a woman, and oh what a woman. As the sun begins to set, here comes an old man resplendent in forty pounds of formal-dress turquoise. With the loudspeakers squawking like a chicken espying a hawk, he whispers into the 1930s chrome microphone, "An' our nex' dance is gonna be th' Butterfly Dance." He limps away on the cuffs of his jeans.

Unlike a ballet recital, where the act is announced, the curtains part, and the dancers wobble out, here at Puyé, as at other tribal dances, the announcement of the dance may precede the dancer's appearance by anywhere from twenty minutes to forever. Where is the dancer? Tidying up the camper, perhaps. Air temperatures over 100 degrees are common, so last-minute repairs to sweat-streaked body paint are needed. If a dance belt, which belonged to the dancer's grandfather, breaks on the way to the arena, the dancer would not appear at all, for the spirit of the belt would

need to rest. Dancers delay because a good song is playing on "Tony Lujan's Indian Hour" on radio Taos, KKIT (after Kit Carson).

Sometimes a dancer does not hear the loudspeaker and must be summoned by footrunner. And then always, of course, the dancer must speak to all relatives on the way to the arena, and most certainly stop to allow the little nephews and nieces a look. How awed the little children are to see a towering *Katsina* spirit who looks suspiciously, a little at least, like Uncle Tomás or a corn dancer who seems to strongly resemble Aunt Yazie. Lastly, there is the ubiquitous possibility that the dancer is still out on the Tesuque highway, legs dangling out the maw of a pickup truck while the muffler smudges the air for a mile downwind.

While awaiting the Butterfly Dance in giddy anticipation, everyone chatters about butterfly maidens and the beauty of the Zuni girls who danced in ancient red-and-black garb with one shoulder bared, bright pink circles painted on their cheeks. They laud the young male deer-dancers who danced with pine boughs bound to their arms and legs.

Time passes.

And passes.

And passes.

People jingle coins in their pockets. They suck their teeth. The visitors are impatient to see this marvelous butterfly dancer.

Unexpectedly then, for everyone is bored to scowls, the drummer's arms begin drumming the sacred butterfly rhythm, and the chanters begin to cry to the Gods for all they are worth.

To the visitors, a butterfly is a delicate thing. "O fragile beauty," they dream. So they are necessarily shaken when out hops Maria Lujan.* And she is big, really *big*, like the Venus of Willendorf, like the Mother of Days, like Diego Rivera's heroic-size woman who built Mexico City with a single curl of her wrist.

And Maria Lujan, oh, she is old, very, very old, like a woman come back from dust, old like old river, old like old pines at timberline. One of her shoulders is bare. Her red-and-black *manta*, blanket dress, hops up and down with her inside it. Her heavy body and her very skinny legs made her look like a hopping spider wrapped in a tamale.

She hops on one foot and then the other. She waves her feather fan to and fro. She is The Butterfly arrived to strengthen the weak. She is that which most think of as not strong: age, the butterfly, the feminine.

Butterfly Maiden's hair reaches to the ground. It is thick as ten maize sheaves and it is stone gray. And she wears butterfly wings—the kind you see on little children who are being angels in school plays. Her hips are like two bouncing bushel baskets and the fleshy shelf at the top of her buttocks is wide enough to ride two children.

She hops, hops, hops, not like a rabbit, but in footsteps that leave echoes.

"I am here, here, here . . .

"I am here, here, here . . .

"Awaken you, you, you!"

She sways her feather fan up and down, spreading the earth and the people of the earth with the pollinating spirit of the butterfly. Her shell bracelets rattle like snake, her bell garters tinkle like rain. Her shadow with its big belly and little legs dances from one side of the dance circle to the other. Her feet leave little puffs of dust behind.

The tribes are reverent, involved. But some visitors look at each other and murmur "This is it? *This* is the Butterfly Maiden?" They are puzzled, some even disillusioned. They no longer seem to remember that the spirit world is a place where wolves are women, bears are husbands, and old women of lavish dimensions are butterflies.

Yes, it is fitting that Wild Woman/Butterfly Woman is old and substantial, for she carries the thunderworld in one breast, the underworld in the other. Her back is the curve of the planet Earth with all its crops and foods and animals. The back of her neck carries the sunrise and the sunset. Her left thigh holds all the lodgepoles, her right thigh all the she-wolves of the world. Her belly holds all the babies that will ever be born.

Butterfly Maiden is the female fertilizing force. Carrying the pollen from one place to another, she cross-fertilizes, just as the soul fertilizes mind with nightdreams, just as archetypes fertilize the mundane world. She is the center. She brings the opposites together by taking a little from here and putting it there. Transformation is no more complicated than that. This is what she teaches. This is how the butterfly does it. This is how the soul does it.

*Pseudonym to protect her privacy.
"*La Mariposa*, Butterfly Woman," © C. P. Estés 1992, 1995, *Women Who Run With the Wolves* (pp. 206–210).

HOMAGES TO THE TWENTY~ONE TĀRĀS

TIBETAN

Translated by Stephan Beyer

O M! Homage to the holy and noble Tārā!
Homage, TĀRE, quick one, heroine,
removing terror with TUTTĀRE,
savioress, granting all aims with TURE,
the syllables SVĀHĀ: to you I bow!

Homage, Tārā, quick one, heroine,
whose eyes flash like lightning,
born from the opening corolla
of the lotus face of the Lord of the triple world.

Homage, Lady whose face is filled
with a hundred autumn moons,
blazing with the laughing beams
of the hosts of a thousand stars.

Homage, Lady whose hand is adorned with a lotus,
a lotus blue and gold,
whose field of practice is charity, striving,
austerity, calm, acceptance, and meditation.

Homage, Lady abiding in infinite victory
in the crown knot of the Tathāgata,
served by the sons of the Conqueror
who have attained every single perfection.

Homage, Lady who fills all quarters of space
with the sounds of TUTTĀRE and HŪM,
trampling the seven worlds with her feet,
able to summon all before her.

Homage, Lady worshiped by Indra, Agni, Brahma,
by the Maruts and Viśvêśvara,
honored by hosts of spirits,
of ghosts, celestials, and the walking dead.

This is the single most important praise of Tārā in Tibetan literature. The capitalized words are mantras, *sacred syllables used to invoke the presence and power of the goddess.*

OPPOSITE: *Vajra Tārā,* 12th century. National Museum of India, New Delhi.

227

OPPOSITE: *White Tārā*, Tibet
or Mongolia, 17th century. The
Asia Society, New York, Mr.
and Mrs. John D. Rockefeller
3rd Collection (1979.52).

Homage, Lady who destroys the magic devices of others
with the sounds of TRAT and PHAT,
trampling with right foot up and left extended,
blazing with a blazing mass of fire.

Homage, Lady who annihilates the heroes of Māra,
TURE, the terrible lady,
slaying all enemies
by frowning the brows of her lotus face.

Homage, Lady holding her hand over her breast
with a gesture that symbolizes the Three Jewels,
her palms adorned with the universal wheel
radiating a turbulent host of its own beams.

Homage, Lady whose diadem spreads a garland
of shining and happy beams,
subjugating Māra and the world
with a laughing, mocking TUTTĀRE!

Homage, Lady able to summon before her
all the hosts of protectors of the earth,
saving from all distress by the movement
of her frowning brows and the sound of HŪM!

Homage, Lady whose diadem is a crescent moon
blazing with all its ornaments,
ever lit by the beams
of Amitābha in her piled hair.

Homage, Lady placed amidst a garland that blazes
like the fire at the end of the world era,
annihilating the army of the enemy
in her joyous posture of royal ease.

Homage, Lady who strikes the earth with her hand,
who pounds upon it with her feet,
shattering the seven underworlds
with the sound of HŪM made by her frowning brows.

Homage, Lady blissful, virtuous, calm,
whose field of practice is calm nirvana,
possessed of SVĀHĀ and OM,
destroying great sins.

Homage, Lady who shatters the bodies of enemies
in her joyous posture,
the savioress manifested from HŪM
in the mantra arraying the sound of ten syllables.

Homage, Lady who strikes with the feet of TURE,
whose seed is the form of the syllable HŪM,
shaking Mount Meru, Mandāra, Kailāśa,
and all the triple world.

Homage, Lady holding the deer-marked moon
in the form of an ocean of gods,
dispelling all poison
with the sound of PHAT and twice-spoken TĀRA.

Homage, Lady served by the ruler of hosts of gods,
by the gods and horse-headed celestials,
dispelling contention and bad dreams
with the brilliance of her joyous armor.

Homage, Lady in whose eyes is the brilliant light
of the sun and the full moon,
dispelling terrible fevers
with TUTTĀRE and twice-spoken TĀRA.

Homage, Lady endowed with the strength of calm
by the array of the three Truths [OM ĀH HŪM],
destroying the hosts of evil spirits, the walking dead,
TURE, the most excellent lady!

This is the praise with the basic mantra,
and these are the twenty-one homages.

TANTRIC PRAISE
OF THE GODDESS

——————◦◦◦——————

HINDU

Adapted by Jalaja Bonheim

*Tantra is a branch of Hinduism and Buddhism in which worship of the goddess
plays a crucial part. The following stanzas are to this day recited regularly in many
Hindu temples. They convey the understanding that all things—those that give us
pleasure as well as those that give us pain—are manifestations of the goddess.*

Salutations to the goddess who dwells in all things as
the energy of infinite goodness,
salutations again and again.

Salutations to the goddess who dwells in all things as
their innermost nature,
salutations again and again.

Salutations to the goddess who dwells in all things as
the light of consciousness,
salutations again and again.

Salutations to the goddess who dwells in all things as
intelligence, salutations again and again.

Salutations to the goddess who dwells in all things as
sleep, salutations again and again.

Salutations to the goddess who dwells in all things as
hunger, salutations again and again.

Salutations to the goddess who dwells in all things as
desire, salutations again and again.

Salutations to the goddess who dwells in all things as
chaos, salutations again and again.

Salutations to the goddess who dwells in all things as
fierceness, salutations again and again.

Salutations to the goddess who dwells in all things as
change, salutations again and again.

Salutations to the goddess who dwells in all things as
beauty, salutations again and again.

Salutations to the goddess who dwells in all things as
compassion, salutations again and again.

Salutations to the goddess who dwells in all things as
peace, salutations again and again.

OPPOSITE: *Rainbow Boddhisattva,
Vijali,* 1992. World Wheel Site 9,
Shoto Terdrum, Tibet. Courtesy
of the artist.

IX ● GUARDIAN OF THE SOUL

Apuleius' Vision of Isis

ROMAN

Translated by P. G. Walsh

This is an excerpt from a novel called The Golden Ass, *which was written in Latin by the Roman writer Apuleius—in fact,* The Golden Ass *is the only Latin novel that has survived in its entirety to the present day. The fact that a 2nd-century Roman author would have written such a glowing tribute to Isis attests to the wide popularity of this goddess.*

OPPOSITE: S.O.S., Evelyn de Morgan, late 19th or early 20th century. The De Morgan Foundation, London.

A sudden fear aroused me at about the first watch of the night. At that moment I beheld the full moon rising from the sea-waves, and gleaming with special brightness. In my enjoyment of the hushed isolation of the shadowy night, I became aware that the supreme goddess wielded her power with exceeding majesty, that human affairs were controlled wholly by her providence, that the world of cattle and wild beasts and even things inanimate were lent vigor by the divine impulse of her light and power; that the bodies of earth, sea, and sky now increased at her waxing, and now diminished in deference to her waning. . . .

But scarcely had I closed my eyes when suddenly from the midst of the sea a divine figure arose, revealing features worthy of veneration even by the gods. Then gradually the gleaming form seemed to stand before me in full figure as she shook off the sea-water. I shall try to acquaint you too with the detail of her wondrous appearance, if only the poverty of human speech grants me powers of description, or the deity herself endows me with a rich feast of eloquent utterance.

To begin with, she had a full head of hair which hung down, gradually curling as it spread loosely and flowed gently over her divine neck. Her lofty head was encircled by a garland interwoven with diverse blossoms, at the center of which above her brow was a flat disk resembling a mirror, or rather the orb of the moon, which emitted a glittering light. The crown was held in place by coils of rearing snakes on right and left, and it was adorned above with waving ears of corn. She wore a multicolored dress woven from fine linen, one part of which shone radiantly white, a second glowed yellow with saffron blossom, and a third blazed rosy red. But what riveted my eyes above all else was her jet-black cloak, which gleamed with a dark sheen as it enveloped her. It ran beneath her right arm across to her left shoulder, its fringe partially descending in the form of a knot. The garment hung down in layers of successive folds, its lower edge gracefully undulating with tasseled fringes.

233

Stars glittered here and there along its woven border and on its flat surface, and in their midst a full moon exhaled fiery flames. Wherever the hem of that magnificent cloak billowed out, a garland composed of every flower and every fruit was inseparably attached to it. The goddess's appurtenances were extremely diverse. In her right hand she carried a bronze rattle; it consisted of a narrow metal strip curved like a belt, through the middle of which were passed a few rods; when she shook the rattle vigorously three times with her arm, the rods gave out a shrill sound. From her left hand dangled a boat-shaped vessel, on the handle of which was the figure of a serpent in relief, rearing high its head and swelling its broad neck. Her feet, divinely white, were shod in sandals fashioned from the leaves of the palm of victory. Such, then, was the appearance of the mighty goddess. She breathed forth the fertile fragrance of Arabia as she deigned to address me in words divine:

"Here I am, Lucius, roused by your prayers. I am the mother of the world of nature, mistress of all the elements, first-born in this realm of time. I am the loftiest of deities, queen of departed spirits, foremost of heavenly dwellers, the single embodiment of all gods and goddesses. I order with my nod the luminous heights of heaven, the healthy sea-breezes, the sad silences of the infernal dwellers. The whole world worships this single godhead under a variety of shapes and liturgies and titles. In one land the Phrygians, first-born of men, hail me as the Pessinuntian mother of the gods; elsewhere the native dwellers of Attica call me Cecropian Minerva; in other climes the wave-tossed Cypriots name me Paphian Venus; the Cretan archers, Dictynna Diana; the trilingual Sicilians, Ortygian Proserpina; the Eleusinians, the ancient goddess Ceres; some call me Juno, others Bellona, others Hecate, and others still Rhamnusia. But the peoples on whom the rising sun-god shines with his first rays—eastern and western Ethiopians, and the Egyptians who flourish with their time-honored learning—worship me with the liturgy that is my own, and call me by my true name, which is queen Isis."

OPPOSITE: *Isis* from the Sarcophagus of Ramses III, 12th century B.C.E. Louvre, Paris.

234

Index of Goddesses

Literary Credits

"Spider Woman Creates the World" from *Grandmothers of the Light* by Paula Gunn Allen. © 1991 by Paula Gunn Allen, reprinted by permission of Beacon Press, Boston.

"Eurynome" reprinted by permission of Open Court Trade & Academic Books, a division of Carus Publishing Company, Peru, IL, from *Tell It by Heart* by Erica Helm Meade. Copyright © 1995 by Open Court Publishing Company.

"The Making of the World" from *The Journal of American Folklore*, Vol. 1, 1888.

"Coatlicue" translated by Edward Kissam. Reprinted by permission of Edward Kissam.

"The Myth of Ngalyod" from *Time Before Morning* by Louis A. Allen. Crowell, 1975. © Louis A. Allen.

"Coadidop" from *The Mythology of South America* by John Bierhorst. Copyright © 1988 by John Bierhorst. By permission of Morrow Junior Books, a division of William Morrow & Company, Inc.

"Huiio the Rainbow Snake" from *Watunna: An Orinoco Creation Cycle* by Marc de Civrieux, edited and translated by David M. Guss. Copyright © 1980 by David M. Guss. Reprinted by permission of the author and the translator.

"Homage to Tara" from *Cult of Tara: Magic and Ritual in Tibet* by Stephan Beyer. University of California Press. Copyright © 1973 by permission of The Regents of The University of California.

"Hymn to Gaia, Goddess of Earth" from *Homeric Hymn to Gaia*, translated by Jules Cashford. Reprinted by permission of Jules Cashford.

"Grandmother Spider Gets the Fire" from *Grandmother of the Light* by Paula Gunn Allen. © 1991 by Paula Gunn Allen. Reprinted by permission of Beacon Press, Boston.

"Traditional Praise of Oya" from *Oya: In Praise of an African Goddess* by Judith Gleason. Copyright © 1992 by Judith Gleason. Reprinted by permission of HarperCollins Publishers, Inc.

"Frigga, Eostre, and Holde" from *Myths of Northern Lands* by H. A. Guerber. American Book Company, 1895.

"Pele The Volcano Goddess" from *The Storyteller's Goddess* by Carolyn McVickar Edwards. Copyright © 1991 by Carolyn McVickar Edwards. Reprinted by permission of HarperCollins Publishers, Inc.

"Two Water Goddesses" from *African Mythology: An Encyclopedia of Myth and Legend*. Copyright © 1990 by Jan Knappert. Renewal copyright © 1995 by Diamond Books. Used by permission of HarperCollins Publishers Ltd.

"Anancy and the Hide-Away Garden" from *Anancy-Spiderman* by James Berry. Text © 1988 James Berry. Reprinted by permission of the publisher Walker Books Ltd., London.

"The Story of Shiratamahime" from *The Mystery of Things: Evocations of the Japanese Supernatural* by Patrick Le Nestour. © 1972, reprinted by permission of John Weatherhill, Inc.

"Hymn to Usha, Goddess of Dawn" from *Hymns from the Rig-Veda*, translation and Sanskrit calligraphy by Jean Le Mée, copyright © 1975 by Jean Le Mée. First published in 1975 by Alfred A. Knopf, Inc. Used by permission of Jean Le Mée.

"Hymn to Selene, Goddess of the Moon" from *The Homeric Hymns* (pp. 68-69) by Apostolos N. Athanassakis. © 1976 by The Johns Hopkins University Press. Reprinted by permission of the publisher.

"Sun Dreaming" from *Land of the Rainbow Snake*, arranged and translated by Catherine H. Berndt, © 1979. Originally published by William Collins Sons. Courtesy The Estate of C.H. Berndt, The University of Western Australia.

"Hymn to Nut" (pp.24-25), translated by Jules Cashford from *The Myth of the Goddess: Evolution of an Image* by Anne Baring and Jules Cashford. (Viking, 1991). Copyright © Anne Baring and Jules Cashford, 1991. Reprinted by permission of Penguin Books Ltd.

"Where the Frost Comes From" from *Wise Women of the Dreamtime: Aboriginal Tales of the Ancestral Powers*, collected by K. Langloh Parker, edited with commentary by Johanna Lambert, published by Inner Traditions International, Rochester, VT 05767. Copyright © 1993 by Joanna Lambert.

"Amaterasu" told by Jalaja Bonheim. © 1997 Jalaja Bonheim.

"Nananbouclou and the Piece of Fire" from *The Piece of Fire and Other Haitian Tales* by Harold Courlander. Copyright © 1973, 1992 by Harold Courlander. Reprinted by permission of The Emma Courlander Trust.

"Lady of the Evening" from *Inanna: Queen of Heaven and Earth* by Diane Wolkstein and Samuel Noah Kramer. Copyright © 1983 by Diane Wolkstein and Samuel Noah Kramer. Reprinted by permission of HarperCollins Publishers, Inc., and Diane Wolkstein and S.N. Kramer.

"Shining One" from *The Inland Whale* by Theodora Kroeber, copyright 1959 by Indiana University Press. Reprinted by permission of the publisher.

"Hymn to Aphrodite" by Sappho, translation © 1994 Jane Hirshfield; first appeared in *Women in Praise of the Sacred*, published by HarperCollins, 1994; used by permission of Jane Hirshfield.

"Aphrodite and Anchises" from *The Homeric Hymns* (pp. 47-49) by Apostolos N. Athanassakis. © 1976 The Johns Hopkins University Press. Reprinted by permission of the publisher.

"Freya" from *Myths of Northern Lands* by H.A. Guerber. American Book Company, 1895.

"Hymn to Hathor" ("Prayer to Hathor as Goddess of Love") from *Hymns, Prayers and Songs*, translated by John L. Foster. © Society of Biblical Literature, 1995. Reprinted by permission.

"Hymn to Hathor at the Temple of Dendera" from *Ancient Egyptian Literature, Three Volumes* by Miriam Lichtheim. University of California Press. Copyright © 1973-1980 by The Regents of The University of California.

"Oshun Acquires the Art of Divining" from *Jambalaya: The Natural Woman's Book of Personal Charms and Practical Rituals* by Luisah Teish. Copyright © 1985 by Luisah Teish. Reprinted by permission of HarperCollins Publishers, Inc.

"Prayer-Song to Laka" from *Unwritten Literature of Hawaii*, Smithsonian Institution, Washington, 1909.

"The Birth of Lakshmi" told by Jalaja Bonheim. © 1997 Jalaja Bonheim.

"A Supplicant Speaks of the Goddess Kwan Yin" by Richard Kell from *Control Tower* published by Chatto & Windus, London, © 1962.

"At last love has come..." by Sulpicia from *A Book of Women Poets From Antiquity to Now* by Aliki Barnstone and Willis Barnstone, editors. Copyright © 1980 by Schocken Books, Inc.. Reprinted by permission of Schocken Books, distributed by Pantheon Books, a division of Random House, Inc.

"The Hungry Woman" from *The Hungry Woman: Myths and Legends of the Aztecs*, edited by John Bierhorst. Copyright © 1984 by John Bierhorst. By permission of Morrow Junior Books, a division of William Morrow & Company, Inc.

"The Curse of the Goddess Macha" from *The Serpent and the Goddess* by Mary Condren. Copyright © 1989 by Mary Condren. Reprinted by permission of HarperCollins, Inc.

"The First People and the First Corn" from *Daughters of the Moon* copyright © 1993 by Shakrukh Husain. Originally published in the UK by Virago Press Ltd. under the title, *Virago Book of Witches*. Used by permission of the Virago Press Ltd., London.

"Erzulie Ge-Rouge" from *Divine Horsemen: The Living Gods of Haiti*, 1970, by Maya Deren. Republished by permission of the Estate of Maya Deren.

"Descent of Inanna" told by Jalaja Bonheim. ©1997 Jalaja Bonheim.

"Baubo: The Belly Goddess" from *Women Who Run With the Wolves* by Clarissa Pinkola Estés, Ph.D., Copyright © 1992, 1995. All performance, derivative, adaptation, musical, audio and recording, illustrative, theatrical, film, pictorial, electronic and all other rights reserved. Reprinted by kind permission of the author, Dr. Estés, and Ballantine Books, a division of Random House, Inc., and Rider Books, London.

"Hymn to Athena" ("Hymn to Pallas Athena") (pp. 343-344), translated by Jules Cashford from *The Myth of the Goddess: Evolution of an Image* by Anne Baring and Jules Cashford. (Viking, 1991). Copyright © Anne Baring and Jules Cashford, 1991. Reprinted by permission of Penguin Books Ltd.

"Arachne and Athena" told by Jalaja Bonheim. © 1997 Jalaja Bonheim.

"Durga the Warrior Goddess" told by Jalaja Bonheim. © 1997 Jalaja Bonheim.

"In Praise of Kali" from *Grace and Mercy in Her Wild Hair* by Ramprasad Sen. Translated by Leonard Nathan and Clinton Seely, © 1982. Reprinted by arrangement with Shambhala Publications, Inc., 300 Massachusetts Avenue, Boston, MA. 02115.

"calming Kali" by Lucille Clifton copyright © 1987 by Lucille Clifton. Reprinted from *good woman: poems and a memoir 1969-1980* by Lucille Clifton, with the permission of BOA Editions, Ltd.

"Enheduanna's Praise of Inanna" excerpt from Hullo and van Dijk, *Exaltation of Inanna*, Yale University Press, as quoted in *A Book of Women Poets from Antiquity to Now* by Aliki and Willis Barnstone. Copyright 1980, 1992 by Schocken Books. Reprinted by permission of the publisher.

"Artemis and Actaeon" told by Joanna Goodman. © 1997 Joanna Goodman.

"How the People of Today Have Two Stories" from *The Storyteller's Goddess* by Carolyn McVickar Edwards. Copyright © 1991 by Carolyn McVickar Edwards. Reprinted by permission of HarperCollins Publishers, Inc.

"The Joy of Sumer" from *Inanna: Queen of Heaven and Earth* by Diane Wolkstein and Samuel Noah Kramer. Copyright © 1983 by Diane Wolkstein and Samuel Noah Kramer. Reprinted by permission of HarperCollins Publishers, Inc., and Diane Wolkstein and S.N. Kramer.

"Isis and Osiris" from *Isis and Osiris* by Jonathan Cott. Copyright © 1994 by Jonathan Cott. Used by permission of Doubleday, a division of Bantam Doubleday Dell Publishing Group, Inc. Reprinted by permission of William Morris Agency, Inc., on behalf of the author for UK and British Commonwealth rights.

"Ayiasma" (p. 42, 26 lines) in *Gunnar Ekelof: Selected Poems*, translated by W. H. Auden and Lief Sjoberg (Penguin Books, 1971). Copyright © Ingrid Ekelof, translation © W. H. Auden and Leif Sjoberg. Reproduced by permission of Penguin Books, Ltd.

"Why Desire Has No Body" told by Jalaja Bonheim. © 1997 Jalaja Bonheim.

"Praise to Vishnu" from *Sanscrit Love Poetry* by W.S. Merwin. Copyright © 1977 by Columbia University Press. Reprinted with permission of the publisher.

"The Story of Akewa the Sun and Jaguar Man" from *Sun Stories* by Carolyn McVickar Edwards. Copyright © 1995 by Carolyn McVickar Edwards. Reprinted by permission of HarperCollins Publishers, Inc.

"Caitlin of Kilcummin" by Carolyn White. Originally appeared in *Parabola*, Vol V, no. 4, 1980. Used by permission of the author.

"How Ogun Broke into Seven Pieces, Oya into Nine" from *Oya: In Praise of an African Goddess* by Judith Gleason. Copyright © 1992 by Judith Gleason. Reprinted by permission of HarperCollins Publishers, Inc.

"Mbaba Mwana Waresa" from *The Storyteller's Goddess* by Carolyn McVickar Edwards. Copyright © 1991 by Carolyn McVickar Edwards. Reprinted by permission of HarperCollins Publishers, Inc.

"Au Co." Reprinted from *A Taste of Earth and Other Legends of Vietnam* by Thich Nhat Hanh (1993) with permission of Parallax Press, Berkeley, California.

"In Praise of Sophia" from *The Jerusalem Bible* by Alexander Jones, ed. Copyright © 1966, 1967, 1968 by Darton, Longman & Todd, Ltd. and Doubleday, a division of Bantam Doubleday Dell Publishing Group, Inc. Used by permission of Darton, Longman & Todd, Ltd. and Doubleday, a division of Bantam Doubleday Dell Publishing Group, Inc.

"Tabernacle of Peace" from *The Dream Assembly: Tales of Rabbi Zalmon Schacter-Shalomi*, collected and retold by Howard Schwartz (Nevada City, Calif.: Gateways/IDHHB, Inc. Publishers, 1989) pp. 61-63. Copyright © by Zalman M. Schacter-Shalomi and Howard Schwartz. Reprinted by permission of the publisher.

"The Door to the Soul" from *The Storyteller's Goddess* by Carolyn McVickar Edwards. Copyright © 1991 by Carolyn McVickar Edwards. Reprinted by permission of HarperCollins Publishers, Inc.

"Mary's Dream" by Lucille Clifton. Copyright © 1980 by The University of Massachusetts Press. Now published in *good woman: poems and a memoir 1969-1980* by BOA Editions, Ltd. Reprinted by permission of Curtis Brown, Ltd.

"Our Lady of Guadalupe" from *Grandmothers of the Light* by Paula Gunn Allen. © 1991 by Paula Gunn Allen. Reprinted by permission of Beacon Press, Boston.

"Mother Chant" from *She Who Dwells Within* by Lynn Gottlieb. Copyright © 1995 by Lynn Gottlieb. Reprinted by permission of HarperCollins Publishers, Inc.

"Golden Cloud Woman" from *She Who Dwells Within* by Lynn Gottlieb. Copyright © 1995 by Lynn Gottlieb. Reprinted by permission of HarperCollins Publishers, Inc.

"Litany to Our Lady" Anon, from Donovan, Jeffares, and Kennelly, *Ireland's Women: Writings Past and Present*. W.W. Norton & Co.

"A Heretic's Pilgrimage" by Eva Gore-Booth, from Donovan, Jeffares, And Kennelly, *Ireland's Women: Writings Past and Present*. W.W. Norton & Co.

"Mothers of the Faithful" reprinted from *Atom from the Sun of Knowledge* by Lex Hixon, by permission of Pir Publications, Inc.

"Mystic Hymn to the Wisdom Mother" by Lex Hixon from *Mother of the Buddhas: Meditation on the Prajnaparamita Sutra*. Wheaton, IL, Quest Books, 1993.

From "The Thunder, Perfect Mind" from *The Nag Hammadi Library in English*, 3rd, *Completely Revised Edition* by James M. Robinson, General Editor. Copyright © 1988 by E.J. Brill, Leiden, The Netherlands. Reprinted by permission of HarperCollins Publishers, Inc.

"White Buffalo Woman" from *Goddess: Myths of the Female Divine* by David Leeming and Jake Page. Copyright © 1996 by David Leeming and Jake Page. Used by permission of Oxford University Press, Inc.

"The Bride of Mero" by Joseph Campbell from *The Mythic Image*, Bollingen Series C. Copyright © 1974 by Princeton University Press. Selection used with permission.

"*La Mariposa*, The Butterfly Woman" from *Women Who Run With the Wolves* by Clarissa Pinkola Estés, Ph.D., Copyright © 1992, 1995. All performance, derivative, adaptation, musical, audio and recording, illustrative, theatrical, film, pictorial, electronic and all other rights reserved. Reprinted by kind permission of the author, Dr. Estés, and Ballantine Books, a division of Random House, Inc., and Rider Books, London.

"Homages to the Twenty-One Taras" by Stephan Beyer from *Cult of Tara: Magic and Ritual in Tibet*, University of California Press. Copyright © 1973 The Regents of the University of California.

"Tantric Praise of the Goddess" adapted by Jalaja Bonheim. ©1997 Jalaja Bonheim.

"Apuleius' Vision of Isis" © P.G. Walsh, 1994. Reprinted from *The Golden Ass*, translated by P. G. Walsh (1994) by permission of Oxford University Press, London.

ART CREDITS

The editors gratefully acknowledge the help of the various institutions and individuals who supplied art for this book.

Half Title Page: Tārā, Nepalese, 16th century. The Metropolitan Museum of Art, New York, Purchase, 1966, Louis V. Bell Fund (66.179). *Title page: Head of Hathor*, Capital of Osorkon II, c. 888 B.C.E. Louvre, Paris. Giraudon/Art Resource, NY; *Page 6*: Scala/Art Resource, NY; *Page 8*: Ali Meyer/Bridgeman Art Library, London; *Page 12*: Victoria & Albert Museum, London/Art Resource, NY; *Page 14*: Erich Lessing/Art Resource, NY; *Page 17*: Scala/Art Resource, NY; *Page 18*: Photo by Sisse Brimberg, National Geographic Image Collection; *Page 23*: Scala/Art Resource, NY; *Page 24*: Giraudon/Bridgeman Art Library, London; *Page 26*: Photo courtesy of Larry Garfinkel Publications, Vancouver, B.C.; *Page 29*: Werner Forman/Art Resource, NY; *Page 30*: Vijali's World Wheel Theatre of the Earth, A Mandalah Circling the Globe for World Peace; *Page 32*: Bridgeman Art Library, London; *Page 36*: Photo by Don Wiechec; *Page 40*: Photo by Lynton Gardiner; *Page 42*: Schalkwijk/Art Resource, NY; *Page 44*: Erich Lessing/Art Resource, NY; *Page 50*: ©Bildarchiv Preussicher Kulturbesitz, Berlin/Photo by Swantje Autrum-Mulzer; *Page 52*: Bridgeman Art Library, London. The Arthur Rackham illustration has been reproduced with kind permission of his family.; *Page 54*: Erich Lessing/Art Resource, NY; *Page 56*: Michael Holford Photographs; *Page 59*: Giraudon/ Bridgeman Art Library, London; *Page 64*: Bridgeman Art Library, London; *Page 66*: Bridgeman Art Library, London;

Page 68: Bridgeman Art Library, London; *Page 70*: *Celestial Being* (India), c.1000. Sandstone. Height: 24 ½"; width: 9 1/16"; depth 6 7/8". Williams College Museum of Art, Museum purchase, with funds provided by John T. Winkhaus, Jr., Class of 1935 (69.45); *Page 71*: Bridgeman Art Library, London; *Page 72*: Bridgeman Art Library, London; *Page 73*: Scala/Art Resource, NY; *Page 74*: Bridgeman Art Library, London; *Page 76*: Giraudon/Art Resource, NY; *Page 78*: Bridgeman Art Library, London; *Page 81*: Victoria and Albert Museum/Art Resource, NY; *Page 82*: Bridgeman Art Library, London; *Page 90*: Giraudon/Art Resource, NY; *Page 92*: Giraudon/Bridgeman Art Library, London; *Page 94*: Erich Lessing/Art Resource, NY; *Page 97*: Peter Willi/Bridgeman Art Library, London; *Page 98*: Bridgeman Art Library, London; *Page 100*: Erich Lessing/Art Resource, NY; *Page 101*: Nimtallah/Art Resource, NY; *Page 102*: ©Bildarchiv Preussicher Kulturbesitz, Berlin/Photo by Swantje Autrum-Mulzer; *Page 104*: Bridgeman Art Library, London; *Page 106*: © R.M.N; *Page 109*: Victoria & Albert Museum, London/Art Resource, NY; *Page 112*: Bridgeman Art Library, London; *Page 114*: Bridgeman Art Library, London; *Page 116*: Photo by Don Wiechec; *Page 119*: Erich Lessing/Art Resource, NY; *Page 122*: Photo by Blair Clark, #51400/13; *Page 126*: Bridgeman Art Library, London; *Page 130*: Bridgeman Art Library, London; *Page 132*: *Inanna & Ereshkigal*, Sheryl Cotleur, 1993. Animal bone. Width: 96"; height: 65"; depth: 18"; *Page 136*: Erich Lessing/Art Resource, NY; *Page 138*: Erich Lessing/Art Resource, NY; *Page 141*: Alinari/Art Resource, NY; *Page 142*: Bridgeman Art Library, London; *Page 144*: Victoria & Albert Museum, London/Art Resource, NY; *Page 150*: Photo courtesy of Christie's Images, NY; *Page 152*: Giraudon/Bridgeman Art Library, London; *Page 155*: Photo by Bob Capazzo; *Page 157*: Bridgeman Art Library, London; *Page 159*: Bridgeman Art Library, London; *Page 160*: *Lovers* (Mithuna), India, Madyha Pradesh, Khajuraho style, 11th century. Reddish sandstone, H. 74 cm. ©The Cleveland Museum of Art, 1997, Leonard C. Hanna Jr. Fund, 1982.64; *Page 164*: Nimtallah/Art Resource, NY; *Page 167*: Bridgeman Art Library, London; *Page 170*: Bridgeman Art Library, London; *Page 171*: Victoria & Albert Museum, London/Art Resource, NY; *Page 172*: Photo by Don Wiechec; *Page 175*: Photo courtesy of Patterson Graphics; *Page 177*: Bridgeman Art Library, London. The Arthur Rackham illustration has been reproduced with kind permission of his family; *Page 178*: Erich Lessing/Art Resource, NY; *Page 185*: Photo by Lynton Gardiner; *Page 187*: Bridgeman Art Library, London; *Page 188*: Scala/Art Resource, NY; *Page 194*: Photo Jewish Historical Museum, Amsterdam; *Page 197*: Giraudon/Art Resource, NY; *Page 198*: The Tate Gallery, London/Art Resource, NY; *Page 201*: National Museum of American Art/Art Resource, NY; *Page 203*: Scala/Art Resource, NY; *Page 204*: Bridgeman Art Library, London; *Page 207*: Scala/Art Resource, NY; *Page 208*: Bridgeman Art Library, London; *Page 211*: Giraudon/Bridgeman Art Library, London; *Page 212*: Scala/Art Resource, NY; *Page 214*: Photo by Lynton Gardiner; *Page 220*: Zhang Shui Cheng/Bridgeman Art Library, London; *Page 226*: Bridgeman Art Library, London; *Page 229*: Photo by Susumu Wakisaka; *Page 231*: Vijali's World Wheel Theatre of the Earth, A Mandalah Circling the Globe for World Peace. *Page 232*: Bridgeman Art Library, London; *Page 235*: Alinari/Art Resource, NY; *Page 240*: *Flora*, 1st century B.C.E. National Museum, Naples. Scala/Art Resource, NY.

Every attempt has been made to obtain permission to reproduce materials protected by copyright. Where omissions may have occured, the producers will be happy to acknowledge this in future printings.

Compilation copyright © 1997 by Fair Street Productions and Welcome Enterprises, Inc.

Text copyright © 1997 by individual authors or publishers as noted on these pages. The selections included here have been reproduced as found in translations, manuscripts, or previously published adaptations of oral stories, and, for the most part, have not been edited or changed. If there are errors or omissions, the editors apologize.

All Rights Reserved. No part of this publication may be reproduced, stored in a retrieval system, or transmitted in any form or by any means, electronic, mechanical, photocopying, recording or otherwise without written permission from the publisher.

Produced by Fair Street Productions and Welcome Enterprises, Inc.
Project Directors: Deborah Bull, Alice Wong, Hiro Clark Wakabayashi
Editor: Deborah Bull
Designer: Gregory Wakabayashi
Managing Editor: Susan Wechsler
Assistant Editor: Joanna Goodman
Text Coordinator: Shaie Dively
Production Assistant: Susanne Nally
Photo Research: Photosearch, Inc.

Published in 1997 and distributed in the U.S. by
Stewart, Tabori & Chang,
a division of U.S. Media Holdings, Inc.
115 West 18th Street, New York, NY 10011

Distributed in Canada by
General Publishing Company Ltd.
30 Lesmill Road
Don Mills, Ontario, M3B 2T6, Canada

Distributed in Australia by
Peribo Pty Ltd.
58 Beaumont Road
Mount Kuring-gai, NSW 2080, Australia

Distributed in all other territories by
Grantham Book Services Ltd.
Isaac Newton Way, Alma Park Industrial Estate
Grantham, Lincolnshire, NG31 9SD, England

Library of Congress Cataloging-in-Publication Data

Goddess: a celebration in art and literature / edited by Jalaja Bonheim.
p. cm.
"A Fair Street–Welcome Book."
ISBN 1-55670-621-9
1. Goddess—Miscellanea. I. Bonheim, Jalaja.
BL325.F4.G628   1997
291.2'114–dc21   97-8432

Printed in Singapore by Toppan Printing Company
10 9 8 7 6 5 4 3 2 1

ACKNOWLEDGMENTS

My deepest appreciation goes to Deborah Bull and Susan Wechsler at Fair Street Productions. While I, on the West Coast, gathered myths and stories of the sacred feminine, they, on the East Coast, coordinated them with images and oversaw the making of the book. Like the triple goddesses of old, we spun the threads and wove the fabric of this book while our phone calls and faxes raced back and forth across the continent. Thanks, also, to Joanna Goodman at Fair Street for her dedicted assistance, to Shaie Dively for keeping track of all the pieces, and to Mairead Stack and Helen Dunn for their attention to detail. I am grateful to Welcome Enterprises, especially Greg Wakabayashi, Alice Wong, and Hiro Clark Wakabayashi for their elegant design and production expertise. And, of course, my thanks go to Lena Tabori for her enthusiastic response to the Goddess.

J.B.